"Criminologists will hail this boc
for the two cases described in
importance to the study of "s
from the introduction by **COLIN WILSON**

In Germany, before the last world war, the darker impulses of the 20th century were manifesting themselves within misfits and outsiders - men who, judged by outward appearance, seemed unremarkable human beings, but whose demonic lusts drove them to act as monsters.
Published for the first time ever in English,
HAARMANN - THE STORY OF A WEREWOLF,
by Theodor Lessing, tells the full story of **Fritz Haarmann** - a lowlife black market dealer, whose strange, erotic bloodlust led him to butcher countless young men and boys. The German people began to speak of a "werewolf" in their midst, not realising the monster was a trusted police informer.
KÜRTEN - THE VAMPIRE OF DÜSSELDORF
recounts the deeply disturbing case of **Peter Kürten**.
One of modern history's most infamous criminals, he was driven by a warped sexuality and vampiric blood fetish - making victims of women, men and children.
MONSTERS OF WEIMAR contains, in a new, annotated form, "*the* classic case of a sadistic serial killer".
NEMESIS have also included an afterword on the classic crime films inspired by these grim cases.
In the words of True Crime authority/respected author Colin Wilson, "In no... cases have there been psychological studies that compare with the two in the present volume."

Readers be advised - and also be warned.

MONSTERS OF WEIMAR
This first edition published August 1993
by
Nemesis Books
Unit 4
Millmead Business Centre
Millmead Road
London N17 9QU.

Printed and bound in the UK
by
Woolnough Bookbinding Ltd.

British Library Cataloguing-in-Publication Data.
A catalogue record for this book is
available from the British Library.

Monsters of Weimar

Comprising the classic case histories:

Haarmann - the Story of a Werewolf

Kürten - the Vampire of Düsseldorf

Nemesis wishes to thank
Charles M. Pelts ,
and Franz Rodenkirchen,
without whose kind cooperation
and morbid interests
this disturbing volume
would not have been possible.

CONTENTS

INTRODUCTION by Colin Wilson

Criminologists will hail this book with excitement, for the two cases described in it are of crucial importance to the study of "serial murder". In order to explain why, I must say something about the history of sex crime.

We make the natural assumption that sex crime is as old as history, but this is not strictly true. Sex crime in the modern sense of the word - murder committed for rape - is a fairly recent phenomenon. The reason is simple. For most of its history, mankind has suffered from poverty and starvation. And when you are half-starved, sex is a minor issue. The few sex criminals known to history were men who were in the unusual position of being rich and powerful. In fact, even Roman emperors like Tiberius, Caligula and Nero, with their abysmal record of murder, were not sex criminals in our sense of the word. They simply used their position to indulge their lust. Even the Emperor Augustus, who is known as one of the "goodies" of history, used to get his wife to procure him young children to deflower.

It is much later that we begin to encounter the famous - or infamous - sex criminals of history, and these are so few that Theodor Lessing, the author of the section on Fritz Haarmann, manages to mix up three of them in a single paragraph: "The criminal case of the Marquis de Sade, (who had a perverse desire to torment children, and bathed in hot baths prepared with the blood of gruesomely martyred children) bears not the slightest resemblance to the Haarmann case, since Haarmann was not driven by the urge to torture, but by the urge to kill at the climax of his sexual desire, followed by the dark secret of mutilation..."

In fact, the Marquis de Sade never killed anyone, or even did anyone any great harm (if flogging a prostitute is overlooked) apart from writing pornographic books. The marquis (or rather, marshall) who raped and disembowelled children was Gilles de Rais, burned for his activities in 1440, while it was an aristocratic lady, Countess Elizabeth Bathory, who died walled-up in her own chamber in 1614, who killed servant girls to bathe in their blood. Apart from these two, the record of historical "monsters" is almost completed with the addition of the Italian princeling Ezzelino da Romano, the Wallachian Vlad the Impaler (also known as Dracula) and the Russian Ivan the Terrible - but these three were bloodthirsty maniacs who enjoyed mass slaughter rather than "sex criminals".

The Marquis de Sade, who died in a lunatic asylum in 1814, has the dubious distinction of being a kind of patron saint of sex killers. Sade was born in an age (1740) when nearly all crime was economic - committed out of poverty. The best that can be said of him is that he was an utterly spoilt brat who flew into a violent temper at the least opposition. He had also developed a taste for sodomy and flogging. So when he was thrown into jail for a number of misdemeanours (like blasphemy and administering Spanish Fly to prostitutes), he found it intolerable to be ordered about by people he considered his social inferiors. His rage was so boundless that he wrote a number of books full of appalling tortures. But his major assault on the authority he detested was a philosophy in which he argued that "everything is permitted", that man is a mere animal, religion a delusion, and that therefore everyone should be allowed to do exactly what they like, even to mass murder.

Sade is important because he was a kind of turning point in the history of sexual morals. But an even more important turning point had occurred half a century earlier. A printer named Samuel Richardson had already caused one of the greatest changes in human history when he invented the modern novel; ***Pamela***, the story of a servant girl who resists all her master's attempts at seduction and rape, became a European bestseller in the same year that de Sade was born, and Richardson's imitators had soon turned Europe into a "nation of readers", with lending libraries springing up like mushrooms in every town.

It was, I believe, this sudden tremendous surge in the human *imagination*, created by the novel, that launched the "age of sex *imagination,* created by the novel, that launched the "age of sex crime". All over Europe, thousands of people learned to curl up in a window seat and allow their minds to float away into *other people's lives*. Frustrated spinsters like Jane Austen and the Bronte sisters learned to alleviate their boredom by creating imaginary lovers. The Gothic novel specialised in ruined castles where a virgin was quite likely to get kidnapped and raped among decaying coffins in the family mausoleum. One of the most famous Gothic novels of the period, ***The Monk*** (by Matthew Lewis) is a lurid fantasy of murder and sexual violation. In the same year (1795) Sade was working on his most violent and "sadistic" novel, ***Juliette***, which would land him back in jail for the rest of his days.

Ten years after his death, Sade was the major influence on a new tide of pornography that flooded Europe. In earlier centuries, the pornography had been fairly innocent, confining itself to describing the sex act - often between monks and nuns, or priests and penitents. (De Sade was by no means the first writer to attack the Church.) But this new pornography was quite different in tone. It frequently described violent rape - often in the guise of Christian women being kidnapped and imprisoned in a Turkish harem. But it also lingered blissfully over "the forbidden". Brothers were always seducing their sisters or teachers their pupils, while children peered through a crack in the pantry door at the butler masturbating as he read pornography. Quite suddenly, sex had ceased to be something frank and open, that could be talked about and laughed about in the manner of Boccaccio or Rabelais. It had become steamy and somehow "wicked".

In the first decade of the 19th century there occurred two strange cases that we now recognise as "sex crimes". In 1807 and 1808, two girls vanished in Regensdorf, Bavaria, after visiting a fortune teller called Andrew Bichel. When Bichel's home was searched, the dismembered corpses were found buried in a woodshed. Bichel insisted that he had killed the girls for their clothes, but also admitted: "...while I was opening the body I was so greedy that I trembled, and could have cut out a piece and eaten it." He also admitted to have tried to lure three more girls to their deaths. And since the girls' this was really his motive. Bichel was in the grip of the same obscure sexual fever that later made Fritz Haarmann bite his victims in the throat as he strangled them.

The other case is of the female mass-poisoner Anna Zwanziger. Brought up in comfortable circumstances, she married a drunken lawyer. And while her husband was out drinking with cronies, Anna stayed at home devouring Richardson's ***Pamela*** and other novels. The husband became a hopeless alcoholic, and she was forced to become a kind of high class prostitute to keep her children fed and clothed. When her husband finally died she slipped steadily down the social scale, finally becoming a housekeeper. Then, in 1807, she began a series of poisonings - mostly of employers and fellow servants - with arsenic, which eventually led to her arrest in 1809. There can be no doubt that poverty had driven her partly insane; but it also seems clear that the real motive behind the murders - many of which were quite pointless - was a kind of sadism; the sense of power it gave her to cause death - precisely like the emotion that made Bichel tremble as he dismembered one of his victims. Both Bichel and Anna Zwanziger were executed.

But it was not until the second half of the 19th century that we can clearly recognise the emergence of the sexual criminal. In 1867 a clerk named Frederick Baker lured a girl named Fanny Adams away from her companions in Alton, Hampshire, then killed her in a hopyard and scattered the pieces over a wide area. (We use the phrase "sweet Fanny Adams" - meaning nothing - because he left so little of her to find.) In 1871, a young butcher named Eusebius Pieydagnelle killed six girls with a knife, experiencing sexual orgasms as he did so. In Italy in the following year, a youth named Vincent Verzeni was charged with a number of violent sexual attacks, including two murders - he experienced orgasm as he strangled his victims. (This explains why some of them escaped; he reached a climax before they died - the same, we shall see, was true of the "Düsseldorf monster", Peter Kürten.)

But the first case of sex murder that made headlines all over the world was Jack the Ripper, the "monster" who killed and disembowelled prostitutes in the East End of London in 1888. The horror caused by the first two murders turned to incredulity when the Ripper killed two women in one night - he was interrupted after killing the first, and went off to find another whom he could also disembowel. The final murder - of a woman called Mary Kelly - took place indoors, and the killer spent over an hour mutilating the corpse. This seems to have been the last of the crimes of Jack the Ripper, but the sensation created by them was so great that the "pen name" of Jack the Ripper has become better known than that of any other murderer in criminal history.

Yet, oddly enough, the "age of sex crime" inaugurated by the Ripper began slowly and hesitantly. In the 1890's, a French tramp who earned himself the title "disemboweller of the south-east" raped and mutilated eleven victims; finally caught as he tried to kill a peasant woman in a forest, he proved to be Joseph Vacher, a soldier who had spent some time in an asylum after attempting suicide, and who was obviously mentally subnormal. A few years later, a German carpenter, Ludwig Tessnow, was driven by a compulsion to mutilate children and sheep. And shortly before the First World War, a Hungarian plumber named Bela Kiss, who suffered from compulsive sex urges, killed at least a dozen women and disposed of many of their bodies by sealing them in oil drums - Kiss vanished during the war.

But it was at the end of the war, in Germany, that multiple sex crimes began to occur with a frequency that announced that the Age of Sex Crime had finally arrived. In 1921, a Berlin peddler named Georg Grossman was found in his room standing over the body of a naked girl, who was trussed up like a piece of meat ready for butchering. It soon became clear that Grossman had killed many girls in his flat during the First World War and sold their bodies for meat. In 1924 (as Lessing recalls), a man named Karl Denke was caught when he tried to kill a travelling journeyman to whom he had offered a meal, and the pickled remains of thirty bodies were found in his house. Denke confessed to a taste for human flesh.

But it was when the case of Fritz Haarmann erupted - also in 1924 that the Germans realised that mass murder was turning into a kind of epidemic. This account by Theodor Lessing, who examined Haarmann, is here published for the first time in English, and fills an important gap in the annals of mass murder. Unlike Grossman and Denke, Haarmann was never a cannibal, and many people concluded that he had killed simply to sell the corpses for meat. In fact, as this account makes clear, Haarmann sometimes became possessed by a violent and sadistic urge to kill when he was sexually excited, and often felt shaken and repentant when he found himself lying in bed with a corpse. It is difficult to decide whether the subsequent disembowelling and dissection of the corpse was part of the same sadistic impulse, or whether Haarmann simply wanted to get rid of his victims in a way that would leave them unrecognisable. What *is* clear is that Haarmann was obsessed by murder in the same way as two more recent "serial killers", Dennis Nilsen and Jeffrey Dahmer (also both homosexual), and that he was the first example of this type of sadistic-homosexual killer.

One more interesting fact about Haarmann deserves to be noted. His skull, which is in the Institute of Medicine at Gottingen University, reveals that Haarmann's brain rested directly against the bone in several places, probably due to meningitis in childhood. An enormous number of murderers have, at some point, had violent blows on the head which have produced a change of character: these include the child-killer Albert Fish, the burning car murderer Rouse, the "Gorilla murderer" Earle Nelson, and the multiple killer Raymond Fernandez. Another more recent serial killer, Henry Lee Lucas, experienced a character change after his mother had hit him on the head with a piece of wood. One day, we may know the precise links that connect brain deterioration and violent crime.

The other case in this volume, that of Peter Kürten, is generally regarded by criminologists as *the* classic case of a sadistic serial killer. I first came upon Kürten by accident at the age of 20, when I was working on my first novel ***Ritual in the Dark*** in the Reading Room of the British Museum. The novel was loosely based on the Jack the Ripper murders, although the killer, like Haarmann, is homosexual. Looking up "sadism" in the catalogue, I came across a book called ***The Sadist*** by Professor Karl Berg, and immediately sent in a request slip for it. I quickly realised that here was a case that bore many close parallels to Jack the Ripper,and that since the Ripper had never been caught, I might well use some details of Kürten's psychology for my own mass murderer. It was Professor Berg who had studied Kürten as Lessing studied Haarmann, and in so doing, had created the first detailed study of the motivation of a sex murderer.

Kürten was the son of a drunken workman, who sexually abused his daughters, and often raped his wife in front of the children. Kürten himself was sexually obsessed, and attempted incest with his sister. But his taste for sadism was aroused by a sadistic dog-catcher, who taught him to masturbate the animals and torture them. As a teenager, Kürten soon graduated to having sexual intercourse with sheep and goats, and cutting their throats as he reached orgasm.

But it has always seemed to me that the experiences that turned Kürten into a mass murderer were his periods of solitary confinement in prison at the turn of the century. He admitted to Berg that his masturbation fantasies had to become more and more violent in order to stimulate his jaded senses. In fact, Kürten's sadism developed by exactly the same process as the Marquis de Sade's. Many subsequent cases of sex murder have shown the crucial role played in the inexorable development of fantasy - that double-edged legacy of Samuel Richardson and the Marquis de Sade.

It was not until he returned to Düsseldorf from prison in 1925 that Kürten launched into a career of mass sex murder, interspersed with violent attacks and arson. (Pyromania is another sexual perversion connected with sadism.) He told Berg how, on the day he returned to Düsseldorf, a magnificent blood-red sunset somehow inspired him to begin the "reign of terror" which ended only with his arrest five years later. Readers who get a chance to see Fritz Lang's classic film ***M*** - in which Peter Lorre plays a child-killer based on Kürten - will find that it conjures up something of the atmosphere of panic during those five years.

George Godwin's book on Kürten, here reprinted, was originally intended as an introduction to the English edition of Berg's ***The Sadist***, but was published separately because it was too long. It is an interesting psychological study, but not nearly so interesting as Berg's original book - it is to be hoped that Nemesis will sometime reprint this classic of criminology.*

So the remarkable volume you are now holding contains the first two important psychological studies of serial killers, available to non-medical readers for the first time. There have been many notorious sex killers since that time, from Earle Nelson, Albert Fish, the unknown "Cleveland Torso Killer", Gordon Cummins ("the Blackout Ripper") and Reginald Christie, down to the Boston Strangler, the Yorkshire Ripper and the Hillside Stranglers of Los Angeles. In none of these cases have there been psychological studies that compare with the two in the present volume. They remain memorable landmarks in the history of modern criminology.

Colin Wilson

*** Subsequent to Colin Wilson's introduction, Godwin's essay, *Peter Kürten*, has been interspersed with the main bulk of *The Sadist*, to create this anthology's definitive case history of Kürten**
- Editor.

Haarmann - the Story of a Werewolf

by Theodor Lessing (1925)

(TRANSLATED FROM THE GERMAN
HAARMANN - DIE GESCHICTE EINES WERWOLFS
BY MO CROASDALE)

ABOUT THE AUTHOR:

Theodor Lessing was a noted socialist writer, and a native of Hannover - where Fritz Haarmann committed his crimes. His writings include an investigation of the white slave trade, and works on other social and moral issues. Such social concern inspired his interest in the Haarmann case, which he clearly believed was aggravated by the indifference shown by a city to some of its most vulnerable inhabitants, until it was too late to do anything but take bloody retribution.

Lessing died in mysterious circumstances in the early 1940's, and is widely believed to have been murdered by the Third Reich.

Fritz Haarmann - the "Werewolf" / "Butcher of Hannover"
(far left, in prison uniform)

Part One
Time and Place

Hannover, the capital of the German province of the same name and centre of Lower Saxony, lies at the foothills of the German Mittelgebirge, the central mountain range from where the sandy pine and heather regions of the North German Plain reach to the North Sea coast. The river Leine flows from the Eichsfelde through the hilly hollow of Göttingen between the mountains of the Harz and Weser and reaches the sparse North German plain near Elze, gushing forth between the Hildesheim and Oster forests. At Hannover the river bears to the right and flows into the Große Moor - "vast moor" - near Hudemühlen. The Hohe Ufer, the "high bank" where the river absorbs the Ihme and Fösse streams and hurries on through the old part of the town, probably gave the town its name, recorded for the first time around 1050.

"Honovere", truly "a town in the country", is surrounded by a wide semi-circle of 2500 acres of woodland, known as the Eilenriede. The water-rich marsh, surrounded by hills and woodlands known as the Deister ("thick forest"), pushes its way through an opening to the south. Few other European towns altered their appearance so completely between 1850 and 1900. Until 1866, Hannover was the elegant, protected home of the old English Guelphic kings. The voices of Germany's first lyricists were heard in this lush, green idyll in Lower Saxony, which had slept dreamily for six centuries: Hölty and Bürger, then the early "nightingales" of romanticism; the Schlegel brothers, Lichtenberg and Leisewitz, Detmold and Feder brooded here, and Leibniz, Germany's most knowledgeable thinker. Moriz and Iffland were born here, as were Hartleben and Frank Wedekind.

When Bismarck annexed Hannover for Prussia in 1866, the town had less than 70,000 inhabitants. Then after the victorious war with France between 1870 and 1873, the so-called expansion years, industry progressed dramatically with the result that the pretty little villages of the area such as Hainholz, Döhren, Limmer and List, soon became sooty factory suburbs. A technical college was built, coal was mined from the Wealden, and urban features changed dramatically and completely when the Rhein-Weser-Leine canal was laid and connected to the high "Mittellandkanal", the central land canal, and simultaneously mining began in the vast potash deposits around Hannover. After only a few years one factory, the so-called "Continental" works, where artificial rubber was manufactured, had transformed the tiny suburb of Vahrenwald into a proletariat district of 15,000 people. Breweries,spinning mills, wool mills, the construction factories of the Körtting brothers and Georg Egestorff, and the so-called Hanomag where cars and wagons were manufactured, transformed the village of Linden on the far side of the Ihme into a factory suburb consisting of the families of more than 100,000 civil servants and proletariats. This transformation into a plutocracy, which suffocated the cultures of the old farming families and gentry, was far from unusual, indeed was typical of Wilhelminian Germany. However, true chaos set in when the Prussian reign crumbled, and the young generation, which had run wild during five years of world wars, shaking off the last vestiges of discipline and decency and becoming accustomed to killing and "requisitioning", returned to their totally impoverished home to find 14 million dead... Starvation in the east had wiped out entire areas of the region, culminating in parents eating their children, children eating their parents. There was degeneration, poverty, confusion beyond compare. German money had been devalued to such an extent that only the printing and distribution of increasingly valueless pieces of paper ensured survival from one day to the next. During this co-called "period of inflation", which commenced with the collapse of the German armies in a world war and the storms of the German revolution, Hannover began to grow in its guise of an international transit and black market. By 1918 its inhabitants totalled around 450,000. Just four hours by rail from Berlin and only eight hours from Cologne (where English, French and Belgian control began), Hannover was a most convenient centre for the bartering, black marketeering and other transactions of the time by which thousands lived. The whole world survived on speculation. As money was worthless and survival could only be eked out with material assets, people bought, bartered and stole as never before. And there were Hannover, conveniently situated between where great riches flowed out to Holland and England; Berlin, where the Slavic, Wendish, Polish and Jewish East poured in; and finally Cologne, the bridge to Belgium and France, so conveniently central that hundreds of families put down roots, and hundreds of new haunts of entertainment and depravity sprang up attracting an evil race of dealers, black marketeers, parasites and freeloaders which gradually corroded the old values and solidity of this (as a great poet once said) "palest of cities".

In three areas of the town, the first of which held the railway station, crooks, fences and prostitutes, over whom the town authorities were completely unable to gain any kind of control, traded as never before. At this time of strict bread rationing, when minute amounts of bread, meat and milk were available only after hours of queuing, there was a flourishing trade in stolen and secretly slaughtered working animals; in rabbits, goats, dogs and cats, in potatoes, flour and all kinds of black market goods, and above all in clothing, linen and shoes. At night, crowds of the homeless, the unemployed, the hungry and miscreants of all kinds gathered in the station waiting rooms. A short walk from the railway station along the wide tree-lined alley is the Georgestraße, the main artery of the town, a wide boulevard with linden trees, flower beds, landscaped gardens, pavilions and monuments. And around 1918, in between the famous old "Hoftheater", the court theatre, and the beautiful gardens of the so-called Café Köpcke, there was a second centre of depravity: the "market of male prostitutes", 500 of whose members were registered in police lists, while the chief inspector of police put the total of homosexuals in Hannover at almost 40,000. They lived in their own small world. In one of the most beautiful restaurants of the suburb of Calenberg, the Neustädter Gesellschaftshaus, they held social evenings and balls at which boys and youths danced, dressed in ball gowns. A second, less salubrious meeting-point was the old Ballhof, a baroque ball-room dating back to the time of Germany's royalty. And for the lowest of the low there was one of the oldest, most depraved streets of the Old Town known as the "Neue Straße", the new road, where there was a dance hall known as the "Schwule Guste", where lesbians and homosexuals met at night, gaining admittance only after giving a certain sign. But the third main centre of depravity was the artistic old part of the town, where the river flowed along the so-called High Bank, crossing one of the many bridges to a well-known ancient island town known as "Klein-Venedig", "Little Venice". Crumbling, centuries-old masonry, a Saxon watchtower, and a maze of gables, timbered houses and old ruined alleys, reminiscent of the middle ages, from the centre of which rises the church whereLeibniz is buried, and on the "hill," actually a kind of ramp, there is a Moorish Jewish temple. This part of the town, with its mighty Guelphic castles against which the river washes, was once the smartest part of the town, but with the passage of time - just like the area surrounding the Berlin castle - it became the shabbiest, poorest low dive, the criminal quarter. As with Hildesheim, Brunswick and Goslar, previously a delight for the discerning eye, Hannover became a breeding ground for the poor, the depraved, the murderers, for those condemned to ill fortune.

"Neue Straße", where the former residence of Emperor Friedrich Wilhelm of Brunswick is to be found (which later became the poor-house), runs parallel to the steep river bank. The rear walls of the centuries-old houses with their bay windows and balconies end abruptly on the banks of the river, which is flanked by poor farmyards and modest gardens. Not far away, opposite the Jewish temple, is the so-called "Rote Reihe", the "red row": a cluster of tired, crumbling buildings, in one of which (the one next to the murderer's house) an electrician named Rühmkorff discovered induction electricity. In this filthy, hopeless squalor, in hovels separated from each other by thin paper walls or wooden boarding, lived the poorest of Germany's wretched poor in this miserable time.

The youngsters who had survived the war had learnt that it was "all right" to kill the enemy for a coat or a pair of boots, the "enemy" being everyone else. Thieves and fences had their"exchange" on the "island". Here (in the language of this underworld), the evenings were spent dealing, fiddling and swindling. This is where stolen goods were handled, where "jobs" were pulled. At night, when the moon hung over the ramshackle roofs and grey chimneys and turned the ghostly black river to silver, this heavy, dour, worn down, broken bundle of human suffering crept out of its old boxes to hang over the side or kneel on the old bridge over the stinking lagoon: impoverished, troubled mothers of too many children; tired, numbed men, old before their time. And amongst them the younger people: the vast numbers of whores and their pimps, rip-off artists, con-men, in the local pubs, the "Kreuzklappe", the "Kleeblatt", in the "Deutscher Herrmann", boasting of their deeds whilst the silent stars reflected in the dark waters of the foul river.

The First Finds

On 17 May 1924 some children playing near the "Wasserkunst", the edge of the water near Schloß Herrenhausen, found a human skull. On 29 May the skull of a youth was washed up behind the Leineschloß in the mill race. On 13 June two more were found, and as before: one in the east part of the town on the banks of a river, the other in the west near a mill. The autopsy proved the first two to be the skulls of young people aged between 18 and 20, the one found near the mill on 13 June from a boy aged between 11 and 13. In all cases, a sharp instrument had been used to separate the skulls from the torso. The flesh had been removed, or else had rotted away, as the skulls had obviously been in the water for some time. The scalp had been removed from the skull found on 13 June near the "Wasserkunst". It was thought at first that the skulls originated from the anatomical institute in Göttingen, or that they had been thrown in the Leine in Alfeld, where there was at the time an outbreak of typhoid. Finally the theory was that they had been flung into the river by grave-robbers caught in the act in the cemetery in Engesohde.

However, none of these theories was proven, and a short while later boys playing on a field in the Döhren marshland found a sack containing human bones. On 24 July a scalped skull, obviously decapitated, was found in Garbsen, again that of a very young person. It was impossible to keep these grisly finds a secret. The population had been gripped by horror for some time, and for several years superstitious rumours had been going around: "People are being caught in traps in the Old Town," "children are disappearing down cellars," "boys are being drowned in the river."

It was said that human flesh had been for sale on the market during the time of greatest need. Housemaids in the villages around Hannover refused to go shopping in the town. And the fear that a "werewolf" may be at large in the area increased daily. Between 1918 and 1924 an extraordinarily high number of people went missing; the number registered in 1923 grew to almost 600, and even though most eventually turned up again, Hannover still had a much higher figure than other towns of similar size. Investigations showed that those missing were invariably boys and youths aged between 14 and 18.

On Whit Sunday in 1924, hundreds of people left Hannover and the surrounding area for the "Hohe Ufer", the high bank, and descended on the small paths and bridges in the Old Town, where they started to search feverishly for human remains. Early in the morning of 5 July, after a large number of human bones had been found, the river bed was dammed from the mill to the big bridge over the Leine near the Cleve gateway, and then searched by policemen and municipal workers. This part of the river is in the centre of the town, and due to the heavy traffic in the area is not popular with potential suicides. The finds were terrible. More than 500 parts of corpses were found, which after examination by the court doctor proved to be the remains of at least 22 people, of which roughly a third would have been between the ages of 15 and 20. Approximately one half had been in the water for quite some time, and the joints of fresh bones proved to have smoothly cut surfaces.

In the meantime, due in part to the speedy efforts of Detective

Superintendent Rätz, a friendly young giant, and in part to a series of strange coincidences, the solution was revealed. On 23 June a suspect was taken to the court prison: Friedrich (known as Fritz) Haarmann, born in Hannover on 25 October 1879. He had fifteen previous convictions, and since 1918 had been an informer for the criminal investigation department. He was known to the police both as a "dealer" in clothing and meat, and to the security police and criminal investigation department for many years as a homosexual.

His appearance redefined the conventional impression of murder and murderers.

Personal Description

He was not unsympathetic in appearance: a simple man of the people, with a friendly, open expression; obliging, courteous, and surprisingly fastidious in appearance. Of average height, broad and well built, he had a coarse, rough, shiny full-moon face with strong colouring and small, inquisitive, cheerful animal eyes. The narrow head was round, broad-browed, and flat at the back. The ears were not large, a little lower than eye height, and stood out from the head. The nose was small and as unprepossessing as the rest of his appearance; although slightly noble in profile, it was nonetheless bulbous with wide nostrils. The mouth was small, pert and thick-lipped. The tongue, which darted in and out nervously, was surprisingly fleshy; the teeth were white,strong, sharp and healthy; the chin jutted forward energetically. Over the top lip was a small, well-groomed moustache; the full cheeks were clean shaven. His brown hair, smooth and parted to the left, was thinning. The eyes, somewhere between brown and blue in colour, were cold and soulless; cunning, downcast; rarely still. His expression closed up completely as soon as the atmosphere became embarrassing. The contradiction was obvious: The physiognomy was noticeably tight, "trapped in the grip of the self", but at the same time he appeared to be unbelievably talkative, wanting sympathy, and hyperactive. He talked constantly, his soft, white hands moving all the tir nervousness, plucking and pulling constantly at the long f tip of a finger on his left hand was missing; he claimed it had been bitten off in a fight. His torso was well developed: the neck strong and mean, his chest and back, like his behind, well rounded, like a woman's. The body was coarse, but at the same time slightly feminine. His member was strong; the pubic hair grew, not towards a point beneath the naval, but rounded off above the pubic bone. His plump feet were flat. His voice, mushy, smarmy, and close to a treble, was like the querulous voice of an old woman. His whole disposition was "androgynous", not masculine or feminine, and not child-like, but a combination of all three. His most striking feature (which unfortunately was ignored by the experts, who were not even aware of it) was his many automatisms and stereotypes. (By "automatisms" I mean those expressions which occur involuntarily, "stereotypes" those which gradually become habitual.) Several of his movements were automatic: a certain dodderiness in his walk, the almost coquettish way he wiggled his behind and lower body (particularly as a response to praise or embarrassment). When he became tired his left hand started to rub against a particular spot on his right temple, almost as if it hurt, and if he lost his train of thought he would lick his lips with his thick tongue before (like Sterne's Corporal Trim), "starting again from the beginning".

Another stereotype was the eternal pulling at his fingers, the moistening of his lips, the blinking of his eyes as soon as he was on the defensive. His speech too was full of stereotypical expressions in the low Hannoverian dialect. He had several favourite illusions that recurred, such as the idea that all boys were in love with him; that, far from him being after the boys, they were all after him; that women (whom he despised and regarded as rivals) liked to flirt with him. Although he had not the slightest respect for the property of others and no social feelings (such as sympathy or altruism), he was a gregarious creature. The strongest emotions in his make-up were his lewdness and need of tenderness, feelings that were bound together like the story in the *Mahabharata*, where the man-eater Hidimba, the demon of blood lust, is bound to his sister Hidimba, the goddess of gentle beauty. He wanted to be loved and admired, and was full of ways of drawing attention to himself by sulking and whining like a silly disruptive child. Haarmann loved "feminine" pastimes, such as baking and cooking and darning socks, but would smoke strong cigars at the same time. He particularly enjoyed ground coffee, strong cigars and Harzer cheese (a particularly strong type). His general appearance was far from evil, more of a creature living entirely for the time, self-centred and impulsive; an easily manipulated show-off. He was inherently incapable of holding onto abstract (i.e. imagined) ideas; any impressions he received had to become "reality" immediately. In this respect one could say that his intellect was far less well developed than his reasoning. This "short circuit" between imagination and reality was so immediate that, for example, when talking of decapitation ("chopping heads off"), he mimicked walking to the scaffold and the blade falling; when talking of how he dismembered bodies, his hands showed the cutting movements. He would become sentimental ("I want to be executed on the Klages market-place. My grave-stone will say, 'Here lies Haarmann, the mass murderer.' Hans will visit my grave on my birthday and lay a wreath on it."), and bring tears to his own eyes. When talking about sexual matters he reached automatically for his genital area (even in the courtroom). He was a raw creature, without logic and morals. However, he also lacked logical and moral hypocrisy.

Parental Home and Youth

On 25 December 1921, "Old Haarmann" died, aged 76 in Hannover. Some Hanoverians remembered the miserable, cantankerous and bad tempered old man as an archetype rowdy and miser. He would chase "anything in a skirt," and at night he was to be found rampaging and swanking around the seedy bars of the Old Town. His father too had been a grouser and a drunkard, and there were as many heirs to his ways as there were in Zola's Rougon-Macquarts. "Old Haarmann" had been a railway stoker in his youth but left the service in 1886, having been branded unreliable as the result of an accident in which his train driver was killed. Typically, he sued the railway company, although he could have lived quite comfortably anyway thanks to a marriage of convenience. His wife Johanna Claudius was seven years his senior, and provided him with a dowry of several houses and a small fortune, making him a wealthy citizen in this time of rapid expansion.

He was a wild, quarrelsome, small minded and artful man. His general dissatisfaction worsened when he contracted syphilis in later life and was unable to continue with his womanising (shortly after his marriage there were several occasions on which he took his mistresses to his home). Johanna Claudius was a simple-minded, slightly stupid woman, worn out and old before her time. The birth of her sixth child (the sexual offender) left her sickly and she spent most of her time in bed. Of her six children the eldest son, Alfred, became a decent, lower middle-class factory foreman at the "Continental" works, an upright Philistine and family man. The second son, Wilhelm, was sentenced at an early age for a sexual offence committed on the 12-year-old daughter of a neighbouring innkeeper, and the three daughters, all of whom divorced their respective husbands early in married life, proved to be easily excitable, compulsive creatures. One of the sisters, Frau Rüdiger, died during the war. Haarmann did not get on with the second sister, Frau Erfurdt, and only the youngest sister, Emma, who became Frau Burschel, remained his ally - not that this prevented one of them from prosecuting the other. Haarmann even broke into his sister's tobacconist's shop on various occasions, staging break-ins to which, full of remorse and tearful, he later confessed, or blamed on others.

Friedrich Heinrich Karl Haarmann was born the youngest of six children on 25 October 1879; his mother was 41 at the time of his birth. Little is known of his early years (what is known was obtained mainly from his siblings' stories), but one thing we do know is that the child was spoilt and pampered by his mother. It would be of interest to a psychologist to know that even as a small child he regarded his father (whom he hated and wished dead) as a rival. This loathing of his father continued throughout his life. The two men constantly threatened each other, the father to have his son put in an asylum, the son to have his father thrown in jail for the supposed murder of a train driver. There were physical fights, when each claimed that the other wanted to kill him. However, there were also occasions when they united to carry out some swindle, or to appear in court to exonerate the other. In contrast, the rapture Haarmann felt for his mother was always evident in his relationship towards her, and she was the only person of whom he spoke well and with sentimentality. In all other respects the family unit had broken down. The siblings continued their litigious behaviour towards each other, first over the inheritance from their mother, who died on 5 April 1901, and later over the inheritance from their father.

From anecdotes relating to Haarmann's childhood we can see two distinct traits. To begin with, we know of his feminine (transvestite) tendencies, how he liked playing with dolls, and his passion for needlework, and how he would blush and was easily embarrassed in the company of boys. Secondly, there was his pleasure in causing fear and horror. He would tie up his sisters, and leave dressed dummies lying on stairs to look like bodies; he would tap on people's windows at the dead of night and run away or hide, awakening a dormant fear of ghosts or werewolves. Haarmann started school at Easter in 1886. His teachers described the pretty child as spoilt, mollycoddled, quiet, easily led, generally popular, and dreamy. His behaviour was "exemplary", but his performance was well below average. Twice he had to repeat a school year (in 1888 and 1890). In 1894 he was confirmed as a third-year student in Christ's Church by Pastor Hardelandt. He complained throughout his adult life of the fact that he had had to carry an old hymn book on this occasion, whereas his siblings were all given new ones.

It was decided that he should become apprenticed to a locksmith, but he turned out to be unsuitable for this, and so was sent, together with a number of others, to the training school for non-commissioned officers at Neu-Breisach. He arrived in Neu-Breisach on 4 April 1895: a physically well-developed, strong 16-year-old with a tendency to corpulence, and pretty, regular but expressionless features. He was a good gymnast and an obedient soldier, but on 3

September he was taken to the garrison sick bay with sudden "signs of mental disturbance". He was in fact suffering from periodic lapses in consciousness, or an anxiety neurosis, which was blamed on a concussion contracted whilst performing bar exercises or sun-stroke suffered whilst on exercise. He was released after two weeks as he had shown only temporary signs of hallucination, but was re-admitted on 11 October with renewed signs of disturbance which were described in the medical records as "equivalent to epilepsy". He was discharged on 3 November 1895, having requested his release himself, as he "didn't like it there any more". In 1888 his father had started a small cigar factory and wanted his son to work there. However, the young man had no intention of working for his living, and there were further arguments between father and son.

Meanwhile, Haarmann's sexual development had progressed in bounds. He had been corrupted by an early experience at school (probably when he was around the age of seven), and this turned him into a corruptor of other small boys. His first experience of "love" appears to have been at the age of 16, when one night a 35-year-old mannish woman lured him over the rooftops and into her room through a window. Then started the sexual offences against children of most ages, which became a virtually daily occurrence and continued for the rest of his life. It is regrettable that the pervert was not castrated after his ninth or tenth offence, as this would probably have prevented the murders he carried out in later years.

In July 1896, aged 17, Haarmann was charged, for the first time, with having lured small children into doorways or cellars and performing acts of indecency on them. On 6 February 1897 the Division for Criminal Matters decided to place Haarmann in the "Provinzial-Heil-und-Pflegeanstalt", an asylum in Hildesheim. Here he was found to be suffering from congenital mental deficiency. He was released from theasylum on 25 March 1897 and transferred by the police as "dangerously deranged" to the town hospital in Hannover. In accordance with Para 51 of the Criminal Code criminal proceedings were halted and Haarmann remained in the hospital until 28 May 1897 when at the magistrate's request he was transferred back to the mental asylum in Hannover after having been deemed incurably deranged by the town doctor, Dr Schmalfuß (whom I knew to be a level-headed and conscientious doctor).

Once in the mental asylum, the young man must have suffered some kind of psychic trauma which affected him for the rest of his life. Although I knew Haarmann to be a first-rate actor and never felt inclined to believe more than half of anything he said, I believed his recurring fear of the mental asylum which caused him to plea repeatedly, "Hang me, do anything you like to me, but don't take me back to the loony bin!"

The circle of parasites that in later years took advantage of Haarmann's monomaniacal derangement, hovering around him like hyenas in the wake of a panther, could assume total control over him simply by threatening him with the words, "We'll put you in the mad-house!"

On 13 October he managed to escape from the asylum whilst working in the gardens. However, five days later he was seized at his parents' home and taken back to Hildesheim. He watched and waited, ready to take the first chance to break out again. This presented itself to him when, just before Christmas, he was transferred to the asylum in Langenhagen. Two days later, on 25 December, he escaped again. This time he fled to Switzerland, apparently with his parents' help, where a relative of his mother worked as an artist near Zürich. Needless to say, it is unknown how he managed to obtain the necessary certificate of integrity from the police.

He worked as an odd-job man in a shipyard from May 1898 until March 1899, then for a pharmacist named Dürenberger in Zürich, returning to Hannover in April 1899, where the matter of his escape had been forgotten. He was just 20 years old ....

Haarmann quickly resumed his old ways despite his father's attempts to persuade him to take up some kind of work in his cigar factory. There were fights between Haarmann and his father, in which Haarmann's weak, oppressed mother tried to intervene on her son's behalf. In one of the houses on the Burgstraße owned by old man Haarmann there lived a labourer by the name of Loewert, whose daughter Erna, a large, pretty blonde, was to become Haarmann's "bride". The official engagement was announced on Christmas Day in 1899, with the blessings of both sets of parents, who fervently hoped that this union would put an end to the young layabout's reckless ways. Erna became firm friends with the Haarmann sisters, although the love affair with Haarmann lasted onlythree years. In 1901 she found she was pregnant by the now 25-year-old Haarmann, but arranged for the pregnancy to be terminated by a midwife.

In October 1900 Haarmann was called up for military service. He put an end to his work-shy life, hoping for another chance to become a soldier. On 12 October 1900 he was recruited into Number 10 Rifle Battalion in Bitsch near Colmar. He later spoke of this time as the happiest of his life. His superiors were pleased with him, and his captain, a man named von Gottberg, made him his batman. Lieutenant Fischer said he was "the best marksman in the company".

Haarmann's mother died during his military service, and he travelled to Hannover on leave of absence for her funeral during the Easter holiday in 1901. His father now wanted to put an end to his son's association with Erna Loewert, and wrote to his commanding officer at Bitsch in an attempt to achieve this. However, Haarmann's superiors saw no reason to reprimand the young soldier, who was always so willing to perform his duties.

In the October of that year the company went on exercise and during a particularly strenuous march Haarmann collapsed, after which he suffered dizzy spells and bouts of weakness. As a result, he was admitted to the military hospital at Bitsch on 4 December after"neurasthenia" was diagnosed. A young captain in the medical corps took a fancy to him, and Haarmann spent a little over four months in the hospital. As no one knew quite what to make of his illness, he was transferred to the ward for nervous diseases at military hospital I in Strasbourg on 14 May 1902, where the following diagnosis was made: "The patient has a mental deficiency, which becomes apparent only during systematic examination, as Haarmann otherwise does not give the impression of deficiency. It appears probable that he contracted dementia praecox in 1895, which led to considerable mental deficiency, appearing as congenital idiocy; subsequently there was some improvement. As a result of his mental illness, which has left a certain mental deficiency, Haarmann is to be regarded as unsuitable for service and work."

The 15th Army Corps Command in Strasbourg assumed that Haarmann's earlier illness had been exacerbated by his military service, and in particular by the exertions of the 1901 autumn manoeuvres. Accordingly, by order of 23 July 1902 he was "recognised as being permanently invalided, temporarily unable to work, and permanently unsuitable for use in community service." He was dismissed from the Rifle Battalion in Bitsch on 28 July. According to his transfer records he was regarded as "very good" at his job. Haarmann was now drawing a military pension of 21 German Marks a month, and went to live with his sister, Frau Burschel, in Hannover. His relationship with his father continued where it had left off and in 1902 he sued his father for maintenance, saying that he was unable to work regularly because of his mental state and heart problems, and his military pension was not enough to live on. The father retorted with the remark that his illness was a sham, put on in order to gain release from military service and so continue his relationship with Erna Loewert. He was, so his father said, perfectly fit and healthy; his only problem was that he was too lazy to work. As a result of this, Haarmann's claim for maintenance was rejected. The relationship with his father disintegrated completely, and in February 1903 Haarmann's father initiated legal proceedings against his son, claiming that Haarmann had threatened to beat his father and siblings to death, accused the father of murdering the train driver, Schröder, and had tried to blackmail his brother Alfred. At the same time he applied (contrary to his earlier claims that his son was not really ill) to have his son committed to a mental institute on the grounds of dangerous lunacy. Proceedings were halted on the grounds that, when questioned by the police, the father's statements were not corroborated by the rest of the family. The son now turned the tables on his father and sued him for knowingly making false accusations; when again questioned by the police the siblings now corroborated the father's statements, with the result that these proceedings also had to be dropped. However, as a result of the remarks made by his father concerning his son's mental state, the Hannover police headquarters decided to arrange for Haarmann to be examined by the town doctor, Dr Andrae, who submitted his report on 14 May 1903. In this, he mentioned that "although Haarmann is morally inferior, of little intelligence, idle, rough, irritable and totally egotistical, he is not 'mentally ill' as such, and there is no official reason to have him committed to a lunatic asylum." This action was therefore dropped, and that was how "the Wolf" (at 24 years of age) came to be released into society.

Criminal Career

At first, young Haarmann hid behind his fiancée. With a DM 1500.00 loan from his father he started a fishmongery in Erna's name, which was to keep him. He himself tried his luck as an insurance salesman, but stopped working altogether when, by order of the general commander of the 10th Army Corps in Hannover, he was recognised as being fully disabled and unable to earn his own income; his pension was increased to DM 24 per month. However, by the beginning of 1904 the money he had received from his father had gone and the shop was doing badly. It was at this time that the engagement was called off, which Haarmann explained thus, "I had got Erna pregnant; she was nice to me and wanted to carry on, but I had had enough. She had been with a student called Heinemann. I told her so. She turned nasty and threw me out of the shop, and as it was in her name there was nothing I could do."

The truth of the matter was that Haarmann had contracted gonorrhoea and, as a result of that and his increasing indifference to women, had turned exclusively to male company. However, evidence shows that the first long association with another male was not until the spring of 1905. Haarmann was undoubtedly the passive partner in this affair. His companion (who died in 1916) was forty-year-old Adolf Meil, a count's valet who received a pension from his mistress for having allegedly "helped out" when his master had a stroke in the bath tub, leaving behind a young widow. This is Haarmann's account of the beginning of this association: "I'd been at the fair and was thinking of nothing in particular, when this bloke came up to me. He was wearing glasses. He said ,'Have you been at the fair?' I thought he was a teacher. He took me to the Nelkenstraße. He stopped outside the wreath-binder's in Goslar and said, 'This is where I live.' I went in with him. He made fresh coffee. He kissed me. I was shy. By now it's turned midnight. He said, 'It's late, stay with me.' I did. He did things I'd never imagined. I was frightened. I messed the bed. But later I met hundreds of others like him."

Haarmann managed to avoid justice until 1904, but after he turned 26 he spent one third of the following twenty years either in custody awaiting trial, or in prisons or penitentiaries. There was a rather comical flavour to his first offence. He had read in the paper that the paint manufacturers Laux & Vaubel were looking for an invoice clerk. Although he was not even sure exactly what an invoice clerk was, he sent a glowing application for the job and was invited to an interview. Haarmann promised in all sincerity to do his very best in the job.

Haarmann was tasked with the payment of invoices, but after only a few days his superiors noticed numerous late payments. He apologised, saying he had been ill and promising to improve. There was an apprentice in his office whom he persuaded, with the help of cigarettes and displays of affection, to do his work for him. All Haarmann now had to do was to check the numbers of departing vehicles.

He made friends with the factory cleaner, Frau Guhlisch, an energetic, unprejudiced woman with an equally "unprejudiced" ten-year-old rascal of a son. The three of them formed a kind of pack of thieves. Once work had finished for the day, huge quantities of ultramarine and other paints were removed, with Haarmann working as Frau Guhlisch's "employee" for these exercises. They broke into the lodgings of a neighbour of Frau Guhlisch, and when they had an evening free Haarmann took the young Guhlisch on expeditions to local graveyards, from where they stole necklaces, metals and parts of tombstones.The factory thefts remained undiscovered until after Haarmann had been dismissed as unusable, when customers complained that products which they had purchased when Haarmann was still working for the company suddenly doubled in price once he had left. Between 4 July and 19 October 1904 Haarmann was tried by jury no fewer than four times for grand larceny and embezzlement. Over the following years there was a continuous chain of theft, break-ins, swindling and sexual crimes. Typical of the 20th century penal system, whenever Haarmann was released from jail both his craftiness and his crimes increased.

The preparation that went into his deeds was impressive. For example, there was the occasion when he bought a disinfection system and rented a room, supposedly in order to start up a disinfection business. He then read through the death announcements in the papers and went to the homes of the bereaved, making out he was an "official of the town's disinfection department" and advising people to have the rooms and/or belongings of the deceased disinfected. He then pretended to carry out this work, whereas in reality he used the opportunity for more thieving. If he was offered refreshment he refused, saying innocently, "As an official representative of the council I am not permitted to accept anything." On another occasion he was caught trying to remove a doorknob; his excuse was the knob on his own door was missing and he merely wanted to replace it. His cheek was such that on one occasion, whilst awaiting trial, he stole a jar containing 60 pickled eggs belonging to his landlord. In 1905 Haarmann was sentenced to a total of 13 months' imprisonment. In later years he seemed to carry out or conceal his activities more carefully. As a result of his continued enmity towards his father, who still regarded him as perfctly healthy but workshy and called him a great malingerer, Haarmann was convicted of bodily harm towards his father on 1 November 1906 and sentenced to a month's imprisonment. Their main bone of contention was Haarmann's inheritance from his late mother, which his father claimed he was unable to pay him.

Over the following years there were frequent visits to graveyards, in the company of young Guhlisch (which may have laid the foundation for Haarmann's future indifference when dealing with corpses). Meanwhile, with the help of his brother Alfred, he managed to find a well-paid job at the Continental works.

It may be regarded as Haarmann's good fortune that a year before the outbreak of World War I he was sentenced to five years' imprisonment, thereby managing to spend the war years in prisons in Celle, Lüneburg, Rendsburg and Rawitsch. It is impossible to imagine what deeds could have been perpetrated by someone like Haarmann at a time when the slightest urge to perpetrate evil towards the "enemy" was obeyed. Perhaps this point should also be considered: due to the fact that all available men had been sent to the front, resulting in a labour shortage during the final years of the war, prisoners were released in order to work in the gardens of the manor houses. Haarmann too was released to the property of one Von Hugo, the lord of a manor near Rendsburg. He turned out to be such a success there that the family grew fond of him and did not want him to return to prison. His five-year sentence imposed in 1913 had been under extremely serious circumstances. At the end of 1913 numerous burglaries were carried out in the basement of the elegant area known as the "List". Haarmann was eventually caught trying to break into one of the cellars and arrested. His own cellar was searched, and a huge store of stolen conserves, wine, eggs and meat products found. For some considerable time he had been providing his landlady and his 17-year-old friend Fritz Algermissen with goods, either as gifts or at very low prices, explaining that he was a chemist at the Continental factory and ran an agency for foodstuffs. In spite of strong evidence in ten other cases of serious theft Haarmann swore "by God and on my mother's grave, I swear I am innocent," but refused to appeal when sentenced to five years' imprisonment. Between 1905 and 1912 he spent only a few months out of prison. It was strange that although Haarmann himself admitted that his sexual offences against boys and young men increased to the point where they were practically a daily occurrence as soon as he was released, he was rarely convicted of such misdemeanours, usually because his partners were too ashamed to report him to the police. In 1911 the fathers of four little boys combined and reported him for misdemeanours perpetrated against their sons in contravention of Para175 of the German Civil Code. The proceedings were called off as the boys' statements did not corroborate. However, the most appalling case must have been that of November 1912 when he was sentenced to two months' imprisonment: whilst walking down the street he had approached a completely unknown 13-year-old boy and promised him money if he went home with him, warning him not to tell his parents. His intent was to drag the boy off home and perpetrate homosexual acts against him.

This incident had already been recorded when Haarmann was released from prison in April 1918 to surface briefly in Berlin and then again in Hannover. This was when the first murders took place - more correctly, the first of which he could be proven guilty, although it was to be another six years before this actually happened.

The Revolution 1918/19

Haarmann described the time after his release from Rawitsch prison thus: "After I was released from the clink I went to Berlin, but there was not much happening there so I went back to Hannover. I went straight to Emma's. Her youngest said to me, 'Don't eat so much bread, Uncle. We have to queue for it, and we're all ill.' So I said to him, 'Let me see what I can do, little one.' I went straight to the station. Emma had given me some money. That's where the pushers are. We nicked stuff, all we needed. We got nice and fat again. Emma sold some stuff. But then old man Haarmann went to the landlord, and he split on me. So Emma said, 'Fritz, you'd better go again.'"

Once again circumstances were such that Haarmann was able to give free rein to his old wild urges. The large entrance hall of the main railway station in Hannover became his headquarters, where there was soon a thriving industry dealing in stolen and illegally slaughtered meat and other consumable goods which were unobtainable but indispensable in Germany. In April 1918 Haarmann rented, ostensibly for office purposes, a shop with a small room at the back from a widow, Frau Schildt, at no. 27 Cellerstraße. He furnished the room sparsely with a few pieces of furniture. At first he stayed with his sister, Frau Burschel, but moved into the small room behind the shop at the end of August and started up his "business", which the other residents found increasingly curious and sinister. There was a constant flow of young people in and out of the rooms, carrying sacks of meat. At night the neighbours could hear sawing and banging from the room at the back and assumed that Haarmann was dealing with the meat he had "hamstered" with his illicit trading.

Next to Haarmann's "shop" was a vegetable shop owned by a rather nervous woman, Frau Seemann, whose relationship with Haarmann was somewhat precarious to begin with, but who also managed occasionally to obtain some illicit items at good prices from Haarmann's stream of visitors. This timid woman was probably the first person to have a vague idea of the murderous deeds being perpetrated in the neighbouring rooms. Once when she heard Haarmann hacking away next door she knocked at the wall and called out, "Any chance of anything for me?" Haarmann called back, "Not this time, but maybe next." On another occasion he gave her a sack of bones. "I made brawn from them, but then I thought, they look so white, I'm not touching that." It was to be another six years before it became obvious that at least two people had been murdered in this little room on the Cellerstraße: Hermann, the 14-year-old son of G. Koch, a bicycle dealer, and Friedel, the 16-year-old son of a publican. Although it is not certain whether Haarmann used their flesh in his butchery dealings (possibly a final vestige of human decency prevented him from confessing to this ultimate atrocity), it is certain that his urge to kill struck before 1923, and that he murdered on several occasions between 1918 and 1923. These deeds never came to light. Haarmann, who otherwise had excellent powers of recollection, was as unable to recall the number of his victims as he was their faces (as indeed he was able to push all unpleasant facts from his consciousness). When asked for the total numbers of times he had killed he would answer abruptly, “Maybe thirty, maybe forty; I don’t know.” He confessed only to those crimes for which there was evidence against him, and told the public prosecutor with satisfied derision, “There are some you don’t know about, but it’s not those you think.”

Police Statements

The full horror of the years 1918 - 1924 will be revealed during the trial. However, we must remember what legal and police conditions throughout Europe were at the time, in the days when over a million people starved to death before the eyes of the supposedly “cultured populace”. Germany was without an army. Its proletarian youth had run wild, had been used and abused for many years, and suddenly found itself without reservations and guidance. The populace fought back. Political murder became commonplace. The Treaty of Versailles reduced police power (constabulary, security police and the criminal investigation department), leaving the police forces unable to cope with the returning masses now no longer accustomed to settled forms of respectable existence. The lower police team, whose pay lay between the 4th and 7th salary brackets, consisted of men who spent several nights a week on the streets until 4 a.m., only to return to duty at 9 a.m., who were so badly paid that help and gifts of any kind were received with increasing gratitude - even those received from criminal hands. Superhuman feats were demanded of these justifiably bitter, poorly educated subordinates. The department dealing with sexual crimes consisted in Haarmann’s days of 12 detectives and one superintendent, tasked with supervising approximately 4000 female (of which only 400 were registered whores) and at least 300 male prostitutes. The amount of money provided by the state for police investigations into missing persons was (and is) so derisory that it was impossible to mount a thorough search into disappearances. Any clues in connection with Haarmann’s victims were usually found by private detectives, or else by the missing person's own dependents. The fault undoubtedly lay with the system, and not with individuals. It is clear, though, that in those uncontrollable times the police forces were more dependant than ever on the goodwill and assistance of the "public", and that if no help or assistance were forthcoming they would have to get what help they could from the criminals themselves. "Helpers" of this type were referred to as police informers, snoopers or snitches, and their role was that of a spy in war. They were used and abused.

Between the years of 1918 and 1924 Haarmann regularly provided the police with information, and proved to be particularly usable and useful (particularly in the raid on a pack of criminals involved in counterfeit money; in the investigatiion into the theft of drive belts, and even searching for missing persons). We shall see just how much at home this man was in both worlds, now passing one of his (male) lovers or mates into police hands, and then using his police connections to help the criminal fraternity or, more usually, in his own carefully guarded murderous urges. Almost all his crimes were facilitated by the fact that he became a trustworthy, semi-official person in the eyes of the naïve people (who at the time regarded a policeman as a kind of judge), and particularly in the eyes of inexperienced youngsters aged between 14 and 18 (whom he generally seduced). He scoured the station waiting rooms virtually every night, which he was able to enter as he pleased (thanks to unofficial, or - as many witnesses stated - official police identification), although at night access was normally only granted to passengers in possession of a valid ticket. He was also allowed to pass freely through barriers, as the rail officials recognised him. He would approach young people in transit, or others milling around the station, check their papers, ask them where they were going, and occasionally inform the authorities (railway attendants, security and CID personnel) of anything or anyone suspicious. There were even occasions on which he made telephone calls from the attendant's office and questioned people. Any boys he liked (homeless, runaways, unemployed) were offered food, work and accommodation; they stayed with him for a night, or several nights, when he seduced them and then murdered them in sexual passion.

As he was aware of the regulations, read the wanted persons lists, knew the dates and times of planned raids in advance, and generally behaved like a member of the CID, it was easy for him to protect his favourites and shelter them from the police. By the same token, any who teased or irritated him, or failed to take him seriously, were passed on to the police. The authorities hid the fact that Haarmann used the police (and that he was often used for cheap laurels by the lower officials) behind a veil of silence as successfully as the incredible spying and lying system of the war years was concealed. It was not unusual for a criminal to be used as a "henchman" and become well known to the authorities, but if this person then misused the trust shown in him the institutions withdrew and a public declaration was made: "This man's position was not official; he received no pay; he had no official means of indentification, in short, the authority does not know him." Informers, sneaks, whatever they were called, were not "official". The authorities and the criminal world oblige each other in numerous ways, most being riskier and more dangerous than honest employment. The word "authority" is simply a word, behind which stands human beings.

The truth of the matter is that Haarmann's activities between 1918 and 1924 were possible only because he was under constant police supervision and because no one could imagine such a well-trusted, generally popular, friendly person to be the perpetrator of the most heinous crimes imaginable. If I too were to conceal this fact here, I would be unable to explain the crime. This is the area to which we must give prominence: Haarmann's police activities.

The Sexual Offences

Despite the fact that Haarmann was reported to the police by friends and neighbours on numerous occasions, his many murders remained undiscovered until 1924. Despite increasing suspicion, something else became more and more obvious during the repeated house searches: Haarmann, the habitual criminal, who was constantly surrounded by young people whom he used, or by whom he was used, indulged in every conceivable sexual deviation. His rooms were searched for the missing Rothe in October 1918, and although the boy was not found, a different youngster was there, completely naked in Haarmann's bed. He approached the boys, gave them food and then took them home, where he paid them to perform unspeakable deeds. As Haarmann confessed to other cases of this type, criminal proceedings were initiated against him in October 1918 for assault and battery, which culminated in a nine-month prison sentence in April 1919.

The apartment on the Cellerstraße had meanwhile become too "hot" for him, and he moved to no. 15 Seydlitzstraße at the beginning of December 1918 where he rented other accommodation from a Frau Hederich. He told her he wanted the rooms to store "cigars, chemicals and other things". It was Haarmann's custom to keep a young person as a "general factotum", who kept the rooms clean and tidy and generally performed all the tasks normally expected of a girl. An impoverished young labourer named Friedrich Oswald whom Haarmann picked up at the railway station was taken to the flat and given his own room. As well as keeping house for Haarmann, he was also expected to work for a tobacconist who was a friend of Haarmann's sister, and with whom Haarmann was enjoying a shady friendship. Before long, this flat too was searched by the police when Haarmann was suspected of having killed young Koch, the schoolboy who had been missing since September 1918. However, again the proceedings had to be dropped, although it was established that Haarmann had committed perverted sexual offences against very young boys. He was detained between 2 June and 19 July, but then the proceedings had to be dropped in accordance with Para 175 as the boys' stories changed from their original statements. Before the main hearing in this case, the public prosecutor's office arranged for Haarmann to be examined by the court doctor in order to establish his mental state, Haarmann having claimed at his previous trial, when he was sentenced to nine months' imprisonment, that he was not responsible for his actions and was suffering from epilepsy.

The forensic doctor, Dr Brandt, submitted his report on 12 June 1919, stating that Haarmann was not mentally ill and should be held fully responsible for all of his crimes, particularly the sexual offences.The report was based largely on information given by Haarmann himself, although he had omitted to mention the years he had already spent in a mental institution.

As this apartment was also becoming too "hot", Haarmann moved out in September 1919 and into new accommodation belonging to a Frau Kroell who lived at no. 13 Nikolaistraße. His associations with young people continued. His landlady realised what unspeakable deeds were being perpetrated here and insisted on his moving out immediately. He moved into a different flat on the same street. It was at this time, the beginning of October 1919, that the friend entered Haarmann's life with whom he was to spend the rest of it.

More about the Psychology

We have learnt that in June 1919 the Hannoverian forensic specialist declared Haarmann to be "sound of mind" and "fully responsible for his actions". This report is in marked contrast to the one submitted to the Hannover State Benefit Department by the nerve specialist, Dr Bartsch, on 18 December 1922. Haarmann had been sent to see this specialist by the State Benefit Department with a view to continuing or increasing his invalidity pension. Dr Bartsch decided that the patient had an "extreme mental deficiency" (although he arrived at this view after only a short discussion and IQ test), and actually suggested Haarmann's brother have his "mentally deficient" brother declared incapable of managing his own affairs. It appears likely that the court experts at the subsequent trial (the two court doctors from Hannover and the psychiatry professor in Göttingen) tried to make it seem as if the reports submitted by the psychiatrists in Hildesheim and Langenhagen in 1899, those submitted by the military doctors in 1898 and 1902, and latterly Dr Bartsch's report of 1922, were based on "hysterical simulation" resulting initially from Haarmann's attempts at gaining release from military service, and then his endeavours to be awarded the highest possible pension.

So let us put aside for now the questions of "compos mentis", of "responsibility" and of "madness". Readers must be warned against regarding complicated matters as simple and simple matters as complicated, which medical psychology with its obsession with incorporation and integration and "clinical pictures" and its hard-to-define and aged Greek-Latin expressions (schizophrenic, cyclothymic, hysterical, dementia praecox etc.) cannot help but do. The fact that the emotions of the "superstructure/ego" are in perfect order does not exclude the possibility that the underworld of the soul can be leading its own life with no regard to reason and insight. Illness is not always of a positive nature; it is often only felt as a sense of loss or failure, or as dissociation. The fact that a person simulatesmadness or mental deficiency or hides behind illness does not rule out the possiblity that he may indeed be mad or mentally deficient - indeed, simulated madness (as in *Hamlet*) may cover up a true madness in the way that the simulation of an illness may in itself be the real illness. The merging and overlapping of actual and imagined experiences tends, even in the simplest creature of instinct, to be far more intricate than we suspect. In order to fully understand the following, and in order to understand it so that it will still apply after a hundred years (when today's psychiatry and scientific psychology will have dated), we must agree, soul to soul, to empathise and imagine, leaving behind premature phraseology and scientific explanations. However, it is also essential that we seek no analogies and parallels to the strangest crime of our time, and above all avoid the unbearable "sexual-pathological" prattle about sadism and masochism and so forth. The criminal case of the Marquis de Sade (who had a perverse desire to torment, and bathed in hot baths prepared with the blood of gruesomely martyred children) bears not the slightest resemblance to the Haarmann case, as Haarmann was not ruled by the urge to torment others, but by the urge to kill at the height of his sexual desire, followed by the dark secret of tearing and devouring the flesh of his victims. To dispose of other, stronger life, or be destroyed by this stronger life; to give oneself to death, or to assimilate the other with its killing; to devour and be devoured, these are the two polar axes of the entire cosmic game of life; little is explained by deeming first one pole, and then the other, degenerate in the one-sided excess of erotic power. If a temporary formula is required for what is contained on the following pages, then one should call to mind the age-old Germanic myths of the wolf-figure which became human, the "proto-evil"; the legend of the werewolf (the loupgaron of the Romantics, the Anglo-Saxon werewolf), the "bullet-proof" monster, defenceless only when confronted by holy hands, cursed to bite through the throats of children and to tear them to pieces. Recall the forgotten tales of primeval times, of dragons and dinosaurs ..... think of the lecherous Blutschink that still lives in the Paznauertal, rising from the sea at night to search for its victims whose blood it must suck. Think of the nightmares about our forests; the bloodthirsty Ludak of the Finns and Lapps. The ancient world referred to these murderous creatures as lycanthropes; the following is a case of lycanthropy.

It is most peculiar that in the days when the Haarmann case was being investigated a second case of anthropophagy (cannibalism) should have come to light. In a small apartment block near Münsterberg on the Breslau-Glatz route in Silesia there lived for many years a farmer by the name of Karl Denke, a 54-year-old recluse well known and respected in the parish as a devout church-goer. On 21 December 1924 a travelling journeyman named Vincenz Oliver asked Denke for alms, and was invited into the house. As soon as Oliver had sat down at the table Denke attacked him with a pick-axe, but Oliver managed to escape. Denke was arrested, but hanged himself in in his cell whilst awaiting trial. The police then searched Denke's farmstead, and found papers belonging to numerous journeymen. In the barn they found pots containing salted meat which forensic doctors confirmed was undoubtedly human flesh.

Denke had, over at least 20 years, killed a great number of people, young girls and boys, and devoured or sold the flesh at the market.

The Friend

Picture a tough, wily edible crab in the bottom of the ocean, lodged in the dark cavern of a slimy giant polyp, and you will have an idea of the strange symbiosis of compulsive crime and parasitic intelligence, of madness of mind and spiritual parasitism which irrevocably bound together Hans Grans, young, gentle, and girlish, and the effeminate, rough, bloated Haarmann, Grans's senior by 22 years.

Grans was a pretty, self-centred youngster from a large family with more than its fair share of problems and worries. His parents' small book-binding business and library of old books was in the darkest part of the Altstadt, the Old Town. Hans devoured the books with rapture, and his desire for glamour and the big life increased with each tacky novel. After his second year at secondary school he was moved back to primary school and confirmed in 1915. Whilst apprenticed in a metal works he was already embezzling petty cash and taking forged receipts to the company's clients for payment, and then using the cash for sweets and cigarettes.

The optimistic little good-for-nothing then worked for various industries in and around Hannover and for the Bergmann Electricity Corporation in Berlin. In 1918 he joined the post office as a temporary worker but left after a short while to join up with the Mortar Storm Troopers in Heuschkel, who discharged him on 1 October 1919 for unpunctuality. He returned to his parents, telling them that he intended to join the German Army, but in reality he spent his time in female company. When his father checked whether the boy had applied to join the Army, Hans ran away from home, spending his nights in the dives of the Altstadt and earning his living by selling old clothes on the station. That was how he entered Haarmann's region. One of the other youngsters at the station drew Hans's attention to the "queer".

"Hey, Hans, the other day that queer gave a pretty boy 20 Marks," and young Grans, with the sole intent of earning himself some money, approached the much older man, who took young Hans back to his apartment at no. 46 Nikolaistraße near Kisserow.

"I was crazy about Hans at first. But when I saw him naked I didn't fancy him any more. He's as hairy as an ape. Honestly, believe me; he looked just like an ape. But later he shaved it all off."

The boy stayed with Haarmann and an unusual relationship developed. "He was like my own child; I looked after him like a son. I pulled him out of the ditch and tried to make sure he wouldn't go to the dogs." The two remained together for four years, although Haarmann obviously denied that he was keeping the boy. From time to time he would give Grans English cigarettes to sell; if he could get more for them than Haarmann billed him, Grans was allowed to keep the "profit" for himself. The relationship was undoubtedly sexual, but was also more than that. The ideals that surfaced in Haarmann's deepest soul concerned young Grans, and if it was claimed that it was merely the knowledge that Grans knew of Haarmann's evil deeds and a fear of being given away by him that kept Haarmann enslaved in the power of his young, inconsiderate tormentor and beloved tyrant in later years, it must also be remembered that Haarmann could have disposed of the little upstart at any time, as he possibly did with other accessories to his murders (one often threatened to report the other to the police, and on several occasions they faced each other with knives at the ready shouting "Murderer" at each other, but always crawling back together again).

Judge and jury had a straightforward understanding of the relationship: "Grans knew of the first murder, the killing of Friedel Rothe, and in order to keep an accessory's silence Haarmann took Grans in and became his foster father." We shall see that these two creatures, balanced on the edge of human society, were bound together by improbably complicated emotions and were capable neither of living together fully, nor of survival without the other. At the time Haarmann took his young boyfriend in he was about to start the nine months in jail to which he had been sentenced on 23 April 1919. In order to avoid this, he quickly moved addresses, omitting to re-register with the police. He spent the December and January living in lodgings belonging to a widow, Frau Birnstiel, on the Fusilierstraße; Grans moved to the nearby Bronsartstraße.

Haarmann had several disagreements with Frau Birnstiel, and when he physically abused her she reported him to the police, whereupon he was arrested and detained to serve his nine-month sentence. He remained in jail until 3 December 1920, during which time (from March until December 1920) young Grans was left to his own devices. He hung around in questionable company and was reported several times for theft and once for unnatural sexual acts, but each time proceedings had to be dropped due to insufficient evidence. Finally, on 27 November he was arrested for trying to sell a misappropriated bicycle on the "market" run by receivers of stolen goods on the Hohe Ufer. He was released on 1 December as there were no grounds for suspecting he would abscond, and two days later Haarmann returned from prison. They celebrated their reunion in their local, the "Dicker Fritz", but then on 5 March 1921 Grans was arrested for receiving stolen goods and sentenced to three weeks' imprisonment; he received a conditional three-year suspended sentence.Between December 1920 and the end of August 1921 there followed a period of uninterrupted bliss. Appearing on the outside as two well-dressed, decent gentlemen, they stayed at first in a private hotel which was under religious management, and later rented lodgings in a small, middle-class inn, the "Fürst zur Lippe" on the Osterstraße. Here these apparently upright citizens lived a good life, telling people they ran a draper's shop. It was quite touching when the inn-keeper, a Herr Wiedemann, and his daughter, a Frau Koch, appeared in court and stated that it was impossible to think anything wicked of these noble and kind gentlemen. When the two men returned from their day's work in the evening they always brought a little toy or some sweets for Frau Koch's three-year-old daughter, and even when it was discovered, after the two "noble" gentlemen moved out of the inn, that all the laundry had disappeared, no one could imagine Herr Haarmann and his young "employee" having done the deed. In reality, however, their "business" consisted of Herr Haarmann begging items of laundry from the houses in the smarter areas of town with stories such as he was a needy war invalid exiled from Upper Silesia collecting items for the "Herberge zur

Heimat", supposedly a hostel for exiles, or he was looking after his 76-year-old father, and more of the same. He would ask politely whether it would be possible for him to buy any old items of clothing or laundry they may have; usually he was given all sorts of things which Grans would then take and sell to the junk dealers on the Burgstraße. Disposing of the day's acquisitions in this way usually provided them with a daily income of between DM 30 and DM 60, of which Grans spent his share on women and card games. In between these times they would perform "guest appearances" in Hamburg or Berlin.

They were eventually arrested on 10 January 1921, but Grans managed to lie his way out whilst Haarmann was sentenced to three weeks' imprisonment for begging. As the newspapers now contained warnings about the two swindlers they had to change their approach: Haarmann went into back yards and gardens to steal washing from the lines, Grans then unpicked the initials and sold the laundry. On 31 August 1921 they were again caught red-handed, and again the cunning fox managed to wriggle out, whereas the old wolf was sentenced to six months'imprisonment, which he served between November 1921 and March 1922 at the Jägerheide Prisoner Labour Camp on the Müggenberger Moor near Celle.

Prior to this the two men moved apartments again; this time to the house at no. 8 Neue Straße - the house where the majority of crimes were committed. At the heart of the haunted area!

Psychological Comments

There is a story about a pillar of capitalist society who was honoured by the mayor and other council representatives on the occasion of his 70th birthday. After the officials had their say the septuagenarian opened his speech of thanks with the following words, "I thank you, gentlemen, for the honours you have bestowed on me. You are correct: I have lived amongst you now for forty years - and you can't prove a thing!"

This is a picture of an archetypal civilised society, its head in the ground, honourable and upright on the surface. Grans was such a creature, his soulless intellect devoted to himself and his own survival, but no different to that educated but doomed civilisation that lived off the marrow of the earth, semi-aware of the hypocrisy but not really seeing it. Entire plant and animal worlds and millions of people were sacrificed, children withered away at looms, in mines, at machines; wherever you looked, "civilisation" was surviving off the life of something else, but mankind was an ostrich, pretending it was not its concern.

Grans understood Haarmann's wild, sick urges and realised that he could thereby ensure his own power and control over his much older companion. There is no doubt that he was fond of his "silly old fool," and that he was very grateful to him, for Haarmann provided him with somewhere to stay, with a home. And above all, Haarmann was a cunning teacher, an experienced swindler who had seen life. Still, Grans occasionally felt sympathy for the older man who had put himself at the mercy of the youngster with an unscrupulous craving for life; needing, in the cold hell of his loneliness, someone to love.

"I had to have someone I meant everything to. Hans often laughed at me. Then I got mad and threw him out. But I always ran after him and fetched him back. I couldn't help it; I was crazy about the boy."

Haarmann did love Grans, and Grans took advantage of it. Whenever the older man was in one of his rages, the younger boy would hold him around the waist and put his tongue in the older man's mouth. This turned Haarmann to putty, and he submitted totally to the boy. Hans would also permit Haarmann to kiss him, always making sure he held the older man tightly by the arms, as he knew of Haarmann's tendency, when gripped by passion, to go for the neck, to suck at it and choke his partner. Grans was the cleverer by far; tough but gentle, girlish, but with an iron taciturnity. Before embarking on their riskier escapades he would have to resort to "Dutch courage" and was often blind drunk, whereas Haarmann avoided alcohol, to which he was over-sensitive and which made him tired.

There are two typical traits to Grans's character. A born pimp, he was always surrounded by a number of girls who were in love with him and had to obtain money for him. On one occasion, he told a pretty, young creature about to go out with an engineer to take the unsuspecting man's wallet and give it to him, Grans. When the theft was found out only the girl could be punished: Hans swore she had given him the wallet as a gift.

During the inflation, when there was a thriving market for stolen goods on the island near the "Hohe Ufer", there was much trafficking in stolen silver and gold. Grans took this opportunity to obtain items in fake gold and silver ("rip-off goods") from two large companies, and then joined the group of thieves. If there were any arrests, the whole group was liable to be punished - with the exception of Grans, as he was able to prove that his goods had been purchased legitimately. The fact that he was able to sell his goods at a higher price was evidence of people's stupidity; the others may have been selling real gold, but it was stolen. He was offering fake jewellery, but at least it had been purchased "legitimately".

Hugo

During the course of some of the illegal dealings at the railway station, Grans made a second friend in an extremely talented youngster who had also opted for street trading: Hugo Wittkowski. He was a charming, dark-haired boy; slim and nimble, with lively but somewhat dreamy eyes, a sensual mouth and an intelligent face. Haarmann grew to loathe Wittkowski, who was far more dexterous and generally a "deeper" character than the older man, for a variety of reasons. The initial reason was jealousy: Wittkowski "alienated" Grans from Haarmann, and the two younger men took advantage of Haarmann; they would borrow money from him and either not repay him at all, or else pay back tiny amounts at irregular intervals. The main reason, however, was that Wittkowski (who had absolutely no homosexual inclinations) brought a large entourage of women into Haarmann's apartment. Two years later the three men appeared in court together. Haarmann had hatched a devilish plan (which the court was appallingly slow to uncover) to cause the deaths of all three of them, himself and the two younger men: the one he loved above all others, and the one he hated more than anyone else. On this occasion, Haarmann hissed at Wittkowski, "You've always been after me! You offered yourself to me hundreds of times! But I didn't want you. You're not good enough for me," to which the other man replied mockingly, "I only love women."

The House of Murder: No. 8 Neue Straße

Haarmann heard from an acquaintance of Wittkowski, a man by the name of Alwin Köhler, that Köhler had a room somewhere which he had used for storage purposes and no longer required. The landlady, an elderly spinster by the name of Rehbock (who shortly afterwards married a Herr Daniels) did not hesitate to let the room to Haarmann from 1 July 1921. Haarmann told her he also intended to use the room for storage purposes, and that "his young man" (Grans) would be sleeping in the room for security reasons.

The old house was situated beside the river. It had a wide gateway leading past the house to the yard and neighbouring outhouses. Haarmann's room was directly to the right of the entrance to this gateway. Next to the room was a staircase leading to the upper floors. The room faced the road and had two high windows which were separated by a narrow pillar. A wardrobe measuring 1.9 x 1.25 x 1 m had been built into the space beneath the stairs in the wall opposite the windows, which was the wall between the room and the staircase. This was where the corpses were kept. Later, one of the boards was removed from this wall cupboard and sent for forensic tests: there were plenty of traces of human blood on it. Above the cupboard and directly beneath the ceiling - the room was 3 m high - was a window, 30 cm high and 60 cm wide, through which it was possible to see into the room from the landing. Next to the door to the corridor was a gas stove, behind that, in the window corner, the gas meter. A labourer's family by the name of Bertram lived on the opposite side of the gateway. The house was densely populated: the lavatories were situated in the right hand corner of the yard, and there was a water pump against the wall in front of them. The River Leine flowed along the far wall of the house, so Haarmann was unable to reach it from his room.

When he moved in on 1 July 1921 all he had with him was a rickety bed and a wash stand; the landlady had left a few items of furniture in the room. Haarmann and Grans used the room together as a living room, much to the displeasure of the unobliging landlady. However, Haarmann disappeared on 31 August, leaving Grans on his own in the room. Grans told the landlady that "his boss" had gone away on business; later his story was that "the boss has gone on a rest-cure to Jägerheide" [a spa town]. In reality Haarmann was serving his six-month suspended sentence in Jägerheide.

During this period Grans lived it up in the disreputable room, which became a dosshouse for young hookers looking for business in the low dives: Dörchen, Elli and Anni. The hookers were only too pleased to pay Grans "room money". Down-and-outs of all kinds passed through the room; there were drinking sessions and knife fights and scenes with the landlady, who wrote to complain to Haarmann in the "sanatorium" in Jägerheide. Haarmann wrote back in indignation, asking the landlady to look after his "young man" until his, Haarmann's, return and to keep things in order. On his return Haarmann would chase the young man away for his disgusting behaviour. At the same time, Haarmann was conducting an exchange of correspondence of a more tender tone with Grans. However, the landlady had finally had enough of the goings-on, and at the end of February 1922 she threw Grans out and locked him out. Haarmann returned on 1 March 1922. He broke into his room and found it empty. Grans and Wittkowski had taken and sold everything that had been in the room, and had even drawn out and frittered away Haarmann's military pension. Fortunately, the landlady had removed her furniture in time and stored it safely. Haarmann ranted and raved and cursed to the empty room; Frau Rehbock then insisted that he too leave, and when he refused she went to the arbitration services - who, after Haarmann had submitted several skilful, well-written petitions, sided with him and he was able to stay in the room, against the landlady's wishes, until June 1923.

Haarmann's first problem was to furnish the room. His brother Alfred gave him a small amount of money as a part payment of their mother's legacy with which Haarmann bought some furniture. Shortly afterwards Grans reappeared on the scene, and in spite of his previous activities was given a warm welcome. He stayed with Haarmann until 9 April, but was then put in prison from 9 April until 30 July. It should not be supposed that their life was particularly dismal; it was in fact a lively, eventful, idyllic time. There was a constant stream of young boys and youths in and out; schoolboys, homeless, unemployed, runaways, and visitors from the hostel "zur Heimat". There was much bartering, dealing, drinking, singing and feasting. Haarmann was regarded by all as a good protector and "youth hostel" warden. In the cupboard under the stairs where he hid the dead bodies, there were pots with meat, sweets of all kind, cheeses, cold meats and chocolates for his pretty boys - next to the current corpse. Often, three or four would spend the night, fornicating in turn. Elli, Dörchen and Anni were regular visitors. Dörchen, an energetic and resolute little thing who was beautiful (in spite of the syphilis and the whoring) kept house for Haarmann; she tidied the room, made coffee or chocolate for whoever was there, and spent many long afternoons sitting on Haarmann's bed, talking to him. "Herr Haarmann could do anything. We darned socks together and patched our clothes. He could even make brawn and sausages. If we were sewing or darning we would smoke cigars; Herr Haarmann would hold me round the waist and tell me, 'Dörchen, you're the greatest! I'll marry you yet, you'll see.' But he was only joking, because he didn't really want me - he only liked the boys."

But there were days and nights when Haarmann would let no one into his room and sent visitors away. On these occasions the two windows facing the street and the landing window were carefully covered, and the keyhole in the door was plugged; this was when he was busy dissecting a corpse. Needless to say, it is difficult to understand why no one else in the over-crowded environment (in particular the three whores and the stream of boys) did not become suspicious. But bear this in mind: there were many other things going on at the same time, and there was no reason to suspect murder. The criminal's sexual preferences and thefts were common knowledge on the "island", so much so that the street urchins, Hannover's "Buttjers" [kids] and "Binken" [fools], would call out rude names after him, such as "Pittenwieser" , or would offer themselves to him for money, "Fritz, let's do it! Fritz, take me too! Fritz, what'll you give me for it?"

Haarmann remained at liberty from 1 March 1922 until June 1924 (thanks, perhaps, to his activities on behalf of the police), and over these two years he enjoyed an excellent income. To begin with, on receipt of a certificate from Dr Bartsch (who declared him an invalid and unable to work) social services increased his military pension. He then started doing the rounds of the houses with his certificate of disability and introduced himself, in a modest and friendly manner, as a "buyer of used clothing." He was always given a vast number of items, including, on one occasion, five pairs of boots from the same person. These clothes were then sold on to Jews by the "Pupenjungens" [lover boys], but mainly by Hans Grans. Haarmann's busy career as a criminal flourished in the years 1922 to 1924 (when he also received his share of his mother's legacy). One of the Hannover police force's best police officials, Inspector Müller, became Haarmann's special benefactor. Müller subsequently said that he had judged Haarmann to be a tactful, thoroughly nice person and had tried to help him to lead a better life after his release from jail; he had indeed been like a father to him at times, while Haarmann, outdoing society's own hypocrisy, played the repentant lamb and reformed sheep.

Haarmann performed his services for Müller in the following way: he would find out from his numerous contacts amongst all kinds of dubious characters when a robbery had taken place in the criminal quarter and arrange for the thieves to go to his "cavern" on the Neue Straße, saying he would stash the stolen goods away there for them, or offering to buy them. However, he would secretly pass this information on to the inspector, who would despatch some guards to Haarmann's apartment at the given hour, raid the place and return to the police station with the perpetrators in handcuffs. For appearances' sake, Haarmann too would be handcuffed and arrested so that his treachery was completely concealed from the criminal fraternity. Conversely, he would use his police knowledge to help the "darlings" he picked up at the railway station or in the hostels on his night-time journeys around the town, telling them to "stick with me if you've been up to mischief." He would also pass useful tips on to the dealers and thieves in the Altstadt, the old part of the town, and was indeed a kind of custodian of the law and information office for all criminal matters. The only difference between Haarmann and the lower police officials was that he was ... more intelligent.

There was a barber's shop near Haarmann's apartment where the entire neighbourhood went to be shaved and prettified, and all sorts of little dealings were arranged "en passant". Fridolin Wegehenkel, a tall, blond, weedy man with a serious, worried expression, and his wife Josephine, née Gerke, 48 years of age, and their married daughter, Frau Stille, formed the nucleus of Haarmann's "family contacts". Christmas and New Year were celebrated with the Wegehenkels. Haarmann, Hans and Hugo sang "Silent Night" at Wegehenkel's and lit the candles on the Christmas tree. Wegehenkel's shop was where they made their rendezvous and where they met to chat at midday. Madame Wegehenkel, a sweet, suffering, sickly person, slowly became Haarmann's confidante. She acted as a commission agent for the brisk business in old and new boys' and youths' clothing - which was an excellent way of disposing of the dead boys' belongings. Haarmann would also give one victim's clothes to the next, thereby successfully covering his traces. The whole area regarded him as a benefactor of the homeless, and being generally aware of his homosexual tendencies, tended not to ask the origins of the coats, jackets, trousers and underwear he provided on a daily basis. No one imagined that they originated from a succession of murders, so we shall accept that no one in this dreary world realised what Haarmann was up to in his cavern. However, it is equally certain that no one wanted to know what was going on and that it was in everyone's best interest not to look too closely - making everyone in the neighbourhood a kind of accessory. Haarmann was regarded by one and all as a "gentleman" who helped them to earn money in these needy times, who helped them in numerous little swindles and shady dealings (and they all had something to hide), and who, as they were all aware, had free access to the police station - he even received visits from important people such as Detective Superintendents Müller and Olfermann. On one occasion, a young lad offered a ham for sale in Wegehenkels' shop which he had obviously obtained illegally. Soulful Madame Wegehenkel sent him to "the criminal Haarmann", who interrogated the young thief and confiscated the ham, which Wegehenkels cut into joyfully for "Whitsun, when the cuckoo calls". Haarmann was furious when they omitted to share it with him. On another occasion hundreds of bags of flower seeds were offered for sale and again "the criminal Haarmann" appeared at the right time and confiscated them, whereupon the young thieves disappeared hastily.

So should it be surprising that the Wegehenkel couple, who incidentally also pulled the occasional fast one on Haarmann, turned a blind eye to the rumblings that there may be something seriously amiss in Haarmann's activities? Haarmann's hour of glory struck when he himself became the head of a detective agency, in effect an independent police force, which happened thus. A large manufacturer of office books, Edler & Krische, was commissioned by the German Reichsbank to print paper money during the period of inflation. Somehow some of the paper went missing and was subsequently used to forge DM 50 notes which suddenly turned up within the company. The company turned to the "Detective Agency of Former Police Commissioners," which was headed by Border Police Commissioner Olfermann, for help in solving the mystery. He was tasked with finding the forgers and advised to contact Haarmann, who had proved so helpful as an informer on earlier occasions. Haarmann provided Olfermann with some useful tips with the result that Olfermann decided to retain the contact.

No other character involved in the criminal proceedings made quite the same impression as Police Commissioner Olfermann (retd.), who was civil servant to a Herr von Willms and head of the detective agency "Heimschutz" which was founded by the "Niedersächsische Adelsbund" [the nobility of Lower Saxony]. He was a tall, unyielding, thin, dignified man whose chest was swollen with moral indignation, dressed in a black frock coat and dark kid leather gloves, his eyes hidden behind gold rimmed spectacles. His every movement was that of the irreproachable, honourable, stern civil servant who, under oath and with sonorous pathos, denied being closely acquainted with Haarmann and maintained a safe distance from the criminal until it was proven, finally and irrevocably, that he had actually received gifts and money from Haarmann on numerous occasions, that he had cooperated closely with Haarmann on several cases and finally, on resigning from his detective agency on 1 April 1923, suggested casually to Haarmann that the two of them start their own detective agency. Haarmann, who always had one eye open to the opportunity of earning himself some money, had cleverly wormed his way into the trust of this upper-class, none-too-choosy gentleman.

They frequently held their "consultations" in cafés or restaurants, and on these occasions Haarmann would boast of his criminal connections and the police alike and of new "methods" he applied to the solving of crimes. They finally started their own detective agency, the "Amerikanisches Detektivinstitut Lasso", the "American Detective Agency Lasso" (the same agency Haarmann employed to catch his victims). Haarmann had a rubber stamp made and Olfermann made some identification cards with a photo, bearing the words, "The holder of this pass is a detective of the "Lasso" agency and is working on behalf of the Hannover Police. The holder will appreciate the assistance shown to him during the performance of his duties. Lasso Detectives."

Haarmann put this "identity card" to great use on his patrols around the station even after the friendship with Olfermann ended in June 1923, and it was to prove invaluable during the criminal proceedings as obvious evidence that Haarmann had been working as a “private detective” and not with official police support when choosing his victims at the station.

There is a much darker aspect concerning the seedy origins of Haarmann’s income between 1922 and 1924. Even if we were to succeed in understanding the complexities of the man we are left in the dark on two issues, the first one being that Haarmann, who usually explained everything garrulously, was unusually reticent in describing the actual murders, the second one his mysterious meat dealings. His story was that he obtained his meat from a stranger, a butcher named Karl, although details concerning the man’s whereabouts varied. On one occasion, Haarmann said the man was based in Ricklingen, on another in Ronnenberg, and on yet another he said he traded with Karl in the market-hall, where the meat was on offer at half the usual price of horse meat, and which was chopped into small boneless pieces or sold as mince. Haarmann provided the Wegehenkel family and their friends with meat and also used it to pay his washerwoman Johanne Alsdorf (a poor, wasted, deathly pale woman who occasionally sold items of clothing for him). Finally, when he moved into lodgings with the Engel family on the “Rote Reihe”, Haarmann’s meat was served in the restaurant there.

But was there nobody in the Neue Straße area who took exception to or questioned these shady going-on? Well, yes; several reports were made to the police and Haarmann’s accommodation was searched on various occasions, but it appeared that all the “demons of darkness” were in league with Haarmann.

Directly opposite Haarmann’s apartment was a tobacconist’s where he went every day for his cigars and cigarettes. The shopkeeper, Christian Klobes, a vain and choleric but astute character, was always highly suspicious of all the activity in the neighbourhood. One evening, when he and his neighbour, a plumber by the name of Lammers, were having their usual little chat outside the front door, Klobes said, “Karl, things aren’t right here! All those youngsters - I think he lets them in but they never come out again.”

Lammers replied, “Well, if you want to know what I think, I think he’s selling boys to Africa, to the Foreign Legion.”

That settled things for a while, but one day Klobes decided to tackle his strange neighbour. At lunch-time Haarmann came into the shop to buy his cigarettes, and the shopkeeper spoke to him.

"Tell me, you always seem to have such a lot of youngsters visiting you. Do you run some kind of employment agency?" Haarmann looked at Klobes with distrust, and then pointed suddenly to a woman passing by, saying hurriedly, "Oh, I need to talk to her - she's a friend," and was gone. However, the tobacconist watched Haarmann as he walked past the woman without talking to her, turned round the next corner and was gone. Haarmann never went into the tobacconist's again.

The man was full of cunning. When his landlady, Frau Rehbock, tried to lock him out of his room after an argument, he broke the window from the outside and climbed in through it. In order to avoid paying for the repair he pretended to run after a young lad running down the road, smashing the window in passing and then shouting out, "Stop that boy! He's broken the window!" Then he climbed in through it.

The tobacconist, the plumber and a woman in the neighbourhood decided to watch what was going on, wanting to find out what "that criminal is up to." Walking down the lane at night one could see shadows moving up and down behind the curtains, and on several occasions the observers were able to see what appeared to be naked people moving around. At other times they could see a dimmed gas-light. The windows were well covered, but the neighbours could hear muffled hammering, banging and sawing, almost as if bones were being hacked or meat being prepared in the room - which incidentally housed a mincing machine. The stream of youngsters often brought with them poultry or rabbits, and occasionally dogs they had caught, which were then slaughtered in the room (Haarmann always behaved as if he were unable to watch these events), but nothing much was thought of these noises. However, after seeing a number of "missing persons" announcements in the papers, the neighbours decided to make mental notes of the faces of the youngsters seen in Haarmann's company on the "island". On one occasion the son of a senior civil servant in Darmstadt disappeared whilst travelling through Hannover. The courageous tobacconist went to the police station and asked to see a picture of the missing youngster. Lo and behold - it was one of the people he had seen with Haarmann. An immediate search was made of Haarmann's rooms, but it was as if all the demons of the underworld had gathered round to conceal the crime. The boy's clothes were found and Haarmann confessed immediately to having had sexual relations with him, but denied any knowledge of the young man's whereabouts. A few days later the missing person returned to his parents' house in Darmstadt.

Herr Klobes subsequently reappeared at the police station to report something suspicious but was treated as a nuisance, as a result of which he lost his enthusiasm for his "detective" work. However, just at this time he and his wife saw something which could easily have led to a discovery. They often observed Haarmann leaving his apartment in the evenings, laden with packages or sacks, and one warm May evening they decided to follow him as he carried a heavy sack along the banks of the Leine. He disappeared behind a bush, and then they saw him throw the sack into the river. There is no doubt that the crimes would have been revealed in the course of time had Haarmann not moved apartments again, this time on 9 June, to no. 2 Rote Reihe where he rented an unfurnished attic room from a Frau Engel.

Grans did not accompany Haarmann on this move. He was in prison from April until July for embezzling a valuable stopwatch stolen from a barracks. On release he loafed around for a while, spending the occasional night with "Uncle Haarmann", but then finally moving in with his friend Hugo Wittkowski at no. 14 Burgstraße where they rented a room from a labourer's family by the name of Krohne. They obtained a trading licence and started trading in fake jewellery on fairgrounds and in public bars. Apart from that they generally "hung loose" and received money from their "brides". The relationship towards Haarmann became more distant and increasingly hostile.

On the "Rote Reihe" ("Red Row")

The house was a 250-year-old, half-timbered double-fronted house, one of which was opposite the "Rote Reihe" and the Jews' Temple, the other facing the Bäckerstraße [Baker Street]. The Engel family ran a small tavern on the ground floor. The way to the attics was through a very narrow hall and up a narrow, angular, very steep flight of stairs. The third floor faced the Bäckerstraße, the fourth the Rote Reihe. There was a narrow ramp up the hallway, and the door to the room where the murders were carried out was at the far end on the right. The room was tiny - only about 2.5 m by 2.5 m. Tests carried out later showed that the floor and all the walls had been saturated with human blood. To the left of the door was a small bay-window facing the Rote Reihe. The roof dropped away steeply on either side of the window. In the wall opposite the door was a little alcove with a shelf in it, and next to it the blood-soaked, green upholstered camp-bed. There were small tables next to the wall either side of the door; a wash-stand and two chairs completed the décor. Obscene or tacky postcards had been stuck to the walls, and from a chain hanging down between the table on the right and the bed Haarmann had suspended a cooking-pot that could be heated from below; the room had no stove. There was a glory-hole beneath the bay-window.

Other occupants used some of the rooms on the floor for storage purposes, and a married couple, Herr and Frau Lindner, were Haarmann's neighbours. Their kitchen was adjacent to his, separated only by a thin wall. There was a tap in the hall and the toilets were in the yard, overlooked by numerous windows ....

Let us look more closely at the other inhabitants. There was a small, shrewd terror, a woman with the physiognomy of Margarethe Gottfried whose picture was often used to illustrate criminal works. This was thrice-married Elisabeth Engel, née Bräutigam, 50 years of age, small, thin, above average intelligence, mother of eight children (only one of which survived: Theodor Hartmann, labourer at the "Continental" works, an 18-year-old, sly, somewhat foppish individual). At the time Elisabeth was married to another labourer,

Wilhelm Engel, a pompous, coarse character, but good-tempered and phlegmatic when sober, who was also a marshal for the Social Democrats.

How did Haarmann and this faithful follower come to meet? In the spring of 1923 Frau Engel went to a horse slaughterer on the "island" to buy meat. There was none to be had, but near the shop she bumped into Detective Haarmann whom she knew by sight (she was a cleaner at the police station). Haarmann offered her a pound of horsemeat (at the time 60 Pfennigs a pound) for the price of 35 Pfennigs. A friendship developed, and they were soon on familiar terms. They went to the cinema together and generally "pulled jobs" and "fiddles". Haarmann gave the woman second-hand items of clothing (he dealt in used clothing and had a commercial licence); in exchange she undertook to sell the other items of clothing (which had all, without exception, belonged to his victims). Herr Engel and his stepson were bigshots in the local cycling and athletics club, and there were many other members who were only too happy to purchase a tie, a hat or a pair of trousers at a good price. "One good turn deserves another."

Haarmann provided the family with cheap meat for their pub, and in April, after yet another argument with his landlady Frau Rehbock, he asked Frau Engel whether she could provide him with lodgings. She told him that there was a room in the attic which he could have. On 9 June he moved into the hovel near the Jews' Temple, where over the next few years more than 20 people were murdered in an over-crowded, dog-eat-dog garret. (Imagine what ritual murders and pogroms would have been carried out by the people had Haarmann been a Jew.)

Separated from Haarmann's room by a thin wall was his neighbours' kitchen; these were a married couple named Lindner. When Haarmann moved into the building he made a point of immediately informing his fellow residents that he was very particular where cleanliness was concerned and would not be using the toilet facilities that were shared by five families, but would instead take his bucket out to the toilets and empty it there. His metabolism must have been extraordinary: he was seen carrying a covered bucket to the (permanently blocked) lavatories every fifteen minutes, then returning to his room, stopping off at the tap in the hall to get water. He could then be heardscrubbing and mopping without cease (apparently Frau Engel never entered his room).

Frau Lindner was a young, blond woman; slim and genteel. Her husband was a glassworker; a small, benign, swarthy lout. They shared their accommodation with a spinster who occasionally received gentleman callers. There was also a little dog called Fuchsie, who sometimes got a bone from Haarmann.

Frau Lindner loathed Haarmann and was annoyed by the constant stream of young boys trampling across the hall, which gave rise to a great deal of heated arguments. The Lindner couple also became quite violent towards each other, with him shouting "You whore!" at her, and her belabouring him with a broom-handle. Down on the ground floor, the Engels had their slanging matches when Herr Engel had been "boozing". Grans had once spat in the road in front of Frau Lindner, which culminated in Haarmann and Frau Lindner having a slanging match on the stairs. Haarmann then apologised and said, "May I introduce you to each other?" My neighbour, Frau Lindner, and this is my loyal employee who has been with me for many years, Herr Grans." From that time on they greeted each other again.

When Herr Haarmann had his groups of visitors, Frau Lindner, the spinster and an unknown, refined gentleman who was visiting would watch through a crack in the door and soon realised that there were some decidedly suspicious deeds being perpetrated. Apart from that, life was most enjoyable. Huge platters of meat were cooked in the Engels' kitchen. There was much singing and drinking in Haarmann's room. The Lindners frequently called the constabulary or the vice squad, and on one occasion Frau Lindner and a CID assistant spent a whole night standing near the Jews' Temple watching Haarmann's light. But as luck would have it there was never anything particularly amiss whenever the police went to investigate him.

Haarmann was also extremely impudent. One night, after several complaints from the neighbours, the police arrived to search his room. Haarmann refused to open the door, calmly informing the officers that in accordance with Para 106 it was not permitted to search private property between the hours of 22.00 and 06.00 hrs. "Please come back at 6 a.m.," he said. Needless to say, when the police returned they found nothing amiss. The neighbours observed that, "There's no point in trying to report that policeman's pal and his goings-on."

On the second floor lived a Frau Fobbe, a big, strong, energetic and courageous woman, a spiritualist and healer and sworn enemy of Frau Engel on the ground floor. On the third floor was Frau Mühlhan, who looked like a kindly old owl, and read tarot cards for the girls. These two good women were convinced: "Herr Haarmann works for theMidnight Mission. He looks after the homeless. He takes them to the employment agency and makes sure the poor lads get something hot to eat."

On one occasion they were downstairs in Frau Engel's kitchen making brawn. Haarmann brought in a bowl containing chopped-up pieces of meat, which he had covered with a cloth, and poured it into the boiling water. He strained the fat from the cooked meat (which he claimed was pork), heated the drained-off fat again, and then poured it into bottles. The meat was put through a mincer and then returned to the dish. Just before Christmas 1923 Haarmann also made sausages in skins he claimed were sheep's intestines, in the Engels' kitchen. Haarmann regularly joined the Engels at meal-times and shared the sausage with his hosts; the sausages were well seasoned and tasted like brains. The Engels also received a portion of the brawn and the rendered lard. However, they stopped buying their meat from Haarmann after the middle of April 1924, as they felt unwell after eating it and they no longer enjoyed the taste of it. Nothing could be discovered concerning the origins of the meat. Haarmann's fellow residents said they frequently saw him leaving the building with parcels of meat, but he rarely arrived with them.

Apart from that Haarmann led an exemplary life and was most

generous with his money. He took his "darling" Grans to good bars, sometimes leaving tips of DM 50 or even DM 60 a day. Occasionally they were accompanied by Dörchen and Elli, when they would drink only brandy and champagne.

The Discovery

In the months of May and June 1924 the quantity of skulls and corpses found was so great that there was a serious danger of national panic breaking out. Press announcements appeared giving details of the skulls in the hope of obtaining clues from the general public. At the same time the number of police reports that had been issued against Haarmann over the years were called to mind, as was the disappearance of the two schoolboys in 1918; Haarmann had already been suspected of their murders. The following course of action was agreed upon: as Haarmann already knew all of the town police officials, two young policemen from Berlin would arrive at the railway station, pretending to be homeless. They would approach Haarmann and watch what he was up to - and maybe even catch him red-handed if they were really lucky. But once again events conspired against them. The last boy Haarmann had taken off to his apartment was 15-year-old Karl Fromm. A dull, dense boy, he had been approached by Haarmann at the railway station on 18 June and had then spent several days at Haarmann's apartment. On the night of 22 June, Haarmann and Fromm met near the railway station and started to argue; Fromm was cheeky and supercilious, and whether it was in order to get away from the boy, or to "vent his spleen", or for another reason (which will be discussed shortly), Haarmann had the unbelievable nerve to go to the railway police and insist they arrest young Fromm, claiming Fromm had told him he was travelling on forged papers. The boy was arrested straightaway. It was two in the morning. However, once at the police station Fromm reported that Haarmann had kept him, Fromm, in the apartment for several days and nights and had repeatedly performed unnatural sexual acts on him. On awakening one morning, Haarmann had apparently held a knife against Fromm's throat and asked the boy whether he was afraid of death. On seeing how frightened Fromm was, Haarmann had laughed and said he was only joking; if anybody ever tried to hurt the boy, he was to scream and shout as loudly as he could.

It so happened that a member of the vice squad who was at the police station at the time was aware that the police were hoping to arrest Haarmann. This police officer therefore decided to take the dangerous vigilante now, before Haarmann's suspicions were raised and he was able to take cover. Haarmann was taken to prison on the morning of 23 June. He later claimed he had only arranged to have Fromm taken into custody because he knew he was going to kill the boy and had became gripped by the terrible fear that he was not going to be able to resist the urge to kill for much longer. If Haarmann was to be believed (and seeing him it was difficult not to), then this, the first time he was seized by any kind of "moral" scruples, was to prove his downfall. This was 22 June; it was not until 29 June that the beginnings of a confession were obtained.

The Confession

Once Haarmann's various landladies, fellow residents and numerous witnesses had been questioned, but above all, once several hundred items of clothing and linen found in Haarmann's room or confiscated from his acquaintances or voluntarily donated as exhibits had been collected, taken to the police station and shown to dependents of the missing persons and subsequently identified as the property of the missing children, there was such a vast amount of incriminating evidence against Haarmann that it was impossible to doubt that he was the mass murderer the police had been seeking for so long. However, it was still impossible to prove that he had been responsible for even one of the deaths. The many items of clothing and property found in his possession which were later identified as having belonged to the numerous missing persons were, so he said, all due to his business of trading and dealing in used clothes. He admitted to having had sexual relations with them but claimed to have no idea of their whereabouts and gave simple explanations for the traces of blood found in laundry,beds and clothing. He showed remarkable skill at wriggling his way through the inquisition; once again, achieving a successful conviction would have to be left to chance.

One of Haarmann's victims was a young man named Robert Witzel whose parents had besieged the police seventeen times over the year, hoping to find out more about their son's disappearance. (Five further murders were carried out between the time this family first reported Haarmann and his arrest.) When the first skulls were found in the pleasure garden of the Königsschloß, Witzel's father, who was a works manager at the "Excelsior Works", was called for by one of the company's engineers, one Ferdinand Meldau, who wanted to ask about Robert's way of life. Meldau was a man who liked to occupy himself with questions in connection with sexual-pathology, and hoped that if Herr Witzel went to see the skulls he might recognise his son's skull (his son's teeth were noticeably uneven). All that was known was that the young man had visited a circus the night before his disappearance, which led the police to assume that a lust for adventure had made the boy decide to run away with the circus. However, Robert's parents were convinced that their son's best friend Fritz Kahlmeyer, an extremely forward, stubborn and sly young man, well-built and with girlish features, knew more about the circus visit than he would say but was either too scared or too ashamed to tell. Herr Witzel made one last attempt, however,when Fritz asked to borrow Robert's elder brother's bicycle as he had an important errand to run.

"You can borrow the bike," he was told, "if you tell us who took Robert to the circus on 26 April." The answer came: "A police official from the railway station."

The reason for the boy's silence was understandable: he too had been approached by Haarmann, who had sexually abused the youngster and subsequently procured him for homosexual "society gentlemen".

Now they had the second piece of evidence, and the third when some items of clothing belonging to Robert were found in Haarmann's apartment, but despite this Haarmann still did not confess. Then the following incident occurred.

Herr and Frau Witzel and young Kahlmeyer were sitting outside the police director's office, once again intending to discuss their suspicions with Police Commissioner Rätz, when a shrewish female and a young man walked past them. Frau Witzel grabbed her husband's arm, exclaiming, "That man has Robert's jacket on!"

The other couple hurried out of sight when they realised she was referring to them, but Robert's parents rushed after them, accompaniedby a policeman, caught up with them and demanded to know where they had obtained the clothes. Instead of replying, the young man answered with another question, "Would your name happen to be Witzel?" He had found an identification card bearing that name in the trousers which belonged to the jacket, the suit having been obtained from Haarmann. The shrewish creature was Frau Engel, Haarmann's landlady, who happened to be in the police station making enquiries concerning Haarmann's military pension.

Haarmann was now presented with all the evidence against him: The parents, the skull, the clothing, young Kahlmeyer, Robert's clothes which his parents had identified and which had had the identification card bearing their son's name, but which had been returned to and destroyed by Haarmann. In the face of these facts, and with his sister's encouragement, Haarmann admitted for the first time that he had strangled, bitten and throttled young people in the grip of rabid sexual passion.

Haarmann was now subjected to that type of questioning which is as much a part of modern criminal justice as of medieval times, by which the toughest and stubbornest criminals are worn down by incessant questioning, sleep deprivation, physically weakened by force-feeding laxatives, or else by a "strict therapy", and finally broken. They are then given relief, refreshment, encouragement and comfort commensurate with the "unburdening of the conscience." Haarmann broke after seven days of maniacal rages and uncontrollable crying and asked for Pastor Hardelandt (by whom he had been confirmed) to whom he would confess. However, the clergyman was prevented from hearing Haarmann's confession by his duty to observe confidentiality. Finally Haarmann forced himself to confess to the superintendent and the examining magistrate. Although more and more crimes were revealed, Haarmann was adamant that the skulls which had been found in the river were not his victims', as he always chopped their skulls into tiny pieces. He showed the officials and the court doctor the areas in the George gardens near Herrenhausen where he had thrown parts of the corpses into the shrubs and bushes and bones into a lake. He showed them the skeleton of a young man, 16 years old, with the joints still slightly greasy and slippery; these were recognised as being the remains of Haarmann's last victim, Erich de Vries, whom he had killed on 15 June. Now more and more people stepped forward who had obtained clothing or meat from Haarmann, Grans, Frau Engel or Wegehenkel, and thus more and more evidence was provided of Haarmann's murderous activities until he gave up trying to deny anything at all, but simply said, "Add it to the others."

His character also changed at this time. Where at first his behaviour had been chatty but reserved, he now opened up, becoming increasingly helpful and childish; it was only when faced by the parents of his victims or if he felt otherwise threatened, or if he was talking about the act of biting through the throat or his shady meat dealings that the poisonous little lights would extinguish and, whining or sulking, he would withdraw into himself again. The general impression was that he felt relieved of a terrible burden by being able to talk about the darkness and all-consuming fear of his uncontrollable sex life. He actually began to put on airs in his confessions, full of pride at having duped "mankind" (of whom he always spoke badly).

Haarmann remained in the court prison until 16 August 1924, after which he was sent to the Provinzial-Heil-und-Pflegeanstalt in Göttingen for examinations of his mental condition. Privy councillor Professor Schultze completed his investigations on 25 September 1924 and Haarmann went back to the court prison for further observation. His trial by jury in Hannover opened on 4 December. There were 60 volumes of files.

As a result of information obtained from Haarmann, Hans Grans was arrested on 8 July, and the two men met on several occasions before the trial began; at these times Haarmann appeared troubled, whereas Grans came across as quietly disapproving and indifferent. Grans was accused not only of having known of Haarmann's killings, but of having provided the victims or having suggestively driven Haarmann to murder on at least two occasions as he wanted the victims' clothes for himself.

Part Two
The Trial

The Court

The court house in Hannover was built in the 1880's. It is a tasteless renaissance construction with an old-fashioned room with seating for approximately 150 and a glass ceiling which throws a matt light onto the faces beneath. The audience (numbering 80 on the day in question) was seated on the northern side; they were mainly the dependents of the court officials or the curious who had obtained their tickets after spending hours queuing or paying large sums of money for them. The public was cordoned off by a barrier, in front of which were several benches for witnesses and preferential seats for official representatives; senior president Noske, council chairman von Velsen, chief of police von Beckerath, Dr Weiß, the representative from the ministry of justice; representatives of the social services for minors; medics and the police. The jury was seated at the southern end of the room. In the centre of the long table were the president and district court director Dr Bökelmann, and to the right of the long table Dr Wilde, the public prosecutor. Next to him was the second prosecutor Robert Wagenschieffer, then two judges: district court judges Harten and Kleineberg. To the left were deputy prosecutor Jasching and the court stenographer named Hoßfeld. Behind the green table were six jury members and two supplementaries, surrounded by the higher court officials. The members of the jury were: a farmer by the name of Wesche from Hüpede, a carpenter named Harse from Bodenwerder; a tailor, Herr Untorf, from Pyrmont; a smith named Heise from Engelbostel; a post office employee from Holzhausen named Ahrens, and a Herr Ackmann from Kreiensen, a basket weaver. The dock was on the window-side of the wall, to the left of the room. The accused were flanked by two security policemen and a CID assistant. The two official defence lawyers, counsellor Benfey appearing for Haarmann, and barrister Lotze for Grans, were seated in front of the dock. Five experts, two court chemists (named Lochte and Feise from Göttingen), and the psychologist and privy councillor Schultze, also from Göttingen, forensic counsellor and police doctor Schackwitz and the prison doctor, forensic councellor Brandt, were also present.

Opposite them near the door were 21 members of the press, nine representing local papers for the Hannover area, five representing the telegraph offices, and three reporters from outside the district, one American and one French correspondent and four artists.

It was a provincial court with no dramatic experts in criminal law, soul-searching psychologists or well known writers. The court was tasked with dealing, in accordance with Para 263 of the Reich code of criminal procedure, with an "unsettling criminal case which had distressed the whole of Europe, within 12 - 14 days and without causing a public outrage."

The president of the court was ideally suited to this task. He was an abrupt, upright, self-assured character of whom Fritz Reuter gave the following assessment: "He exercised a brisk justice; he had as much idea of sitting quietly, observing and introspective, as a sergeant in the army."

The public prosecutor was more contemplative and intellectual, generally a more aware person, of an aristocratic nature, refined, but so completely lacking in fanatical ethical justice that one wanted to sigh with Zarathustra, "O, I wish there were a madness with which you had been injected, and that your madness were called truth or justice!"

Of less importance was the second prosecutor, a fraternal, sympathetic, honourable man with a passion for poor "legal-speak." The serious, dignified attendants failed to utter a single syllable during the entire proceedings, and the jury served more for decoration than anything else, dozing in their seats and unable to comprehend even a single detail, or to picture the scenarios in their imagination. This court, however, was impressive in comparison with the totally inept defence, which was in itself virtually a sentence for the two accused before the trial had even started. As they had no money to pay for a proper defence, each had to have an official defence. A highly respected criminologist in Berlin had offered to defend the werewolf free of charge but Haarmann, who was inherently afraid of "communists" had been told that his Berlin solicitor had communist contacts. (The parliamentary representatives Katz and Gohr claimed that in the days of the Revolution Haarmann had been used as a political informer or spy against their party. If that were true, any fear of "communists" would be psychologically easier to explain). At the last moment he asked to be given any official defence at all. Two young solicitors turned the difficult and delicate task down, and then a lawyer and notary was chosen, who had turned old and grey over the course of countless pathetic provincial cases and who was completely incapable of even fully comprehending one of the most difficult tasks in criminal law (the springboard for a strong criminal talent), never mind of evaluating it objectively. Haarmann's lawyer would be able to "defend" him only if, by his penetrating understanding of human nature, he were able to illustrate to the jury the need and inevitability of compulsive madness, or if by "blaming" society, or the times, or conditions, he in turn became the accuser of the police and of the morality of the town of Hannover - indeed, became judge over all of society. This lawyer was incapable of either ethos or psychology. As the expert in criminal law from Berlin had intended to call in a psychologist, both to counter the expertise of the court and for the defence, and had wanted me to attend as an expert, I suggested to Haarmann's official defence that the possibilities of psychoanalytical, characterological and phenomenological explanations be explored for which I suggested the following: Ludwig Klages (as the town's leading citizen), Alfred Döblin, Sigmund Freud, Alfred Adler and Hans von Hattingberg; I preferred to attend in my capacity as the representative of several leading journals. The written reply came: "I do not know what psychological questions could be asked."

If therefore no hope existed for psychological penetration of the case, then perhaps a strong factual ethos may have helped to clarify certain aspects. Haarmann's lawyer, however (an old member of a fraternity, representative of the National Liberals and a candidate for a leading seat on the council), in a typically provincial manner, took the opportunity of playing the "Wilhelminian and Bismarckian ages" against "the Republic that has spawned monsters such as Haarmann". A certain judicial sobriety protected Grans's defence, who was a grandson of the philosopher Lotze, against such tasteless small town parochialism. However, he also lacked any forensic talent, psychological interest and clarity of logic; he was a pleasant fellow in the pub, but was powerless and slightly presumptious in this, the most awesome criminal case of the time. More hopeless even than the jurists' shortage of distinction and far-sightedness was the total lack of strong, independent minds in the crowds of listeners and reporters. The decision whether to allow "writers" into the court had been made carefully, as there were numerous aspects of the case which were not to be revealed. Above all, it was made abundantly clear from the outset that any talk of misdemeanours on the part of the police and the authorities was forbidden in accordance with Para 263, which was why any witness or parent of a murdered child was silenced as soon as the slightest mention of police transgression was made. A public scandal was feared - and an invasion by the masses hanging around in the streets outside, kept away from the court building by a police notice and already excited by the parliamentary elections which coincided with the trial, had to be avoided. Only the harmless line writers from the small local papers and the telephone reporters from the large agencies were present plus two independent writers who had been given permission to attend (the word of the Ministry of Justice had to be obeyed ...) were in court, the latter being the sexologist Magnus Hirschfeld and the criminologist Hans Hyan.

Professor Schultze, the psychiatry professor from Göttingen, stood out from other experts. He was a benevolent father figure with a kindly face who industriously copied out in a vast number of files every single word Haarmann ever uttered. The following gems subsequently sprang from these files: firstly, the accused was abnormal and inferior, and secondly, Para 51 (according to which [the perpetrator's] unsoundness of mind is assumed at the time of the offence) did not apply.

This illustrates clearly the absolute cluelessness of medical psychology and its marked reliance on a state of awareness of one's actions in the face of the subconscious atavistic background of physical urges. According to this type of psychology, "abnormal" applies to Goethe as well as to Haarmann, to Strindberg as well as to the murderer Großmann, but from the viewpoint of the ape, man is just as "inferior" as the ape is from man's viewpoint. However, as far as Para 51 is concerned (with its archaic expressions for freedom of will, responsibility and soundness of mind), any honest psychologist would have to declare: the question whether Para 51 applies is about as pointless as asking whether water should be measured in meters or square rods. A standard is laid down which cannot be used in this case.

However, the second expert, Alex Schackwitz, was seized by a hunch of understanding. He was a matter-of-fact, boyish figure; capable, receptive, open; a "splendid fellow ". Even so, he lacked the reverence - no, he lacked that small amount of poetry or wistfulness which is needed in order to feel the truth behind reality. (Reality as such means nothing! The psychologist must know the person better than the person does himself.) The third expert was a psychologist of the "Hofmann: How does a criminal psychologist investigate blood stains?" type.

As neither the psychology nor the ethos were the actual point of the trial, the question had to be asked: "Why go to all the expense?" The state would have to meet the bill, which would run into hundreds of thousands of German Marks, and the end result was already clear: the death sentence. Whether a murderer is sentenced to death twenty times or ten times makes no difference. It was clear from the start that it would not be possible to solve the case to the satisfaction of all concerned. Only two different points would offer appeasement: the moral or the natural. Suicide (self-judgment by one repentant for his heinous sins against human society), or lynch-law, hastily executed by the offended beings.

One of the best psychologists of the day comforted me with these words during the difficult days of the trial:

"Hopeless! Even the wisest man would pass a misjudgment in court, enclosed in frozen perseverance. One can judge correctly or incorrectly in life, but the law consists of defining the question in such a way that no correct decision can be made.

"What would I do? Let the thirty mothers through the court barrier and do to Haarmann what he did to their children. That would be living justice. Devoured by fire, to die in the flames which cannot be controlled. Strike out at life, and it will strike back regardless of whether you were sound of mind or not, or whether you have improved. That's true, and it's the way it should be, and therefore it's not for the over-sensitive or the self-pitying, but the disgusting balderdash of the death sentence hidden behind the cowardly anonymity of affronted society is simply nonsensical ..."

The Indictment

The opening decree was read. The dealer Fritz Haarmann was accused of killing the following persons intentionally and deliberately:

1. Beginning September 1918 schoolboy Fritz Rothe
2. February 1923 apprentice Fritz Franke
3. March 1923 apprentice Wilhelm Schulze
4. May 1923 schoolboy Roland Huch
5. May 1923 labourer Hans Sonnenfeld
6. June 1923 schoolboy Ernst Ehrenberg
7. August 1923 office junior Heinrich Struß
8. September 1923 apprentice Paul Bronischewski
9. October 1923 labourer Richard Gräf
10. October 1923 apprentice Wilhelm Erdner
11. October 1923 labourer Hermann Wolf
12. October 1923 schoolboy Heinz Brinkmann
13. November 1923 carpenter Adolf Hannappel
14. December 1923 labourer Adolf Hennies
15. January 1924 locksmith Ernst Spicker
16. January 1924 labourer Heinrich Koch

17. February 1924 labourer Willi Senger
18. February 1924 apprentice Hermann Speichert
19. April 1924 apprentice Alfred Hogrefe
20. April 1924 labourer Hermann Bock
21. April 1924 apprentice Wilhelm Apel
22. April 1924 apprentice Robert Witzel
23. May 1924 apprentice Heinz Martin
24. May 1924 traveller Fritz Wittig
25. May 1924 schoolboy Fritz Abeling
26. June 1924 apprentice Friedrich Koch
27. June 1924 journeyman baker Erich de Vries

147 reports were made. It was proven in 38 cases that the missing persons were still alive and in 114 that Haarmann could not have been the criminal, which left 30 cases. Murder was proved in 27 of these and Haarmann was not convicted of three other cases (which were not included in the indictment). Hans Grans, born 7 July 1901 in Hannover, was accused of two cases of instigating murder and a second charge (which was later dropped) of receiving and dealing in stolen goods.

The Accused

"A tailless predatory ape which walks upright on the hind legs, lives in packs, will eat anything and everything, has a restless heart and a lying soul. Thieving, lecherous and quarrelsome but with many varied skills. The enemy of all other living creatures, and his own worst enemy." (Simia homo sine causa, pedibus posticis ambulans, gregarius omnivorus, ingietus cordis, mendax mentis. Furax, salex, pugnax at artium variarum capax. Animalium reliquorum terrae hostis, sui ipsius inimicus teterritmus.) This is the oldest description of primeval man. Self-centred and enslaved, cowardly and foolhardy, brutal and sentimental, but above all vain and lecherous - this is how Haarmann was regarded: a flowing element, in which affected and genuine childishness and affected and genuine mental deficiency complemented each other beautifully. Dedicated to hunger and lasciviousness, "shameless" in every sense, he was nonetheless, even in his play-acting, a piece of naïve primeval nature, unaccustomed to having to account for anything. Haarmann's naïve story-telling, his combination of fiction and fact, was refreshing and liberating after the legal-speak of the jurists, the confused hypocrisy of the authorities, "society's" vanity, hidden behind a guise of science, morality or professional duty, and civilisation's self-righteous, indignant utterance of these living lies. The feeling was that people of the truth also lie. This outstanding actor was right! He had absolutely no fear of that which frightens every civilised person, of death, of corpses, of decay, but in a thunderstorm he would hide like an animal, shivering; though irreligious he would pray to God.

Periodically his childish ways would give rise to sympathy. On one occasion the lights in the room were switched on; speaking to himself he said, childlike, "Just like a pretty Christmas tree." On another privy councillor Schultze (who was somewhat advanced in years) yawned. Haarmann said to him (as if it were he who were watching the professor, and not vice versa), "Well, are you all right to go on, Professor?" Turning to the court he said, "You must understand: he has been ill."

To the journalists he once said reproachfully, "You're not to lie; we know you're all liars," and to the jury, "Keep it short; I want to spend Christmas in heaven with Mother."

My reports dealt with police responsibility and the lack of expertise; they made the court uneasy and when the president (who was becoming increasingly nervous - how could Haarmann be allowed to speak in defence of the police authority?) read out my claims to Haarmann and asked him whether they were correct, Haarmann called out, "It's all lies; the man is lying!", but turned to me and said quietly, "Next you'll be telling us the police are my best friends!", and his eyes twinkled as if he found it all so amusing.

Hans Grans appeared in a totally different light. He was as tough as he was gentle, as unbreakable as he was girlish; always supercilious,courteous and amiable, he was like a fox in the face of death, ever vigilant and constantly on the lookout for a means of escape. He used a long pencil or the forefinger of his right hand to illustrate his evidence in the air, asking sharply advocatorial questions concerning his solidly constructed defence, the purpose of the questions known only to himself. He was far lonelier than Haarmann; he was innocent but nonetheless the more dangerous of the two. Although he was more sensitive than Haarmann, he did not have the same fearful or defensive nature. Haarmann's nature was affected, every minute of the day, by unconquerable demonic powers; the inferiority complex of someone long oppressed, besmirched, derailed, often teased, took advantage of the dark frenzy. And he enjoyed playing his games with the witnesses (his "fences"); each "has something" on the other. He is not afraid to show his claws: "I'll watch you all croak. The witness has a nerve. He needs to be given what-for."

By contrast Grans was too egotistical even for love and revenge; he was unaffected by the heat of the moment. All he understood was self-preservation.

"All I have done is what you can prove, and that is the issue here." I could not believe that a terrible miscarriage of justice would sentence him to death. When I said to his parents, "Don't let your child down once he is in the penitentiary," his father replied, "If I knew he were guilty of that of which he stands accused, I would go myself and report him," and the mother said, "If he goes to prison we'll take him back; if he goes to a penitentiary we will have to disown him - it would be such a disgrace on the family."

What is the emotional relationship between thc two? They are two galley slaves, forged together back to back, the boy feeling neither hatred or revulsion but only the urge to escape from this togetherness by freezing against any contact with the other body. That was why he was unable to build up his defence system against emotions, which would probably have saved his life. The other person was waiting for each friendly word, courting with his desire for revenge. He would retract in a moment everything with which he had cleverly burdened his former loved one were the loved one only to speak some words of sympathy or even of gratitude. But because the boy wanted only to escape from being forged to this already half-cold corpse, Haarmann had only the one desire: to take the one he hated the most, because he loved him the most, with him to the dark land. However, he was so artful in this that only Grans was able to sense it. He always spoke with tenderness. For days he spoke only of "Hans" (whereas Hans referred only to "Herr Haarmann" or "the accused Haarmann"), but with menacing undertones, then begging for companionship. He finally blurted out the following accusation, apparently driven to it by the other's coldness, but in fact it had long since been prepared: "Grans didn't just bring the boys to me for me to kill them. He didn't just use all sorts of tricks to get me going, he showed the boys how to do it. He took advantage of my madness and for days on end he'd try to persuade me to kill boys whose trousers he wanted. He killed too! He did worse things than me! Grans and Wittkowski, his friend, got Adolf Hennies into my room and killed him. They had been arguing over women. Then they took his clothes and laughed when they showed me the body when I got home. 'That's one of yours,' they said. I started to cry and begged them to take the body away. There were no marks on the neck so it couldn't have been one of mine. But they put this one on me, they ran off and I had to cut the body up and get rid of it."

Out of his devilish desire for revenge, Haarmann had spent days working on this incredible accusation (which the court believed). With guileless conviction and naïve insistence. Once it was out and he had achieved his aim of not going to his death alone, the statements against Grans soon became considerably weaker and he started to shrink back again as soon as the other person managed to force out a halfway friendly word. (Wittkowski, who was also accused, surrendered voluntarily to the court as soon as he heard this accusation.) For days afterward the vaguely perceptable emotional subcurrent which emanated from Haarmann's suppressed desire for sexual revenge surrounded the rigid armour around the watchful Grans. But even this was not clear: poor Undine was not only a parasite on life, not only an emotional parasite living off another's madness .... "Certainly I know the only person to have been like a father to me, who offered me love or whatever this dullness is called, is suspected of something terrible, the most terrible thing, and I keep my silence and will not give him up to the hangman, does this have to be a betrayal?" This was something ethical, something with character; this was "greatness". If the community and its authorities are blind, if they cannot control poverty, vice, prostitution, crime, and indeed often help to perpetrate it, should I, 20 years old, outcast and pushed aside, be the only one to see all and tell what he sees? Grans dealt in the clothing of murdered people at the railway station in full view of three police departments. He himself wore the coat which had belonged to Hennies, the jacket which had belonged to Wittig, breeches which had belonged to Hannappel, the shirt which had belonged to Spieker - all murdered.

If the police failed to notice anything, then surely this person, who lived from day to day, also "thought nothing of it". His feelings towards Haarmann were by no means so straightforward that he was merely a fox, living in the trail of a wolf. It is even possible that even the worst of the bad should show his shame by making out he is worse than he actually is. When the hookers who worked for Grans, and whom he wished to impress, were around, he would boast of how he had Haarmann in his sexual power and put his arms about the wild man, who immediately became acquiescent, but at the same time Grans would whisper in pretty Dörchen's ear, "I'm just playing with him." But there is no doubt that not only was the older man pushed around, but the younger one absorbed the depravity of the other, and if Haarmann was bound to Grans by the same love as an old wolf to a young fox, then Grans was bound not only by the gratitude a parasite felt towards his host, but also a certain "laissez-faire": "He loves me. What would he be without me?"

The Witnesses

Around 200 witnesses appeared during the trial, so let us attempt to classify them. First there were the whimpering youngsters, the fences, the pimps, the hookers; those who had run away from the social services or been thrown out of loveless, wretched homes, some suffering, some active in their depravity. The group most strongly represented is that of the "witnesses of imagination". Young people who have read the papers and whose Nick Carter information is fuelled by murder weapons, corpses and devoured human flesh. Two of them appeared, speaking of complicated bondage, sadistic flagellation and torment which Haarmann had supposedly subjected them to. A labourer claimed Haarmann had invited him over for some wine which had almost killed him as Grans had secretly poured some powder into it. A fourth told how he had overheard fabulous stories about African arrow poison (curare) and a fifth of having witnessed insane acts of lasciviousness ... Closely related to this group were the vanity witnesses. They really knew nothing but wanted to have "been there, seen it", wanted to have had their moment of glory, to show their knowledge of human nature and their cunning and so they puffed themselves up but managed only to confuse rather than to help.

The third group consisted of the difficult witnesses. These are the simple, dense youngsters, stubborn souls, the tiniest rogues, against whom Haarmann appeared a giant. Their statements are extracted from them, drop by drop, totally without direction and not comprehending who they were, what they knew or what they were doing. Beside them were the fearful, middle-class, necessary people, dazed and beaten, moaning because each member of the muddy little group imagined the other to be concealing some petty little deed (because every member of this group constantly watches the other, yet will unite against a third). They were still full of humility for "Herr Haarmann", who in their opinion was a "gentleman" and an "official". There were also several figures of elegant, refined society which stayed in the mind: gentlemen in frock coats, civil and practical, skilful, lissom, easily interchangeable. They (members of a "genteel society") move away from the teeming masses; they know that if they appear to associate themselves at all with the burden and the guilt, then justice and society will immediately move away from them. Senior president, council chairman, chief of police, the inspectors - there they sat in their leather chairs, watching this play about mortal anguish; never dreaming, even in their hearts: mea culpa! Along came a well-dressed, genteel little man in little boots and a little shirt, made a graceful little bow to the pressmen and began to speak.

"I would ask the gentlemen not to print my name in their newspapers as this would have a most detrimental effect on my present employment." (He is a dealer in stolen goods.) Along came another little thing, crushed and shattered, wearing prison clothes because he was serving a sentence for robbery, and began, "President, I must refuse to take an oath. I am a follower of Darwin and do not believe in God. I am therefore unable to swear."

A touching interlude was provided by Grans's "fiancée", Elfriede Zwingmann, a poor kitchen girl in the "Erlanger Bierstube." She tried as best she could to exonerate her beloved good-for-nothing. Every word she uttered cried out for mercy, and she was so unassuming that everyone thought: the girl has never had a bad thought in her life. As far as she was concerned Haarmann was a "detective". If a person like that needed money he went to the station and asked the travellers what they had in their bags. If no plausible answer was forthcoming the "detective" confiscated the bags. Later he would sell the contents and live off the money obtained by that means. That was why Haarmann always had enough money. And if he didn't want to give any of it to her Hans, then she would simply give him her own hard-earned, paltry seven German Marks a week; she knew he was unfaithful, but he wasalways nice to her, and good, and when it was proven that he also beat her she said simply, "Only the once, and it didn't hurt."

Dora Mrutzek, another of Grans's lovers, was in marked contrast to this simple-minded little creature. It is hard to understand why she should have been such an obsequious burden on her former lover - maybe it had something to do with her jealous husband? Nonetheless, she was the only woman in the circle of women loathed by the jealous Haarmann with whom Haarmann actually got on. "Herr Haarmann kissed the boys and was a criminal who lived off the money earned from his crimes. Whenever there was a tough job I would take it to Herr Haarmann and my husband [apart from numerous lovers, Dörchen also had a husband] would get jealous and try to hit me. Herr Haarmann would laugh and say, 'Dörchen, I'll marry you,' but he only wanted the boys." Haarmann returned the compliment by telling the court, "And you wouldn't believe what she can drink! She boozed a whole bottle of brandy in the tea-rooms by herself once and wasn't even sloshed."

The Murder Method

The murderer stated the following: "I never intended to kill those youngsters. Some of the boys did come back several times. I then wanted to protect them from me. I knew that if I got going something would happen, and that made me cry. I said to them, 'Don't drive me wild,' because if I went wild I would bite them and suck their necks. Some of the boys at the Café Kröpcke liked to muffle or prevent their partner from breathing. Sometimes we scrapped for hours. It's not easy for me to get going. Lately it's happened more often. It used to worry me; 'Oh God, where's it going to end?' I would throw myself on top of those boys. They were worn out by the antics and the debauchery. I bit through the Adam's apple, must have throttled them at the same time. I would collapse on the dead body. I'd go and make myself some strong black coffee. I'd put the body on the floor and cover the face with a cloth so it wouldn't be looking at me. I'd make two cuts into the abdomen and put the intestines in a bucket. I'd dip a towel in the blood collecting in the abdominal cavity and keep doing that until it had all been soaked up. Then I'd make three cuts from the ribs towards the shoulders, take hold of the ribs and push until the bones around the shoulders broke. I'd then cut through that area. Now I could get the heart, lungs and kidneys and chop them up and put them in my bucket. Then I'd take the legs off, then the arms. I'd take the flesh off the bones and put it in my waxcloth bag. The rest of the flesh went under the bed or in the cubby-hole. It would take me five or six trips to take everything out and throw it down the toilet or into the river. I'd cut the penis off after I had emptied and cleaned the chest and stomach cavities. I would cut it into lots of little pieces. I always hated doing this, but I couldn't help it - my passion was so much stronger than the horror of the cutting and chopping.

"I'd take the heads off last. I used the little kitchen knife to cut around the scalp and cut it up into little strips and squares. I'd put the skull, face down, on a straw mat and cover it with rags so that you wouldn't hear the banging so much. I'd hit it with the blunt edge of an axe until the joins on the skull split apart. The brain went in the bucket and the chopped up bones in the river opposite the castle. Or else I went to the Eilenriede where it's nice and marshy and threw the pieces on the ground and trampled over them. There was probably only one occasion when I was in such a hurry to get rid of the body that the whole skull went into the river. I gave the clothes away, most of them went to Grans. Out of love. I sold the other things to Frau Engel or Frau Wegehenkel. Or somebody else sold them for me."

The anatomists said that by applying pressure to or biting through the larynx and pressing against the vagus and glossopharyngeus at the upper end of the trachea Haarmann may have caused respiratory and coronary paralysis which in turn would have led to defenceless-ness. The fact that it is relatively easy to incapacitate a human by pressing togetherthe nerve stems above the larynx is one of the basic rules of the Japanese art of ju-jitsu. Unfortunately Haarmann was not given the opportunity to demonstrate on an animal. There is also the remote possibility that he may have bitten into the main (carotid) artery and drunk the warm blood, which would explain why the bodies had no bruising. It was also one of his perverse passions to take the sexual member in his mouth and bite it. It is to be assumed that he throttled his victims whilst they dozed, exhausted from the debauchery. It is possible that he may have served the flesh of one victim to another in a meal. Although it was certain that, having become accustomed to killing, he killed not only in the ecstasy of his passion, but also for reasons that were not sexual, it was also true that he asked not what the purpose or aim was, but was instead driven by beauty and sensuality.

On one occasion when, so Haarmann reported, Grans "supplied" him with Wittig (whose clothes Grans supposedly wanted), but whom Haarmann did not sexually desire, Grans allegedly said, "But it's easier to do it to someone you don't love." Haarmann replied reprovingly, "No, that's not true. It's easier to do it to someone you do love."

Haarmann lied in his incriminations of Grans. However, he was not just acting when he appeared in court and uttered his fearful cry, "There are days when any rogue can drive me to do anything at all! Often, after I had killed, I pleaded to be put away in a military asylum, but not in a madhouse. That was the only thing I didn't want to happen. If Grans had really loved me he would have been able to save me. Oh, believe me, I'm not ill. It's only that I occasionally have funny turns. Don't imagine that killing someone is nice. I want to be beheaded. It'll only take a moment, then I'll be at peace."

27 Murder Cases

1. Friedel Rothe, born 17 July 1901 disappeared 25 September 1918

It was 1918 in that miserable period when we Germans had nothing to eat. An inn-keeper and landlord by the name of Oswald Rothe was away at war. His wife, an all too gentle, kind person, was unable to cope with their tearaway of a son, Friedel. He was supposed to be taking school exams, but instead loafed around, spending his time smoking and eating sweets. Because he needed money he secretly sold his father's civilian clothes. One weekend when he was expecting more parental trouble he ran away. He was spotted the same day looking for beechnuts in the Eilenriede. It was not until two days later that his anxious mother received a postcard saying, "Dear Mother, have been gone for two days but will not return until you're nice again. Lots of love, Fritz." His father returned from the war that same day, and the couple immediately set about finding their son, their only child - but without success. However, various friends of the 17-year-old boy were forthcoming with information; these were 14-year-old Paul Montag, a strikingly pretty Jewish boy with steely blue eyes, and his old friends Hellmut

Göde and Hans Bohne. The boys confessed that they had met a "fine" gentleman in a café, a police detective, who had given them presents, taken them into the woods and... seduced them. Friedel had become particularly close to the "fine gentleman." He confided in his friends, "I've been to his flat. We had fun and smoked." On another occasion, "I wanted to go to his flat yesterday, but he was in bed with a woman. He called out, 'Can't open the door; I've got a lady caller.'"

The police were unable to find out more so Göde and Bohne decided to start their own investigation, with some success: they found the home of the unknown man (no. 27 Cellerstraße). Friedel's parents submitted a police report and a plainclothes policeman by the name of Brauns was commissioned with searching the "fine gentleman's" apartment for more information in connection with the missing boy. Brauns surprised Haarmann in the middle of the night and found him in bed with a tall, slim boy (one of Friedel's schoolfriends). The boy was told to get dressed and then taken away in handcuffs. Haarmann too was arrested, and was subsequently sentenced to 9 months' imprisonment for seducing the boy, but there was no evidence to substantiate murder. Needless to say, the rooms were not searched for which Brauns (a typical 'official person', full of suppressed energy) gave the following reason: "I was not told to search the place." Five years later, when the "epidemic" of murders was under way, the police remembered the case, and Haarmann confessed: "Back then, when we were arrested, the murdered boy's head was stuffed behind the stove, wrapped in newspaper. I buried him later in the Stöckener cemetery."

2. Fritz Franke from Berlin, born 31 October 1906 disappeared 12 February 1923

Five years passed during which - apparently - no other youngsters were murdered. (Haarmann was not accused of murdering the young schoolboy Koch 1 [he murdered a total of three boys named Koch]). Two whores from the Altstadt appeared at the police station on Waterloo Square: Haarmann's girlfriends Elli Schulz, a plump, pink piglet, and Dörchen Mrutzek, a long thin beanpole (Grans's mistress). They told a most confusing story and produced two pieces of meat, asking whether they could possibly be human flesh. Dörchen's garbled story was as follows: "Two days ago Elli and I met a nice young man from Berlin, a pianist, at Herr Haarmann's place on the Neue Straße. There was a group of us at Herr Haarmann's. A Herr Hans Grans was there too. Haarmann said, 'You'd better go now. I'm expecting a visitor. Detective Superintendent Olfermann will be here soon for an important meeting.' Grans, Elli and I left to go to the "Schützenheim". The young man from Berlin played the piano there. Elli and I danced with Herr Grans. When it was time for us to go home we walked as far as Herr Haarmann's place with Herr Grans, he whispered in Elli's ear (with reference to the young man), 'Hey, he's going to be trampled on today!' We remembered that later. Next morning I went to Herr Haarmann's as usual to clean. Herr Haarmann opened the door. The pretty young man was in bed, half-naked. He was completely white. I was scared to death and said, `What's up with him?' Haarmann covered the young man up quickly and whispered, 'Shhh, he wants to sleep. Go away and come back this afternoon to clean the room.' So I went away, and I said to Elli, 'Something's odd there.' That afternoon I went back. Herr Haarmann had locked himself in and called through the door, 'I'm busy right now, come back again this evening at about 7!' I went back later that evening and all the windows were open. He had already scrubbed the room and cleaned everything. He was in his shirtsleeves and quite excited. He was sweating and said to me, 'Dörchen, can you smell anything bad?' On the bed I saw the clothes belonging to the man from Berlin. I screamed, 'What's happened?' Haarmann said calmly, 'He's gone on to Hamburg. He wanted to get some different gear. He must have been up to something. I changed them for him, and still had to pay some more on top of that.' Then Herr Grans and Elli came and kept asking, 'What's happened to the man from Berlin?' Haarmann laughed at us and Grans calmed us down. Two days later Elli and I were cleaning Haarmann's room. Haarmann had just been called away by Wegehenkel. So we took the chance and had a look through all the drawers. In the table drawer was a cigarette holder and a wallet belonging to the man from Berlin. We looked in the cubby-hole under the stairs, where we found a bloody apron and a huge pot full of pieces of meat. (It belongs to Frau Wegehenkel, and it holds 25 litres.) We hid two pieces which were covered in hair. Here they are."

However, Dörchen and Elli happened to encounter the same police detective Müller who was using Haarmann as an informer. He listened to them, not disbelieving a word, and then took them to the court doctor Alex Schackwitz who (unfortunately) decided not to look at the samples of flesh under a microscope. He sniffed at it, laughing, "I can't smell it today because I have a bit of a cold! But anybody can tell it's pork skin." A search warrant was now issued and Haarmann's apartment searched but nothing suspicious was found.

What had really happened? The 18-year-old son of a decent, upright publican named Franke from the Markgrafenstraße in Berlin, a perky reprobate of a lad, and his friend Paul Schmidt, a 16-year-old stubborn fellow, had taken "things from home" to the station on the Friedrich-straße and sold them there. With their ill-gotten gains they took themselves off to Hannover where Haarmann detained them on his inspection of the station waiting rooms at 6 a.m. Haarmann sent the less attractive lad off to the hostel with some money and took the other one home with him. It was to be another three days before young Schmidt met the supposed detective at the station again, and Haarmann assured the worried boy that his friend had travelled on to Hamburg. His belongings, which he had left behind, had been given to Grans. So the two hookers were right.

Haarmann claimed that Grans had turned up unexpectedly whilst the corpse was still in the room. Shocked, he simply stared at Haarmann and said, "When shall I come back again?"

3. Wilhelm Schulze from Colshorn, born 31 August 1905 disappeared 20 March 1923

Wilhelm Schulze was apprenticed to a writer. He was the advanced, adventurous 16-and-ahalf-year-old offspring of the late Otto Schulze, who had been a railway carpenter and his decent, simple wife. Schulze left for work one morning and never returned. No remains were ever found. His clothing was found in Frau Engel's rooms. Haarmann had intercepted the boy on the station and taken him home.

4. Roland Huch, born 7 August 1907 disappeared 23 May 1923

Roland Huch was a high school student, the only son of a pharmacist on the Arnswaldtstraße. He was 15 years of age, dark blond, big and strong despite having recently recovered from pleurisy. He had a passion for the Marines and wanted above all else to go to sea. One evening, when his parents were at a concert in the Town Hall, the boy packed his best things in a small suitcase, took some money and said goodbye to his best friend, Alwin Richter.

"Alwin, give my parents my love. I'm going away." When his horrified parents heard what he had done they hurried to the railway police department. Detective von Lonski, the head of the police station, snapped at them. "I can't simply set the whole police force in motion simply because some boy has run away from home!"

However, this time the victim was from a good home, and unusually the court summonsed the police for questioning (which according to Para 263 was not normally allowed). It turned out that not only had the police force failed, but the unfortunate father had not even been able to telephone the railway police in Bremen and Hamburg. He had asked for a policeman to accompany him to the slums of the Altstadt but was told brusquely, "That's not our department!" In fact, the missing persons report had not even been passed on.

This time Haarmann sold his victim's belongings to a dark woman named Bormann who in turn sold them to Alex, the lifeguard at Schrader's swimming pool. A year later Alex produced the things again (the buttons still had the name of the tailor, Brüggemann, on them) - the solitary legacy of young Roland, who had longed for the world outside and ended up at the mercy of a wolf.

5. Hans Sonnenfeld, born 1 June 1904 disappeared May 1923

Hans, the 19-year-old son of a Hannover merchant, Johann Sonnenfeld, had been missing since the end of May 1923. His last job had been in the Sichel factory in Limmer. He had also fallen in with a bad lot at the station, had contracted a social disease and now spent his time loafing around. After an argument his parents took his house key off him and he left in a fit of anger. He never returned.

Hans had confided in his 14-year-old sister, Grete, "I have a boyfriend, and I'm his bride."

The investigations into his whereabouts were unsuccessful. It was only a year later when the other Haarmann murders had been discovered that one of Hans's friends, a lad by the name of Grote (who was one of the railway thieves), went to Hans's parents and told them, "The last time I saw Hans he was with Heinz Mohr. They had sold a carpet to someone in Berlin."

But who is Heinz Mohr? In that motley collection of young layabouts, hobos, social services cases, and pimps, all of whom knew the missing boy well, there is now: Heinz Mohr, psychologically one of the most extraordinary figures in this drama. Mohr was a tall, hectic, loose, undoubtedly refined yet fragile character. He appeared ashamed in court and confessed to having been the missing person's jilted "lover", that they had carried out various swindles together, but then that Hans had suddenly disappeared on their return from one of their escapades. However, a few weeks later, Mohr suddenly spotted his missing friend's double-breasted overcoat - on Haarmann. Several other people, including pretty Dörchen and lovely Elli, the two hookers, as well as Haarmann's fences Engel and Wegehenkel, and even his friend Herr Olfermann, all swore in total agreement, "Yes, Haarmann was wearing a black coat before Sonnenfeld disappeared, and a few weeks after Sonnenfeld's disappearance he was wearing a yellow overcoat with a herringbone pattern and thick quilted lining."

Haarmann, who readily admitted to all the other murders, appeared to be in despair in this particular case, continuously contradicting himself. At first he said he had bought the overcoat from Sonnenfeld (who was well known on the "island"), but later he denied even having owned a coat like this one. This too is strange: Sonnenfeld's tie, which had been a gift from his sports club, and the handkerchief which his mother had embroidered with her own hands, and the boy's woollen scarf, were all found either at Grans's or Wegehenkel's or Engel's homes. This gave rise to the suspicion (since Haarmann denied having anything to do with this case) that the entire group around Haarmann could be involved in Sonnenfeld's (whom they all knew) disappearance. Everything now seemed to revolve around the overcoat, although matters were confused further when Hans Grans claimed that he himself had sold the overcoat for Haarmann, to a man of doubtful integrity by the name of Gravörwilli. Gravörwilli was summonsed and confirmed Grans's statement, but went on the say that the coat had been destroyed: he had given it to his wife Sophie who had cut it up to use as cleaning cloths. Instead of immediately arranging to search Sophie's home, she was summonsed to the court where she swore that Haarmann's coat, which had been sold by Grans, no longer existed. However, an identical coat was found amongst the things carried off by Frau Engel, and was now placed on the court table. Was it the coat or not? Things were becoming more and more confusing, until Grans, the person with the most experience in legal and illegal matters, suggested innocently, "Why not fetch the tailor who made the coat?" Fortunately, the tailor lived nearby, and five minutes later was in court. He confirmed that the coat lying on the table was the one he had made for the Sonnenfelds' son.

But what about the coat which Grans sold on Haarmann's behalf to Gravörwilli, whose wife cut it up for dusters? If posterity never finds out it will be because the Hannover jury court neglected the basics of criminal psychology.

A witness identifies a fabric and names a second witness who will also recognise it. The first witness is immediately despatched by motor car to fetch the second one, which of course invalidates that witness's statement. If an item of clothing is to be identified, then you don't put three or five items of clothing in front of a witness and ask which one it is. You hold the item in front of him and ask, "Is it this one?"

As a result of this error the case became so muddled that the Sonnenfeld murder (which may have been the last one to be carried out at no. 8 Neue Straße) was never solved.

6. Ernst Ehrenberg, born 30 September 1909 disappeared 25 June 1923

Little Ernst was only 13 years old. He was an ordinary child, the son of a straightforward shoemaker who was Haarmann's neighbour. One morning in June the boy was sent to a customer to return some shoes his father had repaired. He delivered them, but never returned home. The school holidays started four days later, and on the last day of term the junior section of the "YMCA" was supposed to be going on a day trip. Ernst and his two brothers, Hans and Walter, were going on the trip. When Hans, Walter and the fourth son, Kurt (who had been allowed to take Ernst's place on the trip) arrived at the holiday home, Ernst was sitting on the window sill in the entrance hall with an empty rucksack. "I went to see Aunt Wiesinger in Meinersen. I've got some wood in a back-basket for Mother." The three brothers replied, "Mother's looking for you. She'll be here soon."

"No, don't let her come here. I've got to go," Ernst said, frightened. The youngest brother accompanied him part of the way to the station and then went home to his mother. She was now completely disturbed and went straight to the station herself. Her boy was gone.

It was another year before some light was thrown on the matter, and that was due to the lad's green school hat. A group of little boys was playing near Haarmann's house when the "gentleman" passed by, carrying a green hat.

"Does one of you want this hat? I took it off a cheeky little chap who was playing football."

Little Willi Liebetreu got the hat. Everybody in the neighbourhood knew the criminal. Once his numerous murders were exposed, the 11-year-old took the green hat to the police, upon which the police went to Haarmann's rooms and found Ernst's green braces which his father had made for him.

But what had happened? Young Ernst had either lost or spent the money he had received for the shoe repair that day. However, he was so scared of retribution that he dared not go home but went instead to his aunt in Meinersen. As the day of the school trip drew nearer he got so homesick that he went to the YMCA hostel to meet his brothers there, but ran away again in fear when they told him that their mother was looking for him. He ran straight into the arms of their neighbour, Haarmann, who took him home and killed him.

7. Heinrich Struß from Egestorf, born 23 July 1905 disappeared 24 August 1923

Heinrich Struß was the 18-year-old son of a carpenter in Egestorf. He had a job in town and lived with his Aunt Schaper in Leinhausen from where he took the train to work every morning. He arrived home every evening at 6 pm and had never spent a night away. However, one Thursday in August he did not return from work. His aunt immediately notified his father, who next morning went to town to see if he could find out anything from the insurance company where his son worked. The answer came: "He's not been here for several days." It was assumed that he had fallen in with a bad crowd, or that maybe he had gone to work abroad. The police were unable to trace him. Latterly the young man had been seen at the cinema, in the company of a girlfriend. It was a year later, when items the police had confiscated from Haarmann were on display at the police station, that his parents saw the green-edged brown half-stockings his mother had made, his tie and even his key ring with the keys to his home, his case, his wardrobe and his violin case.

8. Paul Bronischewski from Bochum, born 14 Aug.1906 disappeared 24 September 1923

Frau Ottilie Richter from Bochum was a careworn, pale, broken woman. Her son from her first marriage, Paul, was missing. He was a perfectly respectable boy, completely innocent, apprenticed to a wood turner. On his 17th birthday he went to Garz on the river Havel in the Magdeburg district to see his uncle, a first-mate named Schwarz, who found him helpful, pleasant and hard working. However, he said Paul had seemed depressed during his stay, and he had the impression that Paul did not want to return to Bochum (which at the time was under French occupation) because of problems with his passport.

On 24 September Paul left Garz for the regional railway station at Wulkau, a distance of 11 km. From there he would travel to the East German State railway station at Schönhausen and then back to Bochum. He obviously ran out of money and never returned home. The police made their enquiries but nothing could be established. A year later, when Haarmann's murders were revealed and the items in his rooms put on display at the police station, Paul's mother and uncle went to Hannover where they found Paul's knapsack, his hiking trousers, his grey cord jacket, his half-stockings which his mother had knitted, and even a towel which Paul's mother had made. Paul had got off the train in Hannover and, with the usual promise of accommodation and work, had been taken in and killed.

9. Richard Gräf, born 13 February 1906 disappeared at the end of September 1923

This is a noble and charming interlude in an otherwise horrible series of events. Five impoverished children, three brothers and two sisters, had been left parentless. The mother had absconded to America with a lover. The father, a sickly casual labourer, was unable to feed his children. He found work in Eisenach but was still so poor that he could not even travel to Hannover to identify his missing son's remains. The eldest son Otto carried the full responsibility of caring and providing for his younger siblings, although only 20 years of age himself. Fortunately he found a young girl to help him, and this young girl, her valiant parents and another neighbour, Frau Hoffmann née Brause, became substitute parents for the neglected children.

A sweet, blond girl appeared in court, a young, decent Hannoverian. She was twenty years old, pregnant, and worked eleven hours a day; her name was Anna Wiedehaus. And this young, tender creature was like a mother to five poor children whose natural parents had upped and away. The second brother, Richard, was 17 years old and had one ambition: to follow his mother to America. One September morning he simply walked out, but returned after two weeks: he had no passport or money and was unable to leave Germany. His belongings had been stolen. He was starving and overtired. Anna gave him some food and he told the following story.

"I've met a gentleman at the station. He knows of a good job for me. I have to go straight back; he wants to talk to me. If I can earn enough money I'll be able to go and join Mother."

He said farewell to his Aunt Hoffmann and his patron, a merchant named Dickhaut, left for the station and was never seen again. The police enquiries were a casual affair as the general feeling was he had probably gone to America after all.

Almost a year later Richard's clothes turned up. The Wegehenkels' son had his suit. Richard's brother Otto identified it: "Yes, that's Richard's suit. I've pressed it often enough, I should know it."

Frau Engel had been careful to take the boy's overcoat to the pawn-broker.

10. Wilhelm Erdner from Gehrden, born 4 February 1907 disappeared 12 October 1923

Wilhelm Erdner was the son of a locksmith, also Wilhelm Erdner, from Gehrden. The 16-year-old used to cycle to his job in the machine factory every morning on his father's bicycle. One Saturday he failed to return. The next morning, his father went to the factory to speak to his son's colleagues.

"Have you seen Will?"

"No," came the reply.

But on the Monday 20-year-old Lunghis, a most peculiar character (a cold, cheeky, blond psychopath, with no arms) who spent his time hanging around Gehrden, spoke to the older man.

"Herr Erdner, I know where your son is. Detective Fritz Honnerbrock took him away. Honnerbrock spends his time in the "Eisbeinecke" near the Goethe bridge - that's where we met him. Honnerbrock's always going around with Wilhelm, I saw him yesterday and asked him where Wilhelm was. He said, 'Oh, him! I arrested him on Schiller Straße and took him to the police station.' Has Wilhelm done something?"

Wilhelm's parents went to the police station to make enquiries about their son, and also to ask about this detective "Honnerbrock", but to no avail. However, a short while later Lunghis bumped into the alleged detective whilst walking down the street and asked him where the younger boy was. The answer came: "I am unable to call this case to mind. I am now on duty. Please come to the 'Eisbeinecke' at 7 p.m. thisevening and we shall be able to discuss matters then." But the man never turned up, and neither did young Erdner.

It was not until the following summer that a first clue was found. A bicycle dealer by the name of Rauper, for whom Olfermann and Haarmann had worked as detectives, bought a bicycle in the October through one of Haarmann's connections. This happened thus: Haarmann turned up in Rauper's shop on 20 October 1923.

"Rauper, do me a favour. There's a young man outside, nice fellow, but no job and in a bit of a spot. Buy his bike off him, will you? There's a good chap." Rauper allowed himself to be persuaded. It was an old bike, dark blue, no freewheel. The young man who was supposedly poverty-stricken was... Grans.

The bicycle dealer overhauled the bike, but kept the brake lever which was made from aluminium bronze. He remembered this incident when more was revealed about Haarmann's murders and took the brake lever to the police. It belonged to the bike on which young Erdner cycled to work. Shortly afterwards his grey trousers were found. Haarmann had given them to Frau Stille, the Wegehenkels' daughter.

11. Hermann Wolf, born 9 June 1908 disappeared 24 or 25 October 1923

Hermann was the somewhat neglected son of locksmith Christoph Wolf from the Kleine Wallstraße. He accompanied his elder brother (they were both unemployed) to the "employment exchange"; afterwards they went and hung around the station. The younger boy said, "Karl, wait, I just have to go out for a minute. I'll be right back." Karl waited, but Hermann never returned. He was not reported missing for another six days. His father claimed the boy had said to him, "I've been talking to a criminal at the station. I overheard a suspicious-sounding conversation. He said I was to go to the police and I'd get a reward."

Eight months later, once the murders had come to light, Hermann's mother identified some of her son's belongings at the police station. Amongst other things there was a buckle which her husband had made which proved beyond doubt that these were indeed her son's possessions. The pieces of fabric had been provided by Frau Wegehenkel; she had received them from Haarmann for "patching", although a pair of trousers which she had also been given had been sold. The bereft parents ranted against the police and the murderer; the father was manic, aggressive and threatening, which was probably the reason why Haarmann became cowardly and frightened and denied having had anything to do with this case. He even went so far as to say that he could not have killed anybody on that day (24 October) as it was his birthday and he had got drunk in the Altstadt; he was always sober when he committed his crimes. Alcohol numbed his sexual drive.

Haarmann told the parents, "I have my standards. I wouldn't have gone for such an ugly chap as the one in your picture. You say he wasn't even wearing a shirt. And his trousers were tied to his legs with string. Ugh! You should be ashamed of yourselves, letting your boy run around like that! There are thousands of pieces of fabric around like the ones you're showing me. Don't you go imagining things. Your boy was far from good enough for me."

Haarmann had to be acquitted of this crime.

12. Heinz Brinkmann from Clausthal, born 20 Oct. 1910 disappeared 27 October 1923

13-year-old Heinz was the son of the widow Frieda Brinkmann from Clausthal in the Harz mountains. During the school holiday he was supposed to be visiting his brother Richard, a fusilier in the German army at his barracks in Hannover, and then travel on to visit his Aunt Emma in Uelzen. His concerned mother accompanied him to the station; the train was due to depart from the Frankenscharrerhütte at 1.59 p.m., arriving in Hannover at 6.30 p.m. The boy never arrived. His poor mother was not satisfied with the missing persons report ("Contact us if you hear anything"), but went directly to a detective agency. It was established that the boy never got on the 1.59, but left the Lautental station at 5 p.m., arriving in Hannover at approximately 11 p.m. It was not possible to determine where he spent the night. However, several months later the following clue came to light. One night in October 1923, a man from Bremerhaven, Hermann Otto, who worked for the youth welfare organisation, was on Hannover main station. Between 11 p.m. and midnight he witnessed the following incident which he was unable to forget. There was a slim, young boy, around 14 years old, in the entrance hall. He had a thin, bony face and was wearing a brown corduroy suit. He was carrying an empty rucksack and had his hat in his hand. There was an older person standing next to him. They were approached by a well-dressed gentleman, who spoke to them. Otto had noticed these two men on previous occasions when he had been travelling through Hannover at night and had had to wait on Hannover station for his connection. He had been surprised that it was possible to enter the waiting rooms without a ticket, but this gentleman obviously walked in and out freely and approached any and all youngsters between the ages of 16 and 20. Otto asked a station official whether this gentleman also worked for the youth welfare services and got the following answer, “No, he’s a detective.”

It was Haarmann. Eight months after little Heinz disappeared, when the murders became known and all the clothes that had been found were put on display, his mother and aunt went to Hannover where they identified Heinz’s corduroy suit, rucksack and underwear. ”I recognised his trousers straightaway. Richard wore them first and there was a small inkspot on them. Old Frau Dieckmann, who lives near us, sewed the lining and I put in my old cambric.”

Once again the trousers had been found with Frau Wegehenkel. Her own little son Rudi had been wearing the trousers but when things started to get a little hot she gave the suit to a lithographer, who took it to the police. The boy had arrived in Hannover late at night, too late to travel on to his brother that same night, so he stayed at the station. Haarmann was “on duty” and promised the boy somewhere to stay for the night, then killed him.

13. Adolf Hannappel from Düsseldorf, born 28 April 1908 disappeared Martinmas 1923

The carpenter Jakob Hannappel and his wife Marie, pleasant, decent people, received a parcel from their 17-year-old son at Martinmas. It contained, cake, flowers and sausage. Adolf was a loyal, affectionate person who always received glowing reports from his teachers and later, when he was an apprentice, from his master.

Early in 1923 Adolf contracted TB of the peritoneum. When he was discharged from hospital he was sent to a nursing home in Watersloh for recuperation, from where he was finally discharged in the September. However, he was advised that carpentry would be “too difficult, too tiring; stay in the country. Go for something less strenuous.” So, in October 1923, Adolf was apprenticed to a head dairyman named Rudolf Dehne, a coarse, somewhat blunt fellow who worked in Linsborn near Lippstadt. The estate and dairy belonged to a widow, Frau Sürmann, who thought Adolf “a dear fellow, but ‘e ‘as a gun, like them 'comminists'. And ‘e’s still growin’. ‘E’s eatin’ me out of ‘ouse an’ ‘ome”.

So it was agreed, with regret, that Adolf should leave. He was to go to Hannover and ask for a good job at the Wenger dairy on the Ballhofstraße. If there was nothing to be had there he would go on to his uncle in Hamburg.

On 10 November (Martinmas) Adolf sold his pistol and used the money for the rail fare from Bennighausen to Hannover. No one ever heard of or from him again. The parcel his parents received for Martinmas was the last contact he had with them. And yet, once the enquiries into his disappearance got underway, several people said they had seen him in the third-class waiting room on the station - such a strapping, decent young German was not easily overlooked. He sat quietly on the large travelling trunk he had made himself, wearing smart new trousers; several people noticed the little spirit level next to him. Some saw Haarmann approach Hannappel and talk to him; others saw Grans and young Hannappel struggle to the left luggage department with the heavy trunk. The three of them were also seen going into the town together in the direction of the Café Kröpcke, but nothing further could be establishedafter that. It was not until the following July that Adolf's clothing turned up, his box calf boots, his braces and sweater and the spirit level were again found in the Engel circle of family and friends. A police official at the station (such irony!) had the olive green hat with a dark green band (a present from his colleague Haarmann) and Hans Grans was wearing the smart new trousers. Everyone had bought something from Haarmann - at a good price, too - or been given gifts. This case was made simpler by the fact that Haarmann confessed to it. However, it became increasingly complicated as more and more witnesses claimed to have seen Grans pointing Hannappel out to Haarmann and bringing about the friendship between them. Haarmann used this fact to his own advantage and against his former lover: Grans had ordered him to kill Hannappel because he wanted the trousers and the contents of the travelling trunk; Haarmann himself was not particularly attracted to the young man as he never paid any attention to clothing. But Grans carried on and on, first pleading, then threatening and then cajoling, until Haarmann finally capitulated.

Now Grans's main witness for the prosecution, the barber in Hannover penitentiary, turned out to be such a hypocrite that nobody, even in such a motley collection of rogues as was present at this trial, would ever be able to forget. A smooth, smarmy person who had lost a leg in the war and walked with the aid of a stick, told (puffed up with moral indignation in spite of his own criminal record) of what he had seen at the station. He had read the newspapers and was therefore aware that Haarmann was erotically dependent on Grans. Everything else was misrepresentation with the aim of "having his say". He knew how Wittkowski, Grans and Haarmann had perfected a "murder system", complete with signals and secret marks, Wittkowski operating from the platform, Grans from the vestibule and Haarmann from the waiting rooms. He knew how Hans and Hugo selected the victims and then sent them to Haarmann, who throttled them.

The rest of his fabrications consisted of stories about his "wealth", of successful business deals he had made, and assured the assembly: "A German who has experienced our time of glory and shed blood for the Fatherland in the war does not lie!"

However, it gradually became clear that Grans had not killed, nor provided "victims". Nonetheless there were still vast discrepancies between Haarmann's and Grans's stories. It was proved that Grans, and not Haarmann, collected the travelling truck from the station (immediately after Adolf had been killed), and that he helped himself to the majority of the contents.

On leaving the Court, Adolf's distressed parents asked whether they could have a few items of their son's clothing as a memento, and the mother remarked with despairing bitterness, "Grans can keep the trousers if he thinks they're so elegant!" Grans (woe betide the judges!) was sentenced to death.

14. Adolf Hennies, born 10 November 1904 disappeared 6 December 1923

Nothing remained of this victim other than his coat, which originally had flat, yellow horn buttons. They were taken off and replaced, by an inexperienced hand, with leather buttons. The coat was confiscated from the Burgstraße in the apartment shared by Hans Grans and Hugo Wittkowski and put on display in the police station. Six months later, several independent witnesses (the first of which was his widowed mother, Auguste Hennies, née Habekost, of no. 3 Perlstraße; a dull, heavy woman) identified it as having belonged to 19-year-old Adolf. She recognised its cut, colour and the lining in the sleeves.

The next witnesses to recognise it were Frau Hennies' lodger, Willi Eisenschmiedt, a plausible, quiet old gent who shared a room with Adolf and recognised the coat as being the one he had seen in his wardrobe; his brother, who was a labourer, and a close friend Willi Rackebrand also recognised the coat, as did staff at the clothes shop where the coat had been purchased on hire purchase. There was no doubt that the coat had belonged to Adolf Hennies, but where had Grans got it from? Grans claimed he had bought it from Haarmann on hire purchase and in fact still owed Haarmann some money for it. Haarmann's story was different; "One cold, snowy afternoon Wittkowski and Grans came to my room, asking to use it that night for a meeting. I agreed and went to the pub, the "Schwule Kessel" [a meeting-place for homosexuals near theHoftheater] for a few hours, then went on to the station. I stayed there until morning. When I got back to my room I found a dead body there, completely naked. Hugo and Hans were just tying some clothes into a bundle. I said, 'What's going on?' They said, 'One of yours.' I thought, there're no marks on the neck. Mine all have love-bites. They stuck to their story and ran off, leaving the coat behind. Grans collected it next day and gave me 8 Marks for it. I had to cut the body up and get rid of it. I don't know who it was. But it was this one that the coat belonged to."

On the second day of the trial Haarmann became increasingly tearful as he made his accusations against Grans. He told the investigating judge that he had bought the coat and given it to Grans, warning him that he thought the coat was 'hot', which was why Grans immediately changed the buttons.

Adolf's mother had the following to say, "My son was a very respectable young man; he never spent a night away from home. That was the first time he hadn't come home. He occasionally went to a dance with his friend Wedemeyer, but we always knew where he was. He confided in Wedemeyer that he had a soft spot for a young lady he had used to run errands for when he was working at the Ahrberg butchery. He'd always wanted to invite her to go to the cinema with him, but he was too shy." At the time of his disappearance Hennies was without work and looking for new employment. On the day he disappeared he applied for a post as a travelling salesman, selling soap for a merchant known only as "G", on the old Celler Heerstraße (as this was near the notorious homosexual district, there were several stories abounding about the "soap factory"). There is no firm indication that Hennies knew Haarmann particularly well, but he did tell both his brother and his friend, "I've met a police official who can find work for me and has promised me some clothes."

It is to be assumed that Haarmann made these promises to Hennies in order to lure the unsuspecting young man into his apartment, although this was never proven. I have a simple explanation why Haarmann tried to blame this particular case on Hugo and Hans: the coat was indeed a matter of dispute between the three; they actually physically fought over it. Grans and Wittkowski did not want to pay Haarmann for it, so Haarmann applied his "compensatory" imagination resulting from his jealous hatred to this (convenient) case against Wittkowski, and the hatred caused by suppressed or rejected sexual attraction against Grans. The most notorious of all criminal cases, that of the French marshal Gilles de Rais, has several similar "compensations".

Haarmann was not convicted of this case as there was no proof of his guilt; he was acquitted.

Interlude
The Keimes Case

At this point I am inserting a murder case which is the most peculiar of Haarmann's crimes, but for which he was not tried. It was undoubtedly the most mysterious for the psychologists.

First a few lines of introduction from a long letter written by Herr Georg Koch, a merchant in Hannover (whose 14-year-old son Hermann may well have been one of Haarmann's victims).

"As the father of 14-year-old Hermann Koch, who disappeared in 1918, I would like to provide some counter-evidence to the statement made by the police to the effect that they had not received sufficient information concerning the criminal. Haarmann admitted having kept company with my son. This fact is also obvious from a note of apology Haarmann sent to my son's school when he provided cause for my son's absence. When the police were obviously unable to provide any information in connection with my son's disappearance and released Haarmann from detention, I transferred the case to the Sebastian Detective Agency which, after extensive enquiries, proved Haarmann had committed the murder. In spite of this, a retrial was rejected. This was in November 1921. However, in the meantime the same detective agency proved that Haarmann was guilty of another murder case (Keimes) and on 11 May requested that he be tried on this charge. No reply was received to this application either, although several people (Rehbock, Klobes, Lammers, Lindner) made several reports between 1922 and 1924."

So what exactly was the Keimes case?

On 17 May 1923, the 17-year-old son of a married couple named Keimes, an extraordinarily pretty young boy, disappeared in the southern part of the town. The parents turned to the police who, despite numerous requests to do so, failed to publish notification of the missing person in the newspapers. Three days later the family put their own announcement in the local papers, promising a substantial reward to anybody who could provide information concerning the young man's whereabouts. Several days later a man (later recognised to have been Haarmann) appeared at the family's door, claiming to be a criminologist interested in the case and asked for a picture of their son.

"If your son is still in Hannover, I shall solve the case within three days,' he promised. Whilst the mother had gone to find a suitable picture the man stayed in the room with the missing boy's sister; after the man had left the sister said he had "been laughing hysterically". The boy's body was found in the canal an hour away from Hannover on 6 May 1922 (not for another seven weeks). He was naked and had been strangled. There was a rope around his neck and a handkerchief with a monogrammed "G" had been stuffed in his mouth.

It was assumed (as implausible as it may seem) that there had been a genuine robbery with murder and that the boy had been killed on the spot. It is strange that, after visiting the Keimes family, Haarmann went to the police station and accused Hans Grans of having committed this robbery and murder (an accusation which was dropped when it was established that Grans had been in custody at the time of the crime). As it turned out, the handkerchief in the mouth of the dead body did indeed belong to Grans.

It would appear that this was a case (which would happen again in the later Hennies case) in which Haarmann tried to frame his lover, although he had either committed the murder himself or had been an accessory. It is even possible that he tried to stage the abduction, strangulation and gagging so that Grans would fall for it. Shortly after the huge row between Haarmann and Grans on Haarmann's return from Jägerheide, his room had been ransacked by Wittkowski and Grans, leaving him desperately wanting his revenge on the two men. The Keimes case was never solved. In fact, of the 400 exhibits found in Haarmann's rooms, only 100 were recognised.

15. Ernst Spiecker, born 15 June 1906 disappeared 5 January 1924

Ernst was the result of a relationship during his mother's youth, and she obviously loved him dearly for she found it difficult to make her statement through her tears. One morning in January 1924, the 17-year-old had to appear as a witness at a trial. He wore his best clothes which had been tailored at his step-father's (a fine, sympathetic man) tailoring business. When he had finished at the courthouse he went for a walk with his friend Siegfried Kurth. They parted near the theatre, and Ernst was never heard from again.

This case illustrates particularly clearly what part coincidence can play in the discovery of a murder, and how easily miscarriages of justice can arise.

On the day of his friend's disappearance, young Kurth, the son of an industrialist, was about to emigrate to Argentina. Should it therefore have been surprising that some of the concerned parties thought, with terror and revulsion, that he may somehow be involved in his friend's disappearance? The suspicion could have remained forever had not virtually all of Ernst's belongings been taken to the police station by the familiar contacts amongst the "fences" in the following June. Grans had sold his stockings, sports cap and steel fob watch decorated with horn and was wearing Ernst's shirt at the time of his arrest. He wore clothes belonging to four different victims at the same time, and dealt in clothing belonging to other victims, and this brazen parading could only be explained by incredible cheek or a total lack of guile concerning the origins of these items obtained from Haarmann.

It was proven that Haarmann had known young Spiecker. The son of the Spiecker family's landlord confessed that he and his missing friend had got to know Haarmann, who had given them cigarettes, in the "Schwule Kessel". As in several other cases, Haarmann claimed that he was unable to recognise Ernst from his photograph, nor could he remember him (even though the boy had a glass eye); although he would have to assume Ernst was one of his victims, as the boy's belongings had been found in Haarmann's room. Perhaps it had been the delightful child he, on awakening at midnight one night, had found dead in his arms. Haarmann had allegedly passed out at the sight, or else sheer weariness had caused him to fall asleep again.

"When I woke up early in the morning, the dead boy was next to me. Stiff and cold and blue. I pulled him out of bed by the hands, laid him on the floor and cut him up. I've remembered this case because the dead man had lain there so poorly."

16. Heinrich Koch, born 22 September 1905 disappeared 15 January 1924

This boy was something of a tearaway. His father, a quiet, gentle man, found it difficult to exercise any kind of control over his son. On 13 January Heinrich spent the night away from home and afterwards lied about it to his parents, saying he had spent the night at a masked ball. He left home early on 15 January and was never seen again.

Heinrich spent a lot of his time with others of the same sex and inclination. As he was unable to find other employment, he and his friend, a plumber named Tolle, spent the winter helping slipper maker Otto Moshage, a strikingly intelligent and noble looking man. Ernst told Moshage that he wanted to leave home.

"My parents are always on at me. But I've got a friend. He's a waiter in the Reichshof. He lives in the Altstadt. He gave me 50 cigarettes. I've spent the night with him before."

Moshage was aware of what went on at the station and the theatre and he had also seen Koch in Haarmann's company. He asked the boy what his friend's name was and the boy became embarrassed. Moshage said, "Come on, tell me the truth now. It's Fritz Haarmann." The boy admitted it was. Haarmann, however, claimed not to recognise the boy's photo, but once again, all of the victim's belongings were found. Theodor Hartmann, one of Frau Engel's offspring from an earlier marriage, had sold Ernst's things to all sorts of shady characters, and as Haarmann said every time he was proved of having committed a murder, "It's probably true."

17. Willi Senger, born 6 July 1904 disappeared 2 February 1924

Willi came from a loveless background. His father was a labourer in Linden who had no time for his children. His mother, a dour, lymphatic bottle blonde, was no better. Willi's elder brother was impassive and uncommunicative. It was a joyless family with little conversation.

For several years Willi, 17 years of age, had hung around the station in the company of the homosexuals. Although he was a good-looking youth, he was also rough and violent. One evening in February he told his sister that he was going on a trip, put on his best clothes and left. His failure to return made little impression on this dull world. "One less mouth to feed." However, when the vast number of murders was revealed in the July of that year, Ernst's family decided to "go and have a look at the things". They found Willi's tie, which his brother Heinrich had made and given to him, and his brown coat. Haarmann claimed he had bought or exchanged the clothes from someone at the station; he had known both Senger and his boon companion, 19-year-old Fritz Barkhof, for years. "They were the greatest rogues of all. I was always afraid of them. Senger was big, strong and rough. I could never have got control over him. For that reason alone I could never have killed him."

It is noticeable that Haarmann never confessed to having murdered anyone he had known for a long time. He would concede to a murder if he was able to say with plausibility when faced with the photograph, "I don't recognise him. Maybe; maybe not," (it was obvious that he always found it difficult to look at these photographs).

There was only one witness to Haarmann's association with Senger: Fritz Barkhof, whom it was difficult to trust. He came across as rough and feminine; vain and embarrassed at the same time. This suspicious character was, unwisely, questioned about Senger's activities in the presence of his family; understandably, several things were left unsaid, either through fear or embarrassment, or to protect the feelings of the missing boy's family. One thing is certain: the two boys belonged to the inner circle of those professionals who offered themselves for sale. Senger told Barkhof that he had often spent the night with Haarmann, and, after Senger had disappeared, Senger asked Haarmann whether he had any idea of where the boy could be. Haarmann replied brusquely, "Don't know him." He responded in the same way to further questions concerning Senger. When asked exactly when he had obtained the coat, Haarmann contradicted himself repeatedly. However, it was proven beyond doubt that he did not obtain it until immediately after Senger disappeared.

18. Hermann Speichert, born 21 April 1908 disappeared 8 February 1924

Hermann was a bright, intelligent lad of almost 16, an electrical apprentice at Mühe & Co. on the Hildesheimer Straße. In January 1924 his parents noticed that he was always clean when he arrived home from work. His father went to the company, where he was told that his son had not been to work for four weeks.

The young layabout was now firmly taken to task, but his response was, "I'm not interested in technology any more. I've got a friend who's going to take me overseas with him." But his father insisted that he return to Mühe & Co the next day.

As the family home was in Linden young Hermann went to his sister's, a Frau Albrecht on the Lavesstraße, at lunchtime (between noon and 2 p.m.). Hermann went there as usual on 8 February. The boy and his sister, a pleasant, decent woman, chatted amicably. He left at 2 p.m. and was never seen again. On 10 February his father notified the police of Hermann's disappearance. No traces were found. In June some items of his clothing, which had been made by his mother and sister, were found in Haarmann's apartment at no. 2 Rote Reihe; other items had been sold by Frau Engel's stepson on Haarmann's behalf. Grans was given Hermann's geometry kit, which an old acquaintance of the boy recognised when socialising with Haarmann on the Georgstraße. At the sight of her son's clothing, Frau Speichert broke down. For the first time ever, Haarmann lowered his eyes.

19. Alfred Hogrefe from Lehrte, born 6 October 1907 disappeared 6 April 1924

Alfred was the 17-year-old son of a train driver, Gustav Hogrefe, and was apprenticed to a mechanic on Schlägerstraße. He regularly travelled on the 6 a.m. train from Lehrte to his job in Hannover, arriving home at about 7.30 pm. On Mondays he went to trade school.

On this particular day he arrived home at 10 p.m. He explained his lateness by having been to a PE class after school which ran from 7.30 until 8.30 p.m. On 1 April 1924 Herr and Frau Hogrefe were informed by the director of the trade school that Alfred had not been attending school. The boy was taken to task by his most unpedagogical parents, and he was extremely embarrassed. His father shouted, "Right! Mother and I are off to Hannover tomorrow to your school. We'll see what happens after that!" Early the following afternoon Alfred's parents went to see the boy's teacher and realised that their son had told them a pack of lies. He had skipped school on the three previous Mondays and had sent notes of apology for his absences to the school himself. It was also revealed that his PE class did not take place after school on a Monday evening, but during the day with the other lessons.

In the meantime Alfred had gone to work as usual (scared half to death that his parents would find out what had been going on), only to leave at 2 p.m., saying he wanted to meet his parents from the station. In fact, whilst his parents were travelling home from Lehrte to Hannover, Alfred went home, packed his bags and left again. Gradually over the following months more and more information came to light about what happened next. After leaving the family home, Alfred met a friend, an apprentice by the name of Wiese, at the station in Lehrte. Hogrefe told his friend he had been "badly treated" by his parents at home and wanted to leave. He then offered to sell Wiese his bicycle. Wiese was a bright boy and got the bike for a good price. He kept quiet about this incident. During the evening of the next day, young Wiese met Hogrefe again, this time on the main station in Hannover. Hogrefe was carrying an imitation leather case and bounced up to Wiese, saying, "Oh boy, I bought this case with the money you gave me for the bike!" Wiese asked his friend where he had spent the night and Hogrefe confessed that he had slept at the station. He asked Wiese in a small voice if he could spend the following night in their hayloft in Lehrte. He was obviously homesick, but was too scared to go home to his strict parents now that they knew of all of his fabrications. This was 3 April. On 4 April at about 8 p.m. another friend from Lehrte, apprentice tailor Farin, met Hogrefe outside Hannover station. He excitedly told his friend how he had run away from home a few days before, had sold his bike and bought himself a suitcase with the money he got for it, which was now in the left luggage department. He was spending the nights with a gentleman he had got to know who was a police official living on the Neue Straße.

Farin never saw Hogrefe again after that meeting. But a third friend from Lehrte saw him: apprentice Wilhelm Köhler who travelled daily to work in Hannover. Hogrefe told him the same story.

"My father's thrown me out. My suitcase is in the left luggage department." (He proudly showed Köhler the luggage ticket.) Köhler saw Hogrefe with Haarmann (whom he knew to be a "criminal" and was called "Fritz") the next evening (around 6 April) sitting talking at a table in the first and second class waiting room. Again two days later (around 8 April) Köhler bumped into Hogrefe at the station and walked part of the way to the Herschelstraße with him, where Hogrefe took his leave. Hogrefe told him he often met up with "Criminal Fritz". However, nobody ever saw him again. The boys who travelled to work from Lehrte all recognised Haarmann, whom they took to be some kind of official, from the station. Apprentice Walter Schnabel, who travelled to work with Hogrefe every morning, later stated that they often saw Haarmann (whose name they did not know) on the station concourse as early as 6 a.m., and that he always looked at them most keenly. An older factory foreman had also seen Hogrefe talking to Grans and Haarmann, but that had been in March. All of Hogrefe's clothes, his check jacket, his imitation sheepskin coat, shirt, scarf etc., were later found at Haarmann's, Frau Engel's or with their "salespeople". This was the first time Frau Engel was caught out. She claimed she had found the dead person's coat in a pile of old clothing and had passed it on to her aunt who made slippers. However, she had given her aunt a different story about its origin. Haarmann stated, "I certainly assume

I killed Hogrefe, but I can't remember his face." (If, before his own death, Haarmann were to write down his memories of those he had killed it would become clear that he suppressed all painful or embarrassing memories.)

The facts of this case were: a frightened boy scared of being beaten, spent eight days hanging around the railway station, lonely and hungry. His own father works for the railway. His companions from his home town, who all travel to town, and several railway officials know the boy and regularly see him at the station in Haarmann's company. However, they also know Haarmann. Nothing was done to apprehend the young runaway and after he disappeared nothing was done about questioning Haarmann.

20. Hermann Bock, born 2 December 1901 disappeared mid-April 1924

This case is the darkest of them all. If Haarmann had committed this particular crime, then there was no doubt that it had been planned long in advance as opposed to having been committed in the throes of passion.

22-year-old Hermann from Uelzen, a labourer, was one of those who hung around Hannover doing nothing at all, not working, spending his time in the Altstadt or at the station. He was blond, tall, strong and bold. Haarmann met him in 1921, "at the station", and occasionally used him as a fence for small jobs, or else as a "commission agent" for the sale of clothing of unknown or shady origin. Bock disappeared in the middle of April, and no one missed him. The only person to ask after him was a lathe operator, Fritz Kahmann (simple, frightened, dour, unsure of himself, with scared little eyes) from the Neue Straße, who had shared Bock's room. He spoke to Haarmann, who was his neighbour, several weeks after Bock's disappearance, "Fritz, do you know where Bock is?" Haarmann replied, "How should I know? He's probably been up to something, maybe had trouble with a colleague," to which Kahmann foolishly said, "But Fritz, you should know where he is. The last time he was seen he was on his way to your flat with his suitcase."

Haarmann became thoughtful, then he said, "Well, I don't understand it. Hermann's a nice lad, knows what he's about." Kahmann, who was frightened, said, "Well, I think we should go to the police and put in a 'missing persons' report." "Goodness," replied Haarmann, "yes of course, you're right. Tell you what - they know me at the police station. I'll take care of it. And I'll telephone the hospitals and the court prison; I'll do that today."

The two of them met up again the following day on the "island". Haarmann began his "report" without delay, "It's all been a waste of time. I've asked everywhere, but no one has seen or heard of Hermann." (Later it was revealed that Haarmann had made absolutely no enquiries about Bock at all, nor had he made any telephone calls ....)

Bock had several other close friends: Paul Sieger, known as Alex, who was a rough, fair haired, brutal fellow; Franz Kirchhoff, a 20-year-old locksmith, slightly disabled with a small head, small eyes, a small nose, thick lower lip and hoarse voice, and finally Hans Ulawski, a tall, thin waiter in the "Simplizissimus", whom Haarmann described thus: "He's the biggest rogue around. He's a magician. Goes around the fairs." These youngsters had all known Haarmann for years, and all believed he was a police official (he often told them that he was "off to the police station for a conference"). They also knew that Bock and Haarmann were (literally) as thick as thieves. He and Haarmann often had meals in Frau Engel's pub, and Bock frequently spent the night withHaarmann although his accomplices testified to the fact that, "he wasn't interested in men, only in girls. He was absolutely normal."

Ulawski had a bride in Czechoslovakia; on two occasions Bock and Ulawski went to visit her. Bock's mother, who lived in Ulzen, was a middle-aged, simple, sickly woman, frog-eyed and hard of hearing. She was not particularly disturbed by the news of her son's disappearance. "The boy came for Christmas. When Herr Kamann wrote to me on 8 April I thought, 'Well, he'll be back again'." The way Bock's belongings were "found" in Haarmann's rooms was most peculiar. When Haarmann had been arrested, Ulawski looked through the items on exhibit in his presence but found nothing. As they were leaving, however, he looked closely at Haarmann and cried out, "You're wearing Hermann's suit!" Haarmann laughed at him and said, "This is far too serious for me to be brought into it." Nonetheless, Ulawski stood firm and as he knew which tailor had made his friend's suit he paid a visit there. The tailor swore under oath that not only had he made the suit Haarmann was wearing for Bock, but Haarmann had subsequently come to him, saying he had bought the suit from Bock for DM 30 and wanted it altering.

Suddenly Haarmann "remembered" - he "may" have bought the suit from Bock after all. However, in the meantime Bock's briefcase had also been found, bearing his full name: Hermann Bock, Hannover. Somebody had tried to scratch the name off, but it was still possible to make out the faded writing. Haarmann had given it to Frau Engel, who had been using it for her market shopping. Hermann's other possessions had disappeared off the face of the earth.

It is not likely that this was a sex murder; Bock had been a friend of Haarmann's for several years and often spent the night in his apartment. It was well known that he was not gay, and he was also past the age Haarmann preferred. Was this a case of someone being disposed of, someone who perhaps knew something and was silenced? Or was it the attraction of the case and clothing? Or had it started out as a spot of fun that had gone horribly wrong? Or all three?

Haarmann was acquitted.

21. Wilhelm Apel from Leinhausen, born 4 June 1908 disappeared 17 April 1924

Wilhelm had always been dreamy and reserved and, as his teachers and vicar confirmed, was easily influenced and intimidated. When he had finished school and been confirmed, his father, Wilhelm Apel, a lathe operator from Leinhausen, obtained an apprenticeship for him with one of the big hauliers, M. Neldel on the Nikolaistraße. He took the tram to work at 6 a.m. every morning and arrived home at around 8 p.m. It appears that he started on the "slippery slope" once he had started work in town. His mother noticed from the beginning of 1924 that he seemed depressed. He spent hours huddled over his books and was unableto look his mother in the eye. His father, who was very strict, followed him one day and caught him in town smoking cigarettes and punished him severely, "You'll stay in over Easter, no matter how good the weather is!"

The following day, 17 April, the boy went to Hannover as usual but never arrived at work and was never seen again. When the items which had been confiscated from Haarmann or sold by Frau Engel for him were checked, the boy's clothes (most of which had been hand-sewn by his mother) were amongst them.

As the boy would have waited for the train home in the waiting room which Haarmann "patrolled", there can be no doubt that this was where they met, an event which would have sealed Wilhelm's fate ...

22. Robert Witzel, born 18 March 1906 disappeared 26 April 1924

Robert was the second son of factory foreman Georg Witzel. On leaving school in July 1921 he found employment with the Mittelland rubber works as a labourer and transferred to the Excelsior rubber works in May 1924.

His best friend was labourer Friedrich Kahlmeyer, who was only 14 years of age, but mentally well developed; quiet, good looking with girlish features. The two youngsters, accompanied occasionally by Robert's elder brother Willi, frequented several of the gay haunts and the "Gesellschaftshaus" on the Calenberger Straße. Most nights they looked out for "friends" near the station or behind Café Kröpcke ("Schwuler Kessel", "Café Wellblech"), sometimes going home with them, where they were often given money and occasionally a meal. This was why they were so well acquainted with Haarmann, who often spent half the night at these meeting points.

They also occasionally had intercourse. With regard to attractive young Kahlmeyer, Haarmann said after his arrest, "I'm sorry I never had Kahlmeyer. He should be got rid of."

On 26 April 1924 Robert Witzel asked his mother for 50 Pfennigs, telling her he wanted to go to the circus. He put on his best coat and left the house at about 4 p.m.; he was never seen again. Some time after young Robert's disappearance Kahlmeyer met Haarmann and asked him whether he had any idea where Robert could be. Haarmann pretended to be shocked and upset, making out he had not even heard the boy was missing. This strengthened Kahlmeyer's belief that Haarmann knew nothing of the matter and helped to explain why this youngster, who was so popular in gay circles never told Robert's parents of their son's homosexuality, whether it was out of shame or fear of retribution, or maybe even fear of Haarmann (who constantly threatened them: "If you ever say anything at home I'll have you locked up" [i.e. imprisoned or put in a home]).

Robert's parents and brother claimed that the skull found in the pleasure gardens on 20 May 1924 was Robert's, saying that they recognised the unusual shape of the teeth (the front teeth protruded and were grooved, and a molar had recently been drilled but not yet filled). However, the dentist who had treated Witzel was not able to recognise the skull, and Haarmann was particularly certain that he had destroyed Witzel's skull. The clothes, boots, underwear, keys etc. which were found in Haarmann's rooms and in those of his fences were identified as definitely being the property of Robert Witzel, and his identity card was found in a pair of trousers worn by Theodor Hartmann, Frau Engel's son; Hartmann returned the card to Haarmann. Haarmann was sure he had killed Witzel the first night he stayed with him and had thrown the remains in the river Leine.

23. Heinz Martin from Chemnitz, born 30 December 1909 disappeared 9 May 1924

Heinz's father, a master plumber from Chemnitz by the name of Georg Martin, had died in the war. Ten-year-old Heinz had been left with his mother and sister. He was a good, decent boy, a pupil at the grammar school until Easter 1924. He had had two important experiences in his short life. The first was in 1921 when he visited

Bremerhaven with a host of other grammar school pupils and the second when the visit was repeated in 1922. Since that time he had dreamt of becoming a ship's engineer. He spent his time making model ships and reading travel stories. He was confirmed at Easter in 1924 and was to start an apprenticeship as a locksmith at a knitwear manufacturer's, but in his dreams he was in the big wide world. His mother was a serious, strict woman who had no sympathy for his grandiose plans, and he opened his heart to a fellow apprentice, Horst Clemens.

"I want to go back to Bremerhaven and go on the big ship again. What is there for me here? I have to tidy the kitchen. Make the bed. Is that a man's job? Just don't be surprised when I leave."

Heinz's relations had given him money as a confirmation present, a total of DM 32. It made him feel rich, and he always had the money with him. "You must save," said his mother. "Give the money to me and I'll put it in the bank." The boy reddened and said, "Oh, it's at work in my tool box." His mother suspected that something was not quite right, and said, "Well, I want to go to the factory tomorrow afternoon anyway, so I'll get it then." That was on 8 May. The youngster left for work as usual on 9 May, and at 2 p.m. went to see his superior.

"I have to go to my grandmother's funeral in Leipzig tomorrow. Can I have a day's leave and a pass?"

"Of course, my boy," said the factory foreman, not suspecting the lie. Heinz packed his things, left and was never seen again.

Two women stood in the court in Hannover, looking like death, consumed by the fire of utmost suffering. They had been looking for the child for eight weeks but were unable to trace him. It was thought he might have tried to get to Bremerhaven to follow his dream of becoming a ship's engineer, but oddly enough there were still DM 20 of his confirmation money in his tool box so he could not have had more than DM 12 on him. But was that why he had run away? Had he been afraid his mother would collect the money in the afternoon and realise some was missing and that he had used the remainder, or part of it, earlier, in which case he could only have a very small amount with him now, or even none at all? He was wearing a navy blue sports cap with a blue linen jacket, a red and white checked shirt and a brown cardigan. It was hardly to be believed that he would have left Chemnitz like this.

When the bodies and remains were found that June the two women travelled to Hannover to have a look at the collection of items taken from Haarmann's surroundings. Amongst more than 400 exhibits they found the clothes which had belonged to their Heinz. The initials HM stamped on the leather of the marine cap proved in a most unusual way that the cap had belonged to the youngster. It was returned to the manufacturer, who stated that the stamped M had a small defect and had been used in only one cap - Heinz's. But how had the boy got to Hannover?

It can only be assumed that he had been abducted by one of Haarmann's helpers, or else that he had got off the train at Hannover on the way to Bremerhaven to look for work, and that once on the platform he had run straight into Haarmann's waiting arms - just like all the other poor victims.

After some initial denial, Haarmann eventually confessed to the crime.

24. Fritz Wittig from Cassel, born 23 November 1906 disappeared 26 May 1924

The Wittig and Hannappel cases were the two which Haarmann claimed he had carried out on Grans's instructions when he was under Grans's influence. He always referred to these two cases as the "Düsseldorfer", Hannappel because all he knew was that he was "from Düsseldorf", Wittig because Wittig spoke - so Haarmann claimed - a Rhineland dialect. But whereas the court sentenced Hans Grans to death for inciting to murder (in accordance with § 49 of the St.G.B., the Penal Code), he was convicted only of being an accessory to murder in the Wittig case and sentenced to 12 years in a penitentiary. The court decided that the reason for Grans's actions in both cases was that he wanted the victim's clothes. However, the case cannot be so clear for the psychologists who know the penetrating multiplicity of motives even in what appears to be the simplest case, and who knows that it is easy to find a motive for a deed in retrospect (wherein lies the placating economy of human thought which I called "logificatio post festum" - "talking after the feast", as it is in the administration of justice, who find that "non quia peccatum sed ne peccetur" - "not because of the sin, but lest he should sin"). So we must endeavour to grasp the depths of this amazing case.

Fritz Wittig was a well-built, well-endowed 17-year-old, 5 foot 8 inches tall, with long, wavy, blond hair combed back. His father, a boiler maker in Kassel, and his young brother-in-law, merchant Hermann Schad, were concerned about the good-looking, talented youngster, who was an apprentice in a distillery, because he associated with young girls from an early age. They were, however, unaware that he also had several homosexual relationships. After an argument with his father, during which his father accused Fritz of being foolish and thoughtless, the boy left Kassel on 27 April, taking with him a black suitcase which belonged to his boss, and went to look for work. On 30 April he went for an interview for employment as a travelling salesman for a confectionary wholesaler, Carl Zwanzig on the Goethestraße in Hannover. As he made a good impression and also had with him his certificate of apprenticeship he was employed to visit the company's clients in the town. He started work on 1 May, was given some samples which he put in a black suitcase (obviously the one he had taken in Kassel) but came back in the evening saying he had been unable to sell anything at all. The same happened the next day, when he also returned the samples and said he had to go back to Kassel as his mother had been taken seriously ill; he also took back his certificate of apprenticeship. However, he returned to Zwanzig's on 3 May, saying he would like to try again and would be back on the following Monday. On this occasion he said he had left the black suitcase and his certificate in Kassel.

On Monday 4 May Herr Zwanwig put together an extensive selection of the company's products which he put in his own suitcase and gave everything to Fritz. Fritz was also given a second suitcase containing a variety of jars and small bottles. He left with both suitcases and never returned to Zwanzig's.

As it later transpired, his story concerning his sick mother and the whereabouts of his suitcase were not true. There was little likelihood of mistaken identity: Fritz had a deformed right arm, and it was obvious that his right hand was unusable. On 4 May his family received a letter post marked Hannover in which he gave his address as "Gasthaus Dißmer, Heiligerstraße", where he had indeed spent one night and taken several meals. Later, they received a postcard post marked Hannover-Bebra station, 14 May. That was the last communication they ever received. The police were unable to help them, and the first traces they had were when they went to Hannover and found several of Fritz's belongings amongst those on display at the police station. There was Fritz's suit, which had been confiscated from Grans, and his notebook which had been taken from Haarmann's rooms. There was a calendar at the end of the notebook on which someone had drawn a line through the days up to and including 23 May. There was also the following message: "I herewith give Herr Grans one grey suit to dispose of against commission. Said suit will be returned to me by Monday evening, 26 May, or else I shall receive payment of 40 Goldmarks. Hannover, 26 May." The figure 40 had been crossed through and "twenty" written above it. This confusing note was written in Haarmann's large, neat, carefully looped script which slanted to the right, indicating a careful, reserved nature, and was signed by Haarmann and Grans. It was obviously an agreement the two had reached concerning the suit which had belonged to the dead person.

It now appeared likely from the witnesses' reports that Wittig had been killed by Haarmann during the night of 26 May and that Grans had collected the suit from no. 2 Rote Reihe on 27 May.

Had Grans known of the murder? Had he incited it? Two witnesses were found who claimed to know Wittig's actions between 5 May, the day he left Zwanzig's with the suitcases of samples they had given him, and 26 May, (probably) the day on which he was killed.

It would appear that on Sunday 4 May Wittig travelled to Bielefeld for reasons unknown. A traveller by the name of Fritz Brinkmann met him on the journey between Bielefeld and Hannover. Wittig told Brinkmann thathe was currently working for the Zwanzig confectionary company, but that he was looking for other employment. Once on the platform at Hannover, Wittig was approached by an acquaintance whom he introduced to Brinkmann as Police Officer Haarmann. This acquaintance then invited Wittig to join him for a drink. Brinkmann claimed he then saw Wittig in Haarmann's company several times over the following days, and also that he had seen Grans with Wittig, walking arm in arm along the Ernst-August-Square. Wittig supposedly told Brinkmann at one of these meetings that he had a chance of employment at the Hamburg shipyard and did not intend to remain in Hannover much longer. On a later occasion, however, he said his friend Haarmann had advised him to stay in Hannover. Tailor Richard Huth, the second witness, said that young Wittig had spent the time when he had been unemployed wandering around the homosexual haunts, obviously seeking "contacts". Huth, an old acquaintance of Haarmann and Grans, claimed that on one occasion he had been in the Café Kröpcke with Haarmann (whom he too understood to be a police official) when a pretty young man had walked up to him and asked for a light for his cigarette. Haarmann discreetly took his leave.

When the young man mentioned that he was unemployed and a stranger here, and that he would be grateful for somewhere to stay, Huth offered him a bed for the night. However, in the meantime Haarmann and Grans again approached the stranger and invited him to join them for a drink. All four of them went to the "Alte Reichshand" on the Große Packhofstraße, where Grans cajoled them into drinking more and more(even though he was paying) and Haarmann begged them to be more careful. After closing time they left the bar and Huth went off on his own to retrieve his hat, which an exciting young female in the Corso- Café had taken from him. He hurried to catch up with them at the station, but found only Haarmann. In reply to his question about where the others were

Haarmann replied that the stranger had gone with Grans. When Huth commented that he had not realised Grans was “that way inclined,” Haarmann replied, “Well, he’s keen on him”; the two men then went their separate ways.

So these are the witnesses for the way in which Wittig was taken in by Grans and Haarmann and, at the same time, chased away from Huth. However, Grans’s and Haarmann’s stories now start to take a slightly different slant. Haarmann (who had had to admit to this murder from the start because his constant refrain of "I cannot remember my victims" would not hold in view of the unforgettably deformed right arm), immediately changed his story, saying Grans had drawn his attention to the young man talking to Huth at the Café Kröpcke with the words, “Look at that suit - I want it. Mine’s coming apart at the sleeves.” At Grans’s urging Haarmann approached Wittig; Grans took care of everything else, persuading Wittig to go with Haarmann, who he said was “very good” and would probably give him something to eat as well, instead of with Huth. Haarmann took the stranger off to the “Rote Reihe”, but whilst they were actually having intercourse became revolted by the useless right hand. In spite of that, Grans was able to persuade Wittig to return time and again. When Haarmann, who did not like the stranger, sent him away, Wittig waited outside the building until he saw a light go on in Haarmann’s room and then called out and whistled until Haarmann finally threw down the door key. (The neighbours confirmed this procedure.) On the third day Haarmann pretended to be out (which Frau Engel confirmed), but shortly afterwards Wittig returned with Grans. Grans came several times a day during this period to ask when he would be getting the suit. Haarmann’s reply was, “I can’t love that person,” to which Grans retorted, “it’s easy with someone you don’t love.” On the fourth day Wittig returned, smiling broadly and saying he had managed to get work in Hamburg; he would be leaving that afternoon between 5 and 6 p.m. However, later that night at the station Haarmann met Wittig and Grans, who had stopped Wittig from leaving. (This is contrary to Brinkmann’s statement, according to which it was Haarmann who prevented

Wittig from leaving.) Grans had taken him to one side and said, "Fritz, you idiot, that suit will fit me. Take the boy. I want that suit so badly."

In order to get some peace from Grans, Haarmann took Wittig home with him that night and killed him. The next morning, while Haarmann was busy disposing of the body, Grans turned up looking for the suit. So that Grans would not see what had happened, Haarmann quickly pushed the body under the bed and went to wash his hands. Grans, however, said, "What's that awful smell?" and "Where's the stuff?" When Haarmann replied, "He [meaning Wittig] isn't here any more," Grans immediately started to search the room. Haarmann stood in front of the bed and gave Grans the key to the trunk which Hannappel had left behind. Grans hugged and kissed Haarmann, saying, "Fritz, you really are the greatest! I can always rely on you." Grans then started to complain that he had had to pay Wittig more than DM 40 for the suit, and that Grans would have to share the bill. Grans immediately gave him DM 8 as a part payment and wrote an IOU in Wittig's notebook for the balance as Haarmann was concerned Grans may try to cheat him.

Grans claimed that these facts were only part of the truth; his version of the story was slightly different: "I didn't go up to the fellow standing at the Café Kröpcke with Huth. Haarmann said to me, 'Hey, I really fancy that one.' I never told Haarmann I wanted another chap's things; Haarmann said to me (in both the Hannappel and the Wittig cases), 'Look at that suit; would you like to have it?' I laughed because I never imagined he'd manage to con the suits out of them. When he did manage it I never dreamed he'd killed to get them. I never did anything to force Wittig to do what I said, least of all to go with Haarmann. But I did get Wittig's suit from Haarmann on 26 May and paid him a deposit for it. Haarmann wanted DM 40 at first, but reduced his price to DM 20 when I asked him to."

An inspection of Haarmann's bed, which had a metal bar running lengthways down the middle, showed that it would have been impossible to hide a dead body underneath it. However, Frau Engel confirmed that Haarmann had regularly asked her to tell Wittig he was out, and had even hidden from him in her kitchen. The stranger, whom she recognised as Wittig in the photo, had been delighted when he told her he had managed to find work in Hamburg and that he would be leaving that same afternoon. But later that night he had turned up again, accompanied by both Haarmann and Grans.

So the whole matter can be summed up with one question: Are Haarmann's proven repeated rejections of Wittig sufficient proof that Grans caused his murder? It must be considered that Haarmann certainly never killed for sexual satisfaction alone. It was possible that he himself had wanted to get hold of Wittig's things (maybe to give them to Grans as a gift or for payment, or maybe to impress him or woo him; perhaps there was another reason). However, it may also have been that a dark fear inside him made him want to hide from Wittig by killing him, but then again he did not actually want to kill him; in addition there was the confusion created by somebody else offering himself (possibly only for financial gain), which served only to heighten his fearsome rage. I am inclined to believe (as I do in several other cases) that Grans had a certain secret, dark knowledge of what was going on, although he in no way incited Haarmann to commit murder and was certainly not an accessory.

25. Friedrich Abeling, born 14 March 1913 disappeared 26 May 1924

Friedrich was 10 years old, 1.10 m tall, with a sweet, round face. He wore his hair in a "bob" and was the image of his 13-year-old sister Alice. His father, Wilhelm Mayhöfer, was a locksmith; his mother Therese was a widow before she married him. Friedrich was a pleasant, quiet child.

Friedrich had been punished for playing truant from school on 25 May 1924. On 26 May 1924 he asked his mother for 20 Pfennigs, saying his teacher was taking the class on a school trip; this turned out to be untrue. He left home wearing nothing warmer than a grey sweater with a green border, and failed to turn up again.

On 17 June some children were playing on the Rautenstraße when one of them, 12-year-old Anni Stümpel, was approached by a man who asked her whether she knew Alice Abeling.

"She's over there," said Anni, whereupon the man went over to Alice and said, "Hello, Alice, I've been to see your mother and I've left my card. Your mother will explain. I'm a friend of your father. I just wanted to see you, to say hello." He shook hands with her and left. No card had been left at the Mayhöfer home. The two little girls were the only people to have seen this man, who turned out to have been Haarmann. They described him as having had a dark moustache, whereas in reality it was blond. Later it was established that he possessed a small, dark false moustache which he wore when he was out on his sexual expeditions.

A child's skull was found in the pleasure gardens of the Leinschloß but it was not possible to establish whether it was little Friedrich's. However, his green sweater was found. It had been lying on Frau Engel's sewing-machine since the end of May, then Grans took it to give to his mother for his little step-brother, Alfred. Haarmann's room neighbour, Frau Lindner, remembered that a little boy (whom she recognised from the photo of Friedrich) had come to the house and asked for Haarmann. Feeling sorry for the child she said, "Go home, little one. He's not a nice man." The little boy turned red and left. It is to be assumed that Friedrich was wondering around because he was afraid he would be punished, and that Haarmann had tried to lure him into his apartment with promises of presents. Haarmann probably knew Alice Abeling from her brother's descriptions and went to find her out of curiosity. Psychologically, this was an odd thing to do but it is undoubtedly proof that Haarmann's constant claim that he was unable to remember his victims' faces was untrue.

26. Friedrich Koch from Herrenhausen, born 4 May 1908 disappeared 5 June 1924

This Friedrich was a 17-year-old locksmith's apprentice. His father was a well-known painter in Herrenhausen. Friedrich disappeared on 5 June. Every morning at 7 a.m., accompanied by fellow apprentice Paul Warnecke, Friedrich took the train to work. The two boys probably met Haarmann on the station.

In the afternoon of 5 June the apprentices Koch, Rubi and Böcker walked through the Altstadt to their training college. Koch was carrying a wax-cloth bag containing his "Duden" text book. On the corner of the "Tiefental" a man whom Rubi and Böcker did not know, but later recognised as Haarmann, tapped against Koch's boots with his walking stick and said, "Well, boy, don't you recognise me?" Koch stopped, waved goodbye to his friends and was never seen again. The only belongings to be found were his bag and "Duden", in which he had written his name on the flyleaf.

27. Erich de Vries, born 7 March 1907 disappeared 14 June 1924

17-year-old Erich was the son of a Hannover merchant, Max de Vries. He was apprenticed to his baker uncle in Celle. He was a healthy, good looking, inexperienced and gullible fellow. At Whitsun of 1924 he travelled to visit his parents, but when he arrived at the house his parents were out, so he went to see his aunt who lived on the Herschelstraße, and who would be able to give Erich a key to his parents' house. He stayed with his aunt until 10.30 p.m. and then left, saying he was going back to his parents' home on the Hildesheimer Straße. However, when his parents arrived home at midnight Erich was not there; they therefore assumed that either he had stayed with his aunt or had not left Celle at all, and bolted the door. Erich turned up at 10 a.m. the next morning and told his step-mother he had rung the bell between 3 and 6 a.m. as he had been unable to unlock the door; the dog had barked but as no one had come to let him in he had left again and had spent the night walking through the Altstadt with two men, one young and one older. This story seemed highly implausible.

On 12 June Erich asked permission to go out with a friend who had recently completed his baker's apprenticeship. On 14 June at around 10 a.m. he went to the Ohe for a swim, which had become a regular habit. His father reminded him to be home punctually because the two intended to go to the master baker to see about employment in Hannover, at which Erich expressed his delight at the prospect of staying in Hannover. However, he never returned home after his swim. His sister, 11-year-old Hildegarde, told her parents that when her brother had gone for his swim in the Ohe on 10 June (she had gone with him to mind his things), she had noticed a man standing on the riverbank, whom she later identified as Haarmann, who had watched the two youngsters closely; paying particular attention to Erich as he climbed out of the water. Haarmann had then approached them, asked them if they knew what the time was, then left.

Erich's suit, which was recognised by the small burn mark on the left leg, his silk gauze socks, his neckerchief, glasses, and the comb which had been a present from his sister, were all found later in Haarmann's apartment. Haarmann finally brought himself to take the investigating committee to the lake at the entrance of the palace gardens where, on four separate occasions, he had taken the remains (carried in Koch's briefcase) and disposed of them.

Haarmann claimed to have met Erich de Vries at the station. It is probable that he used his usual tactic - promising cigarettes - to lure Erich to his room.

Legal Points

The further the trial progressed, the more obvious it became that it is impossible to judge a snake without also putting the marsh from which the snake obtained its nourishment on trial. This, however, was not possible in this jury court for the following reasons: firstly, Haarmann's police statements were all made under pressure of the Hannover police force. He was particularly dependent on Dr Schackwitz, who guided him completely. If Haarmann had been brought to trial in another town, perhaps in Leipzig or Berlin, and if a different - but equally impressive - doctor had gone into Haarmann's cell every morning and greeted him with, "Fritz, what a terrific chap you are to have fooled those idiotic authorities in Hannover for ten years," the whole case would have appeared in a different light. It would then have become obvious that the faulty legal system and poor psychiatry were also responsible for the thirty murders. However, as Haarmann remained in Hannover and was totally dependent on the benevolence of the authorities, he was careful not to say anything during these final days which would be to their detriment. Haarmann was in fact deliberately used to help to exonerate the conditions prevailing in Hannover at the time and was likewise treated carefully as long as his statements to the police and court personnel were favourable.

The second reason was that the only experts permitted in court were those doctors who for professional or official reasons had been involved in the preliminaries of this case, and, like the jury, were therefore hardly in a position to provide "the ideal conditions for completely unbiased jurisdiction."

A) The first expert, forensic health officer Brandt was the same expert who, back in 1908 and contrary to three other non-official medics, proclaimed Haarmann as mentally healthy (this was with regard to his sexual perversions) and had released him from the lunatic asylum. Had he now changed his first report, Brandt would have had to admit to a "share of the blame" in Haarmann's acts of insanity perpetrated since 1908.

B) The second expert, forensic health officer Schackwitz, was the police doctor who in 1924 had been presented with some samples of meat and, perhaps not incorrectly but certainly without exact investigation, had said the meat was "pork". As a secondary police doctor he would certainly not have benefitted from revelations of police complicity, never mind his own.

C) The third expert, privy forensic health officer Schultze from Göttingen, was undoubtedly impartial, but was also familiar with the previous reports (which under English law, for example, is not allowed).

I shall not elucidate on numerous other legal errors which occurred during the course of the trial. Nonetheless I felt it necessary, for the sake of truth, to refer to these basic reservations.

Exclusion of Criticism

It was not deemed necessary to remove the 21 members of the

press from the courtroom, even during those parts of the trial which were not open to the public. As they were all "reporters" no attempts were made to mentally evaluate the terrible deeds, they deliberately misled the public and supplied Germany for weeks on end with the most appalling rubbish. This made an incident which took place on the eleventh day of the trial even more astonishing.

Even during the early days of the trial the proceedings were cut short on several occasions for talks and recriminations against the press, reminding them of their obligations for "factual" reporting (i.e. not to say anything in connection with the parts played by the authorities and conditions prevailing at the time). According to Para 176 of the Legal Constitution, the allocation of seats in court is at the discretion of the presiding judge, who therefore could also threaten to remove anyone found to be presenting "untrue and unfactual" reports. All those present were bound by office, profession or employment. It was highly unlikely that the reporters hired by the media system (with the exception of professional communist protestors who possessed only one relatively uninfluential publication in Hannover) would stir up public thinking and reveal this "Panama of civilisation". This gave rise to one of the most nervous questions asked during the trial: just what part may a reporter play and how far may he become involved in the "public administration of justice" (but not, of course, in "jurisdiction") in a trial which is still pending? I believe that criticism of the court should be restricted in one case only, namely if it is misused to the detriment of the accused. This has happened a hundred times before in Germany, amongst others with Max Hölz, Maximilian Harden, Ernst Toller and Adolf Hitler. Such misuse of political liking and aversion was, of course, impossible in the Haarmann case. It was well known from the start that the "werewolf" would have to be made safe. His case had more to do with convention, the criticism of civilisation and psychiatry than with the law. Any court can easily protect itself against public opinion. It need devote itself solely to the case in hand, looking neither to the left nor the right. It is a heinous crime to scan the papers in order to establish "what kind of press one has", whether one's vanity is being flattered or offended by it. If confronted by those with whom one disagrees, then cooperation is to be sought. Any decent person would prefer this to criticism, so all that is required is human and factual initial contact. The sins committed by the Hannover court against these basic principles were beyond comprehension. Legal activity was more for appearance's sake. Attempts were made to proof-read public opinion and to decide the legal case at the same time. Court ushers provided the court with a constant supply of the day's papers. During those ten days in that overheated room, with people packed together cheek by jowl, unrested, overworked and with emotions running high, no one thought of anything or anyone but himself. Professional ambition, academic arrogance, self-justification and the feeling of "playing God" created a cloud of ill feeling, discomfort, animosity and fear, so that the final eruption was predictable.

At this point I would like to make some personal comments. I attended the trial because of my passion for psychology; at no time did I intend to "lecture" or to play the schoolmaster. The subject was so revolting, so disgusting, that I would never have become involved voluntarily. However, as I had agreed to submit some articles on it for some German publications I was pushed into it and was personally insulted and threatened by the Hannover court. I had been permitted to attend firstly because only a few people had ever even heard of me, secondly because as a college master appointed on a permanent basis it was not expected that I would criticise the authorities of my home town, and thirdly because the least concern of the by-no-means radical press which I represented was the revelation of conditions which were later proven to be so vitally important. I would have shown complete consideration had I seen evidence of a desire for the truth instead of the pathetic display of offended small-town legal ambition, medical self-righteousness and misuse of official power, the play involving a stirred-up ant-heap, endeavouring to dispose of a foreign object by stinging and injecting acid into it. No attempts were made to observe conventional behaviour amongst educated people; as soon as the first incriminating reports were read out in the courtroom there began an outrageous declaration of ostracism: all against one. After several similar incidents and being threatened myself with removal from the court if I continued to voice my opinions, the destructive lightning finally struck on the eleventh day and the experts refused to submit their reports (with which I was already familiar) in my presence, the public prosecutors complained about the adverse effect of my reporting, the defence announced it felt insulted and the president barked at me,"You are here as a reporter, not as an author. We will not tolerate psychologists in court!"

I refused, quietly and factually, to accept this attempt to intimidate me and was ordered to leave the court. The whole incident led to a war of words between the newspapers on one side, with my character being denounced, and the public, the college, students and even the Ministry of Culture being stirred up, and on the other with my actions being compared with Zola's or Voltaire's crime critiques; both incidents being proof that an unnatural, inhumane legal machine may forgive any "tendencies" of that witch known as politics, may forgive any arrogance of that unseeing giant known as knowledge, that it understands the language of intent or purpose - indeed, everything but one thing: the natural emotions of the human heart.

The Death Sentence

After the experts had submitted their reports to the effect that, although Haarmann had a "pathological personality", he had not been devoid of "free will" and "responsibility" when he committed his crimes (so there had been no "absences" or "epileptic equivalents"; there was no "manic depressive insanity", no "madness" nor "dementia praecox"), the summing up commenced. That of the public prosecutor was clear and moderate, combining all the important details; Haarmann's defence, unfactual, pompous and lacking knowledge; Grans's defence, more factual, but clumsy and meaningless. The two accused continued to behave like an old trapped wolf, surrounded and frightened, and a young fox caught in a trap, the wolf crying bloody tears and spouting Biblical quotations, blaming his crimes on the "unfavourable times", claiming that under better conditions he could have been an obedient police dog, saying there was a kind of morality in his immorality; the fox, by contrast, gathering all his strength to escape from the trap with his life, even at the cost of a paw or his trapped tail. Their behaviour towards each other remained the same until the end: the wolf, threatened by the younger creature but still feeling the need for some sense of community; the fox, icy-cold, pale, watching and wary, fighting against this fatal fraternity.

They were sentenced on 19 December at 10 a.m.: Haarmann received 24 death sentences in 24 cases. Grans was sentenced to death for his part in the Hannappel case, incitement to murder, and to 12 years' imprisonment for being an accessory to murder in the Wittig case. Haarmann accepted the sentence, Grans appealed.

The Outcome

Stories of werewolves and vampires stretch back into the dark pre-history of today's nations and have always been linked to sexual myths. In order to explain the reappearance of lycanthropy in the midst of occidental civilisation one must start from such games of nature in which the love-life and a desire for death, the desire to destroy the other and for one's own destruction, murder and tenderness, intermingle as with the loveliest of nature's creatures: butterflies and insects.

As it is to be assumed that within Haarmann there lived a constant desire for his own destruction (I had the impression that he viewed his possible execution as one final orgasm), then it is also to be believed that this person, normally devoid of feeling, experienced a self-extinguishing over-excitement that far exceeded anything he experienced in his ordinary day-to-day life, more helpless and more fateful than the orgiastic state of a civilised person bound by inhibitions for whom love and even crime have become a kind of sexual game and comfortable semi-luxury. The fact that the original, excessively pronounced sexuality of this androgyne and androlyke was now completely exhausted, wholly spent, helps us to understand how he dragged up age-old traits of a forgotten genus from the darkest recesses of his mind, a genus whose urge to bite into and devour (including the taking-in of "foreign" nature in the form of food and drink) was a Dionysian act, based on a primal desire for imitation, of eroticism which obliterated the individual. We do not even know whether the animal urge to tear apart and devour is part of some natural sensual experience; when the wolf chokes the lamb one may also say, he loves the lamb even as he hates. I was reminded of a dog which had to be put down because of a compulsion to attack the necks of certain other dogs (which were always of a similarly degenerate nature to his) and bite through it until he had killed the dog. It was obvious at these times that the creature was sexually aroused. There should be a biological explanation for these cases: psychology should look much further into the dream life, childhood surroundings, the toys, desires and ideals experienced during the formative childhood years, than modern school psychology and medicine do at present.

"Yet each man kills the thing he loves,
By each let this be heard,
Some do it with a bitter look,
Some with a flattering word.
The coward does it with a kiss,
The brave man with a sword!"

This was the final cry uttered by a man abused in prison in Oscar Wilde's "*Ballad of Reading Gaol*". That death and love, Eros and Eris, were originally intertwined, is nature's justice, which requires that the highest confirmation be fulfilment. There is, of course, no need for those consumed by passion to indulge in sex murder when at the highest peak of sublime eroticism, because the power of nature has now become such a power of the soul that it forces fate to kill just as lightning is drawn to a high building or tree. But the fact that so-called higher creatures, and man in particular, temporally survive both theact of love and their own self-fulfilment is undoubtedly at the cost of a reduction in the fulfilling power of erotic life - indeed this recollection may already have occurred during the "process of civilisation", in order for inhibitions even to become effective. Normal, controlled people such as ourselves have withdrawn from the pre-human demon of compulsion more as a result of spiritual (i.e. logic and ethos) withdrawal from the earth's forces, than by sublimation. Due to a kind of error in management a creature such as this monomaniac occurs in a stage of creation where civil rights are held only by the middle temperatures of Eros. Not yet fateful and death-bound with religious, mythical, enthusiastic forces, but on the other hand no longer deep enough that death and sensuality still coincide, it still appears to be forced to show hideous loyalty to the laws of "love death", "hideous" because in a "depraved" civilisation natural form may only appear as caricature and depravity.

Just as the dog represents a typically moral-altruistic creature of a weakened, beaten wolf-nature, so too the morals of civilisation appear to conceal a type of misplaced, "enobled" sensuality, whereby the law of the pendulum reached the highest point on one side only to swing immediately to the other, just as moral fanatics like Torquémade, Dante, Robespierre, have wolfish traits and the wild madman some streak of a Christian saint. This werewolf with radio and electricity, cannibalism in fine underwear and smart clothing, can therefore be regarded as typical for the spirit of occidental werewolves; what was experienced by the elders in five years of heroic war during which murder and any kind of prosperity of spiritual death were in the service of the wolf heart and morale and the oldest realisation became the newest: "Homo homini lupus e natura - a man is a wolf to another man."

In 1914 I treated a man in a military hospital who was famous for having sneaked to the enemy's sentry post and strangled the guard on duty. On his chest this man wore... the Iron Cross.

Whether or not such cases actually involve "insanity" or whether or not a person is answerable to the law appears to be a futile and senseless question. The insanity is often to be found in the actual deed; the conscious superstructure, cut off from compulsive vampirism, remains unscathed. In such cases there is generally a lack of stabilising inhibitions (which are a prerequisite for "soundness of mind"). They are replaced with automatic compulsive reactions (as with animals), the stereotypes which the experts disregarded. One obvious objection can be raised: Haarmann's killings were not senseless. He was not a purely sexual offender (just as Grans was not a purely "intellectual" offender). It is likely that he committed several crimes out of avarice, revenge, fear of being an accessory rather than from sexual compulsion, although the following must be noted in this connection. A compulsive neurosis based on years of semi-insanity will not proceed in a discriminating fashion. For Haarmann, killing was as easy as cleaning his boots. In fact, killing in secret (we shall see shortly that this secrecy was a large part of his compulsion) and possibly also the dealing with human remains (such cases of "necrophilia" are not unknown with infantiles) gradually became gruesomely attractive to Haarmann. At this point I would like to add some profound words by Nietzsche: "Thus spoke the red judge, 'Why did this criminal kill? He wanted to steal.' But I tell you, his soul wanted blood, not theft; he thirsted for the knife's fortune. His poor reasoning was unable to comprehend and hence convinced him, 'What's blood?' it said, 'Don't you at least want to steal at the same time? To take revenge?' And he listened to his poor reason, whose words lay like lead. So he stole as he murdered. He did not want to be ashamed of his madness." (There must have been times when the wolf was ashamed in front of the fox for having killed without 'taking note of the clothes'.)

I want to add the following words of Nietzsche for the benefit of the Hannover court and its experts: "What is this person? A bundle of diseases which reach out into the world through the soul, to where it wanted to make its haul. But this you do not want to hear; it will damage your goodness, you tell me, but your goodness is nothing to me. Much of your goodness, and surely not its wickedness, disgusts me. I wish they had a madness which would destroy them, just like this pale criminal. Truly, I would their insanity were called truth or loyalty or justice. But they have their virtue in order to live long and in wretched contentment. I am a railing beside the river; catch hold of me if you can. But I am not your crutch ..."

I now want to move on to an important point which was also totally ignored by the psychologists of the Hannover court: the apparent lack of a motive in many of these cases. I have already said that the search for motives outside the sequence of events goes beyond the logical-economical desire to artificially narrow the concentrated and immeasurable destiny and make it plausible for comprehensive orientation. In reality, no actions may ever be perpetrated for a particular motive. That is not to say that there is no possibility of actions even if no motives can be found for them; on one occasion a wolf, although not hungry, may attack a lamb, and on another, when an attack would be expected, ignore it altogether.

The most curious uncertainty prevails in those cases where the very darkness and appeal exerted by the secrecy and the "abyss" become the very basis for some actions. This lack of motive is unmistakable in some cases of fatal poisoning, for which I would like to give the following example which I experienced myself in 1915 in the early stages of the First World War.

I was on medical service in a military hospital with 500, predominantly Russian, seriously injured patients. A young man from the Baltic regions was working as an interpreter in the Russian department. Hewas 20 years old, friendly, obliging and appeared to be the ideal male nurse. He was well liked by patients, doctors and nurses alike, and valued as a general factotum. It was noticed over a period of time that a surprisingly high number of Russian patients died without apparent medical cause, and certainly not as a result of their injuries. This epidemic of death continued, and finally suspicions were expressed that the patients may have been poisoned. The bodies were exhumed, and traces of arsenic were discovered in the stomachs. At the same time it was discovered that some poisonous substances had been removed from the poisons cupboard in the hospital laboratory. The senior nursing officer held the keys to the cupboards in the laboratory, and they were released only on a senior doctor's instructions. However, there had been several occasions when trusty Oskar, the young man from the Baltics, had been sent to the senior nurse for the keys, and he may have taken the opportunity on these occasions to remove bottles from the poisons cupboard. When the investigation opened Oskar was nowhere to be found. The building was searched all over, and eventually a pale, shocked orderly reported that he had found Oskar hanging from the rafters in the attic; he was already dead. The investigation proved inconclusive,but no one was in any doubt that this popular, well-loved young man had slowly and without motive poisoned the meals of at least twenty of his fellow countrymen to whom he had not shown the slightest trace of animosity. Not much thought was given to such incidents during the war, and the general feeling was summed up in one word: sadism. This case was explained in the same way as ill-natured children often tend to torture animals, watching their victims' agonised writhing with a mixture of fascination and horror; these emotions actually spur them on.

That medical and scientific self-importance which pleases itself in this game between humans and destiny also had a part in Oskar's dark activities. But by calling this man to mind and his modesty when praised ("There's more to him than meets the eye,") it strikes me as highly likely that it was only the playing with the darkness and the fascination of the secrecy that turned this boy into a mass murderer.

In Haarmann's case, however, the appeal of secrecy came from other roots, namely from that sensuality which could be called a depersonalised love-life. A perfect example for this depersonalisation is masturbation, to which adhere both the loss of personality and emotion and the appeal of seclusion. The greatest torment to which Haarmann could be subjected was to show him pictures of his victims and tell him about them, bringing them closer to him. To him, they were "pretty boys" of whom he wanted to know as little as possible. The desire to conceal the bodies of complete strangers in obscurity, to rend them from limb to limb and devour them, left him if he became increasingly familiar with his victims (as with Grans).In my publication "***The Symbolism of Form***" (published by Niels Kampmann, Celle, 1925) I explained in detail that sexual characteristics have nothing to do with eroticism in the sense of personal life. Quite the opposite is true: truly sensual natures are never strong eroticists and are incapable of nurturing and enduring, fulfilling passion. The fact remains, however, that the "libido" is connected to the tools of the original "close" senses (such as taste, smell, touch, kissing, sucking etc.) whereas the eye and ear, the "far" senses for sight and distance, provide a firmer relationship with the personal and a less tenuous association with general sexual feelings, which gives us several clues to the physiognomical. (The indescribable ignorance with regard to the research into his character was evident from the fact that Haarmann was never examined physiognomically. However, the weaker proportions of the cerebellum in comparison with the cerebrum and the predominance of the close senses over the "far" senses were obvious on sight.)

A kind of compensation can be sought from the strange fact that a fear of contact and closeness tend to develop where a bare, dreamless sexual desire gains predominance. I was struck by the observation that Haarmann fearfully avoided any kind of knowledge of his victims (which is why the psychologists were particularly interested by the Abeling case, in which Haarmann murdered a 12-year-old boy and then went in disguise to seek out his victim's younger sister and recall his facial features). The terrible dreamlessness of his raw sexual life went so far that Haarmann never actually possessed any personal longings other than the most general ones (apart from greed and his sexual drive). His affection for Grans was the only personal, ideal aspect of his life; this was the only relationship in which he rose above the bestial. The mountains of Switzerland, which he saw as an impressionable, receptive youth, left no lasting impression on him. He had absolutely no feelings for nature. To him, a bush or tree was merely a hiding place for his sexual offences. Just like an octopus in the depths of the ocean gradually devours all surrounding life forms, so his impersonal "sensuality" gradually devoured everything deeper and more personal. He occasionally went to the theatre, a circus or the cinema, but this was only ever to see the "pretty boys" and if possible to touch them. He never looked at a book or listened to music and was totally indifferent to politics and public life. He went to sports fields and public baths simply because of the naked young bodies on display there.

The deepest layer in the nature of a sexual offender becomes evident when compared with the nature of a crafty, calculating criminal. Had the truth been sought instead of being excluded from the courtroom, much would have been learnt from this comparison. A brief philosophical observation will serve as an illustration.

Just as light and flame, whilst surrounded by the cycle of life, represent the life-giving, warming primeval forces and may even be the essence of life itself, but become a fearsome demon once separated and freed from nature and the only element in which organic life cannot survive, and which endeavours to devour all life, and which surely will devour at the end of all ends, that is what we humans refer to as the "spirit", whilst surrounded by the cycle of life, that life-giving and warming primeval force, indeed possibly the creative force of life itself, but as soon as the spirit breaks free of nature and departs from the dreaming element of subconsciousness into the conscious world, so it changes into a fearsome demon, a cold joke in which nothing spiritual may survive and which endeavours to devour everything dull and dormant, and which, at the end of all ends, most probably will. This now is the most terrible puzzle of our time, of the destiny of our people, our civilisation: both have broken away and become free. Man as a natural soul and man as a purpose-finding spirit have separated.

The theatre of our hemisphere is the tragedy of a soul which can no longer keep pace with the efforts and values to which it has itself given prominence. The efforts have become bigger and more noble than man himself, or as I said earlier, "The werewolf with a radio and electricity"; that is the symbol of our era. However, such association between the natural elements and the spiritual leads unavoidably to two opposing types of degeneration: on the one hand there is spiritless, senseless, insane nature, and on the other hand there is spirituality without nature or soul. Natural instincts which break through in modern man lack the inherent sense and sensual beauty which pervade all life in those creatures that remained undevoured in the cosmic ring. But where "modern man" has broken out of the natural element and faced the earth in overpowering arrogance, he has become its devil. Haarmann and Grans are typical cases for this hopeless split: here we have the caput mortuum of unbridled bestiality, there the empty intellect, deserted by the last little drops of the soul. It is easy to understand how these two poles grafted together, forming a symbiosis, reuniting artificially in a perverse unit which by its nature was doomed to break apart finally and irrevocably. This double degeneration is typified by the two men's attitude to inebriation and alcohol. Grans is such an empty, hollow person that the dreams or inebriation of the blood do not exist for him outside the purposes and intent of his own egoism. That is why he needs artificial inebriation. It provides him with his only chance to free himself from himself. By contrast Haarmann is such a creature of instinct, so blind with rage, so lecherous, that alcohol, whilst it relaxes others, leaves him leaden and sad. Just as a blind man envies a mute his squint, the mute envies the blind man his croaky voice, so here each admires what is lacking in the other: the wily fox envies the wolf his thirst for blood, the mad wolf envies the fox his calmness and the fact that he would never do anything which is not to his own advantage. Madness and devilry - these are the poles of the "best of all possible worlds" ...

Our Fault

If one tenuous question should be asked in the sequence of events of man's inner life, like a stone falling into the washed-out bed of a river, then we have a wonderfully straightforward formula to hand with which the riddle is solved and the stumbling block disposed of. We talk of "fault" and blame the break in our nature (which actually amounts to a break *with* nature) on unalterable laws, circumstances or destiny.

In my philosophical work of the law ("***Axiomatic Studies***", Leipzig 1914, publisher Felix Meiner) I explained in detail that the expression of just cause amounts to this fault finding (i.e. that logic too has an undercurrent of moral will), whereby (§ 13 "*Epoch of Fault*") man is slowly but surely persuaded to seek the "fault" in himself: "Everyone is guilty of everything, and I am the guiltiest of all."

Just as we can never know another's soul better or differently than we do our own, so we can think of change, improvement and giving fresh heart only as far as we can find in our own life a share of the blame for the other's conduct. As long as this "self-judgement of human society" does not become the prevailing mood for legal finding, all judgment remains a torment, a taking of revenge by those who have been fortunate enough to avoid imprisonment perpetrated against those unfortunate enough to have been put in prison. Because the subjects of, and motives for, everything we do, every minute of our lives (disregarding the massacre of millions, the thieving, plundering, lying and spying perpetrated during the so-called "great periods of history"), are the same as perpetrated by animals, children and criminals. However, as soon as we are able to lay the blame for the evils of our society on others we are relieved of all disturbing experiences of shared guilt and shared suffering. That is why, in ordinary everyday life, we endeavour to investigate an accident which may befall one of our number until we can apportion "blame" to some kind of incorrect behaviour. (That is why the German language has the significant double meaning for the word 'Geschick': fate, destiny or fortune, skill, and 'Ungeschick': awkwardness, clumsiness, carelessness.) But in this we also pass judgment, which we do for our own peace of mind.

Of all the economies of sloth, the "anathema sit" is the most comfortable. To burn, denounce or decapitate, or moral indignation - these have always been the simplest ways of dealing with the awkward congestion of the conscious, in that we are no match for an irrational person.

Unpleasant theoretical matters are best dealt with by closing one's eyes to them, by not letting oneself be touched by them, or by fending them off with some set phrase - or by ordering them from the courtroom. On a practical level, unpleasant self-knowledge is best avoided by dealing with the problematical. The Haarmann trial proved the age-old truth. Future centuries in a spirit of finer legal ethics will find the death sentence as unreasonable as it was fatuous - that a modern court, of which I could make a laughing stock with a few strokes of my pen, were I less responsible, could order me from court because I was "virtually incapable of following proceedings and reporting them factually". The whole barbarism of both our psychology and our ethics was revealed starkly in this criminal trial. The unwelcome plant is always weeded out (the sub- as well as the super-normal), whereas what we should really be aiming for is to love the earth more and plough the fields better.

The lowly-born and ill-cared for; false witness and poor upbringing, bad selection, lack of health care and community spirit, the senseless confusion stirred up amongst the masses by the media, semi-education, party and state politics (itself nothing more than organised crime breeding in the name of the state, which, if discovered, it punishes in private), the poverty, dirt and class struggle - all of this creates, on the one hand, werewolves, and on the other: intelligent parasites. Prison produces homosexuality. A senseless penal system kills any remaining traces of tenderness in them, leaving nothing but the moral spite and arrogance one group feels for another, at best it leaves the individual's feeling of solidarity with other "outcasts of society". However, Nature did not create the evil monsters. They were created by the cage. Man has become so delicate and unsure of his desires that a few days in a cage would lead even the strongest, boldest and cleverest to wickedness or insanity. So we've managed it: our madhouses provide madness, our prisons create criminals.

The death sentence was given on the morning of 19 December. Another court session was held later that day. Judgement was pronounced on the court! Before returning home the parents of the murdered children gathered together in a dark, dingy back room; the humble bereaved, lamenting and accusing. Not one of them had been able to find any satisfaction or justice in the proceedings. Not one of them had any kind of answer to the questions, "How could this happen? Why? What for?" This trial had left nothing but bitter, disturbed, angry, deeply wounded humanity. I had been asked to attend this meeting because the parents had heard me take the court to task and were expecting to bring charges against the court, the authorities, the police and the regional and senior councils. I knew how futile that would be. The parents' appeals and charges all ended up unanswered in the waste paper basket.

All I wanted was to put on paper, as factually as possible, the memories of thirty children who had ventured out into the world for the first time, only to end up in the wolf's jaws. When the book appears in print the pointless end of the pointless drama will possibly have been executed. Humanely, the mildest (because the flame of self-destruction burns continuously behind the compulsive greed of lust), ethically, socio-politically the stupidest of all sentences, and in direct contradiction of the nature of the punishment (not to weed out instinct, but to use and purify).

Behind Hannover station, in the lifeless, most soulless concrete jungle on the Cellerstraße, where the first of these murders was carried out, lies the prison: a vast building, surrounded by a depressing, high red brick wall. At one of the corners of this wall there flowered a fair miracle, known to every Hannoverian: a small birch tree, the gentlest yet toughest tree, so fair and so modest, so severe and so delightful, with such a delicate bark and tough, healthy root - like the children of our own Lower Saxony. As if by a miracle it put down roots in the midst of this treeless concrete jungle right next to the red brick wall, breaking through the horror of our human civilisation and obscenity. This is where the guillotine will stand and the red judge perform his futile duty.

I suggested to the authorities in my home town that this day should commemorate the memory of these thirty children. In olden times, when people still had a sense of communal guilt (something wholly unlike our present juristic concept of collective responsibility), communal spirit was maintained if blood guilt lay over a town: chapel, convent, memorial, tree planting - all to redeem the citizens' reputations. Hannover's oldest building, the lovely Nikolai Chapel on the Klagesmarkt, is supposedly the product of such communal atonement. The day on which the last wolf of our forests is killed should be a day of prayer and repentance for Hannover. The crime against the shame and soul of humanity was so great (not least because of the sensational press reporting) that those responsible for the health of the nation, the clergymen, doctors, teachers would try to channel this awfulness back into dignity and beauty. One should talk to the children in the schools and the adults in the churches. All the bells in town should ring out in warning. And at the hour of the guilty-not-guilty monster's death we shall lay the sad remains of the thirty youngsters in a communal coffin, decorate it with flowers and lower it into the earth at our town's expense, not hidden in a churchyard - no! but in one of our big public squares. And all of us, the whole town, will follow it: senators, clergymen, senior council members, chief of police - not to "pay one's respects" (that we cannot do), but to accept and acknowledge our collective guilt.

There have been kings who ended their own lives on the day their people were defeated. Kant proclaimed the basic principle: "On the day war breaks out the government will immediately resign because it has proved itself incapable of preventing that for which it has been elected." Fortunately there are still officials who leave their office voluntarily when fate proves itself stronger than they are. The men responsible in Hannover proved that they were not gentlemen. People attempted to appease the bitterly angry mood left by Haarmann's trial by a chain of "disciplinary procedures", intended to atone for the guilt of the individual subordinate officials. This farce served only to throw sand in the eyes of a too-patient, long suffering people and should not have been permitted. In this constitutional state, corrupted by informers and sycophants, who would gain from two or three incompetent petty officials being reprimanded or sent to other posts? No! Let us look into ourselves and accept the blame! But after that no one should have the right to ask, "Who is to blame?", no one must be allowed to blame the other. We shall all follow the coffin, in our combined parenthood, that coffin of unfulfilled youth for which we are responsible.

Next to the house of murder, where these children were sacrificed, there is a large tree-lined square. In the background is a church wherein lies Hannover's most intelligent son: Leibniz. This is where we shall lay them, in the ground on this square. We shall fetch graphite from our Harz mountains - or better still, fetch from the Haide one of the large boulders which date back to pre-historic times. This shall serve as a memorial plaque, containing only five words for posterity:

"The fault of us all!"

Epilogue

My book is finished and lies before me, typeset and ready for publication. Hans Grans's appeal has been rejected by the court. The death sentence is final.

Then something happened which, had it been written in a thriller, would have been considered far-fetched and pure fabrication. A Hannover messenger named Lüters found a letter addressed to the bookbinder Albert Grans, the father of the man under sentence of death, marked "Registered" and postmarked Meran, lying on the street. He made sure the letter was delivered to the addressee, who in turn passed it on to me. It was the following 4-page letter written by Haarmann, the mass murderer:

"Hannover, 5 February

Confession of the murderer Fritz Haarmann

I have the opportunity, as I am being taken by car to the police station, to present this letter to the public.

I don't want the court or the police to get hold of this letter because I feel they would withhold my confession from the public and thereby cause an innocent man, Hans Grans, to go to the executioner. May God bless the honest finder and his family for all eternity. This is what I, Fritz Haarmann, who have been sentenced to death, wish for you. I shall make a full confession in prison to the prison padre, Father Hauptmann. So that this letter is also checked by the public and doesn't disappear, hence this letter [sic]. Dr Lotze will have to get the letter from Father Hauptmann. I Fritz Haarmann have written this letter by my own hand to prove that this is my writing my brother Adolf Haarmann-Fortmüller of Asternstr. no. 6 knows my handwriting well. My confession. So help me God, I am telling the truth and don't want to burden my conscience before God any more, I who have been sentenced to death.

Hans Grans cheated on me and lied to me terribly for years, but

I still couldn't stay away from him because I had no one else in the world. Grans should have been a comfort to me in my old age because I always looked after him and I would have had a nice fortune saved by now if he hadn't taken everything from me. Grans wasn't bad, but he was very foolish. He was so foolish where women and booze were concerned, I was just a meal ticket. Grans was too innocent in his debauchery to have much to do with what I was getting up to with the youngsters. Grans had absolutely no idea that I killed he never saw anything. Grans only knew that I was perverse and went around with young people. When things were discovered about my murdering, the police forced me to tell untruths, I was afraid of being ill-treated again so I agreed to everything and said things about Grans that weren't true. I called my sister Emma and brother Adolf for help, they came and I told them in the presence of Inspector Rätz, Emma, Adolf, I am being forced and beaten into telling untruths. I asked Frau Witzel to apply for me to make my statement to the prosecuting attorney, but I wasn't allowed to. So I lied and put the blame on Grans so the police would leave me in peace. I said to myself he shouldn't do that to me, I've been too good to him, the more I fibbed about Grans the better the police treated me. Concerning retracting my statement in court I didn't want to, all I thought about was getting my revenge on Grans, and that I managed to do with the help of the police. I want to say at this point that Hans Grans knew nothing of my previous life. He didn't know that I had ever been in a madhouse, he never threatened me, Grans knew nothing of any murders, never saw anything, had no idea. Nobody believed anything Grans said in his statements, or [they were] twisted so that they went against him. That's why Grans said what he did in court, Haarmann mixed truth and fiction so that they could not be told apart. I, Fritz Haarmann, call upon Heaven as my witness that Grans is innocent. Grans wasn't even guilty of dealing in stolen goods. Grans never brought anyone to me who became one of my victims and had Grans known that I killed he would have prevented it. I can't take this guilt to the grave with me and call upon my mother as witness who is sacred to me and who is with God. Hans Grans has been sentenced unjustly, and that's the fault of the police and also because I wanted revenge, because I had always been good to Grans, it was such a burden. Take my bit of life, I'm not afraid of death by the blade it will be a release,but put yourself in Hans Grans's position, he will question [the existence of] God and justice because of me. May Hans Grans forgive me for my revenge, humanity [forgive me] for my murders carried out when I was ill. I am happy to give my death and blood in atonement in God's arms and justice.

(Signed) Fritz Haarmann"

My first thought was that this letter was some kind of joke (never had I anticipated proof of this kind), but this was not the case.

Troubled by pangs of conscience concerning the only relationship which had ever stirred the deeper emotions within him; troubled by his fear of the police who wanted something from him although all he had was the recognition of his own guilt, and finally tortured by the agony that it was too late to turn, that a public retraction would never be allowed, because otherwise our administration of justice would have to admit their great error and may even declare the trial closed and sentencing final; tormented by all these fears the ill-fated creature attempted in this way to have the case against young Grans reopened as a result of public pressure.

Now the following questions must be asked: Can he be believed? Will he be believed? Because there is always the possibility that a mentally sick person suffering from a 'pseudologia fantastica' would exaggerate in his desire to relieve his own burden of guilt to the same extent as he did in his attempts to incriminate. And it is therefore to be expected that this man would be constantly thinking up devious new ways to delay his execution. However, in my opinion the following points have been proven:

1. The judgment of the Hannover court is wholly unsatisfactory. The authorities failed to make their own guilt/responsibility clearly known.

2. It has been proven that as a result of pressure applied by certain authorities and people, Haarmann's statements were not

what they would have been had he been tried by a different court and made his statements to a different police force.

3. The Hannover court was guilty of a miscarriage of justice. It sentenced to death a neglected young man at the mercy of prevailing conditions, solely as a result of statements made by a man who had been pronounced mentally ill by five different psychiatrists. The evidence against Grans could easily have been explained as circumstantial and the result of the way he lived, and also by his desire to see, hear and know nothing. There were two significant coincidences at this trial. The first was that my being there meant there was an impartial person present who was against school jurisdiction, school medicine and school psychology. This initially aroused my suspicions, but it also brought to public awareness the bias or inappropriateness of the court of justice.

The outcome was undoubtedly a setback for the court of justice and also for its president, but still they should be grateful for it. It maintained our German administration of justice in the face of judicial murder caused by a legal system with no knowledge of psychology and an unbelievably incompetent defence.

If I considered what the outcome would be, then all I could see was one terrible likelihood. Haarmann and Grans were executed. A letter containing the following was found after their deaths.

"I have taken revenge against life. Revenge against the only person I was always good to, but still he withdrew from me when my terrible secret was revealed. So I tried to win him back. I put my claws into him and waited. Because he was unable to love me I killed him. That was also my revenge against the police. They used and abused me, and then went all hypocritical as if I were to be "improved". But when the complicity became known they all dropped me but wanted my help to get their cheap laurels for their "careers". They beat my behind. They squeezed my testicles. (It doesn't show there if you've been abused.) They beat me with a rubber tube (it doesn't leave any marks). They didn't leave me alone until I confessed to what they all wanted to hear. So I let them have their triumph. 'We've managed to find something out,' and with the help of the police they finished off my final work and abused the dearest thing I had. So I fooled them all, just when they thought they had got me round. I managed to make my final weeks pleasant by being pleasant to you. But I still used you as a tool for taking my revenge against life. And thereby I took my revenge on you! Revenge against the court, that doesn't kill by natural compulsion as I do! (Isn't the death sentence also murder?) No! That's murder for just reason and positive right. Thanks to morality! Oh, your morality! Your sentences from the mouths of the literati. You thought more of yourselves than you did of the case. And so you welcomed my lies as long as they promised that the public prosecutor would become the president of the German supreme court, that the director of the district court would become the head of the district court. I took my revenge on the soulless defence, these victims of their robes. Did they burn with the desire for justice? They trembled with fear of the opinion of the times and society. Even the stupidest of them, even a member of the jury, a juror would have to sense the truth, were not everyone blinded by the farce of officialdom in its fancy robes. Oh, and your "science". How can your "experts" admit that there is one far more intelligent than they, but is still driven by impulse and "irresponsible" in the sense of unwritten laws. Finally - revenge against the whole nation! There would have been much pleasure at stoning me without compunction for me doing exactly the same as one individual, whereas you dare only do it as many. So I have no regrets, and could not care less for your clerics and their Christianity. I know you all too well and I know about your "soul". You won't kill me; I'll be back - yes, I shall be amongst you for all eternity. And now you yourselves have also killed. You should know it: Hans Grans was innocent! Well? How's your conscience now?"

This was what I had feared. This was Haarmann's overriding thought in his darkest hour. But this poor creature was truly not a devil, nor was he a personality. He was nothing but a primitive animal that was seduced by the cage and abused by society only to collapse before the cross, and whom the hand of a strong psychiatrist was easily able to convince of the wish for confession and repentance which Schopenhauer called "our second path to Nirvana."

How will this drama end? In a normal constitutional state after publication of this book the ministry of justice would have to quash the sentence imposed by the Hannover jury court and pass the case on to a different jury court for a retrial. This would presumably confirm the death sentence for Haarmann; it would presumably also lift the death sentence given to Grans should he, which is to be hoped, vehemently denounce the con of an "appeal for mercy" (through which the Hannover court would attempt to draw a veil over its transgressions) and insist that he wants not mercy, but justice. However, it is also possible that other judges, lawyers and experts would arrive at the conclusion that Haarmann belonged in a mental asylum. In Grans's case a sentence of one or two years should suffice for his activities in connection with stolen goods, after which he would emigrate, work, and become a man. He would then undoubtedly grow into a respected pillar of this time and society.

Hannover, 8 February 1925

Theodor Lessing

Closing Words on Haarmann and Grans

"A judicial murder has been committed."

A dark point

On 30 June 1924 the beginning of a confession was obtained from the mass murderer Fritz Haarmann. Prior to this the police had been unable to gain any information from him. The realisation that only Haarmann, the police agent, could be the werewolf who was terrorising the town, was the result of private investigations instigated by the dependents and parents, who had hitherto been harshly dismissed by the officials and authorities.

In the corridor outside the room where Haarmann was being interrogated were the parents, unless I am mistaken, of three of the murdered boys and various other people. Yells and crying could be heard in the room, and the people outside shouted angrily, "Bring him out here - we want to lynch him!" The door was locked; those standing nearest to it looked through the keyhole. Three (possibly five) people were in unanimous agreement, "We saw Haarmann with his trousers down. He was yelling, and we were certain he was being beaten." As he was taken off to his cell two people saw that he was carrying a blood-soaked cloth. In the confession he left behind Haarmann stated that he had made the claims against Grans only because he had wanted the police to leave him alone. The Hannover court was therefore obliged to accept the evidence of Haarmann's ill-treatment, although five officials swore that this had not been the case and the parents' keyhole observations were put down as hallucinations or sexual fantasies. Despite this three sets of parents (none of whom would have objected to Haarmann being beaten) made statements supporting his confession. I would like to mention at this point that in December 1924, when the court tried to suppress the report which I had submitted because they found it "unacceptable", the Hannover police department informed me that Haarmann's testicles had been crushed in order to persuade him to confess. I set no particular store by this, although it appeared to be from a credible source. I still believe that various witnesses were mistaken about the ill-treatment. However, I want to make public my shame that a German court tried to hinder the investigations into the truth. The judge shouted at the mother of one of the victims, "It's right that Haarmann was treated like that otherwise he'd still be killing today!" When the woman, whom the prosecutor had decided was an inferior witness, retorted, "The prosecutor is afraid!" she was fined. Another young woman, who was appearing in court for the first time, was understandably nervous and had difficulty expressing her embarrassment at what she had seen. She was shouted at, "If that's all you have to testify you could have stayed at home! All you saw was a pair of trousers that were undone; that's not ill-treatment!"

A detective with many years' experience swore under oath that he had never ill-treated Haarmann, but later could not resist bragging to the parents of one of the victims, "I certainly gave Haarmann something to think about with the rubber hose." The parents were decent folk and defended Haarmann's statement at Grans's trial. The official ended up contradicting himself and finally admitted that he had beaten Haarmann and that there had been a rubber hose on the table during his interrogations. All the officials had hitherto denied the existence of such a hose. I do not intend to criticise our underpaid, justifiably embittered, subordinate official. I do, however, have to criticise an official authority that did not try its utmost to clarify all irregularities. There was a lot of covering-up in Hannover.

The Experts

There were two experts present at Hans Grans's trial: Professor Schultze from Göttingen and the Hannover police doctor Schackwitz. The two men had to decide on the credibility of Haarmann's confessions and statements. Privy councillor Schultze submitted his report first, and the following has to be said of the nature and boundaries of court reports of this kind. The privy councillor says, "The defence has asked me whether homosexuals are particularly inclined towards telling untruths. So yesterday I went again from Hannover to Göttingen to check in specialist literature."

The expert threw specialist expressions around wildly, clarification of which is the most basic objective of psychology. He confused credibility with honesty, honesty with truthfulness, truthfulness with truth and truth with the reality of consciousness, factual reality with evidence for judgement, discernment with sincerity and sincerity with openness. The checks and examinations which he performed on Haarmann concerned the intellect (judgement, memory etc.) but completely ignored the emotional aspect, despite the association between this and assorted intellectual functions. Finally, the learned man expressed his surprise that Haarmann's brain showed not the slightest pathological feature; he would have done better to be surprised by a psychology that imagined an examination of the brain would reveal anything concerning the spirit or emotions. The brain concerns "conscious facts", but it has as little to do with the soul as it does with the study of mankind, with the "looking up of information in specialist literature ..."

Alex Schackwitz, the second expert, had complete control over Haarmann between June 1924 and 15 April 1925, the day of Haarmann's execution. Dr Schackwitz compared Haarmann with a trained animal which is easily intimidated by the threat of pain and rewarded with coffee, cheese or cigars. Haarmann's care and treatment lay mainly with three members of the criminal department: Dr Schackwitz, Inspector Rätz and Assistant Reich, who all testified to their association with Haarmann until the moment of his death. Dr Schackwitz, the expert in the Haarmann trial, was the man who pronounced the meat samples presented to him shortly after Haarmann committed his first murders as pork; this was without having examined it under a microscope. Shortly before he was led to the scaffold Haarmann wrote a letter to Dr Schackwitz. The final words in this letter (indeed, Haarmann's last words ever) were, "You can believe this has been a lesson for him (for Hans Grans). He's no good. But you can't punish him. I'm not protecting him. He had no idea ..." I claimed at the time, and still do now, that, if the Hannover court and the Hannover police had had the pride and courage to recognise their own prejudice, the entire trial against Haarmann would have been different, and that against Grans been impossible.

Address to the Jury

The oasis in the midst of the Grans trial was the summing-up by the defence, Dr Teich. It was a speech given by a man, nothing harsh, nothing exaggerated, measured, careful; words from a man who, although his sympathies are with the authoritarian state and the law, is also a fair and experienced man who has freed himself from all malicious pre-assumptions and subjective emotions, and simply asks, "What is truth?" Meanwhile, had the good Lord Himself appeared in the courtroom and stood protectively in front of the young man, of whom nothing, but nothing at all, could be proven, no God could have saved him in this unpleasant atmosphere of hatred and resentment and anti-justice. I once read the following sentence, written by Oscar Wilde, "Council pleads with the jury to let the accused swing." The two old indictments of instigation to murder and being an accessory had been dropped and a charge of aiding and abetting in the Hanappel and Wittig cases brought in their place (in accordance with § 149 of the Civil Code). Grans's summing-up was, "I expect to be acquitted and to have my honour restored by an impartial court." There was a totally unpsychological attitude towards him, and with those words he finally lost people's sympathy. He was sentenced to 12 years' imprisonment and was stripped of all rights for 20 years. The two years he spent in custody were not counted.

Psychology in the Courtroom

A judicial murder has been committed! I do not write this thoughtlessly. It comes from cold, calm consideration; based on a knowledge of all those involved and of the conditions and circumstances, and after having spent a year weighing up and considering every aspect of the case. I am not saying that Grans was innocent. In my opinion he pimped for Haarmann, and he was a wicked parasite and exploiter. But I am adamant that he did not incite to murder, nor was he an accessory to it. Disregarding this personal conviction, there is no doubt that "circumstantial judgement" is the source of all judicial murders of which Hannoverian Jhering says, "Judicial murder is the true mortal sin of justice."

"There is no room for psychology in the courtroom." I never believed these words which were spoken by Bökelmann, the court president. However, Grans's trial proved to me that they had been spoken in all seriousness. Psychological blunders, which anyone who considers human affairs would notice immediately, were accepted without comment. One witness, who had already aroused suspicion, stated that three years before, when nothing of the murders was known, he had seen Haarmann and Grans signal to each other in an over-filled waiting room. The same witness claimed he had seen one of the victims, Hanappel, sitting on a trunk at a particular point in the waiting room with a spirit level next to him. When it became obvious that this witness could only have learnt of the detail concerning the spirit level from the newspapers because it had in fact been inside the trunk and not next to it, he changed his story, "There was something next to him, something that looked like a spirit level." (Nobody commented on this.) Another witness, a female who undoubtedly loathed Grans, said, "He once told me he was just using Haarmann." However, it was now discovered that Grans could not understand the local dialect, and so the president asked the witness whether he had been speaking in the dialect or in High German. In the light of this new information, she replied that he had been speaking in High German. The state prosecutor permitted himself the following comment, "Grans must have known that Hanappel was to be killed because his suspicions were not aroused when he saw the dead boy's belongings which had been left behind." An endless discussion emanated from this question: Why did Haarmann try to incriminate Grans in the two cases where there is evidence of aiding and abetting? It was obvious that Haarmann only gave evidence against Grans if it was possible to incriminate him; in other cases there was no evidence against him, just as with the hundreds of other attempts by Haarmann to incriminate Grans which were also unsupported. For example, Haarmann accused one of Hannover's most highly regarded industrialists, who had done much to further culture and education in Hannover, of having killed more than forty boys. It was Hannover's loss that this man, and others like him, left the town, much to Haarmann's amusement. Haarmann also accused Wittkowski, Friedrich and Grans of other murders, although it was easy to prove that these accusations were totally unfounded.

It is difficult to penetrate Grans's case, as he is one of those individuals I call "atonal": originally unsuspecting natures which freeze up completely in the face of danger, becoming totally unresponsive. Grans the accused showed no emotion during his trial. A characterologist would realise that he also had no feelings of guilt or responsibility - or else he was a consummate actor. In the court, however, this was evidence of "the cunning criminal's unrepentance". The fact is that there was injustice in Grans's treatment as far as his being an accessory to murder is concerned. Grans's sins were many and included procuring, pimping and the most despicable exploitation of inexperienced youngsters; but of that of which he was accused, "being an accessory to murder", that was not one of his sins. The feeling that he was being unjustly treated left him blind to his real guilt and now, with no play-acting on his part, he felt "hard done by" and that he was fighting for his "honour". Is it psychologically possible that a real criminal would store clothing and other items which he knew had belonged to people who had been murdered, that he would wear the clothes in public even once the general public had become suspicious about the murders? It would have been easy for him to destroy all the evidence of his involvement and cover up the trails. According to one witness, "Grans told me he had Haarmann in his hands, and if Haarmann ever tried anything with Grans, Grans would go to the police." And just what would he tell them? "Haarmann has defrauded the gas works by taking gas illegally." Is that how someone who knows I am guilty of murder would threaten me? I could recite numerous other similar frauds. What is the counter-question? Nothing other than Haarmann's first statement, which the court believed implicitly despite subsequent retractions made in consideration of the scaffold. But this too is psychology: the Hannover jury court was guilty of judicial murder when it sentenced Grans to death (and this it must now admit). The sentence was overturned when Haarmann's confessions became public and when I had been able to awaken the public's conscience. The same court now changed their sentence to 12 years' imprisonment. Any other court would have acquitted Grans. I am not saying that Grans was innocent; in my book I portray him as the worst kind of profiteer and parasite, but still I say he played no smaller part in the murders than did the women Engel, Linderer and Wegehenkel and many little police officials who suspected Haarmann's evil doings and law-breaking without realising they were dealing with murder.

Final Words

I do not want the battle I fought against my native Hannover on the pages of the newspaper "Prager Tagblatt" to be considered an Ephialtic deed against my home town. [In Greek mythology, Ephialtes and Otos were the sons of Poseidon and Iphimedeia who, in a battle against the gods layered the mountains Pelion and Ossa together in order to conquer Olympus. The myth expresses the battle between the traditional deities and Zeus's new religion. "Herostrat, Ephialtes, Cassius will always be the perpetrators of a single deed."] I would have written the same in any other German newspaper had there been one available ... I do not intend to hurt anyone.I am concerned about the validity and ethos of the German administration of justice. Not about people who will have changed completely in twenty or thirty years anyway. In closing, I would like to refer again to the reports in the "Prager Tagblatt". On 15 December 1924 and in accordance with § 176 of the legal constitution, the Hannover court prevented me from attending the proceedings. This was as the result of two sentences having been taken from a report, being quoted entirely out of context and pronounced totally untrue. I then started to doubt the impartiality of the court and so immersed myself in the actual trial. This I have compiled to the best of my ability in my book, "***Haarmann: The Story of a Werewolf***", Berlin 1925. Should there be any errors in the book or in the reports in the "*Prager Tagblatt*" then I would ask that they be corrected in accordance with press rules and regulations. Should anything detrimental to the police or the court be construed from my statements, then please sue me for defamation or libel; perhaps then we would be able to establish what is the truth - which is, after all, what we want. The court chose neither legal path. The court preferred to make my presence there more difficult and to denounce me to the Ministry of Culture, taking disciplinary action against me, an academic teacher, in addition to which I was hounded. There was a total lack of political understanding; all of which continued for many years. However, the following was discovered at the end of the Haarmann - Grans trial. During his summing-up and jury address, Grans's defence quoted from my book. The president in both trials, district court director Bökelmann, interrupted him. "I must ask you not to quote from a book with which we are not familiar." The council for the defence called me as a witness to state that I had indeed written a book which described the Grans trial as a miscarriage of justice. The public prosecutor and the prosecuting attorneys realised that they had not seen the book either. A court usher who owned a copy of it handed it over to the prosecuting attorney who took it, looked at the cover and put it down. When giving the reason for the sentence the president stated that, "The court declines to take note of a book about the Haarmann - Grans case which is supposed to have been written by a local medic. We also decline to be influenced by newspaper reports and articles. We professional judges know in ourselves what we must do. We do not need advice or instruction from outsiders. [Taken down literally by the stenographer.] So ... my denouncement by the Ministry and subsequent years of persecution were the result of two sentences taken from a newspaper report. However, "We are not familiar with the issue, but we do disapprove of it."

I am afraid of these "God-like feelings". Not for me! But scared for the day when the majesty of these three eminent juristic authorities of our good town of Hannover, Messrs. Bökelmann, Wilde and Wagenschieffer, which it undoubtedly will do, collapses. [1926]

Kürten - the Vampire of Düsseldorf

A definitive case history,
comprising *The Sadist* (1932) ,
by Karl Berg, M.D.
(with solely forensic text omitted)
and *Peter Kürten -*
***A Study in Sadism* (1937),**
by George Godwin
(inserted in italics).

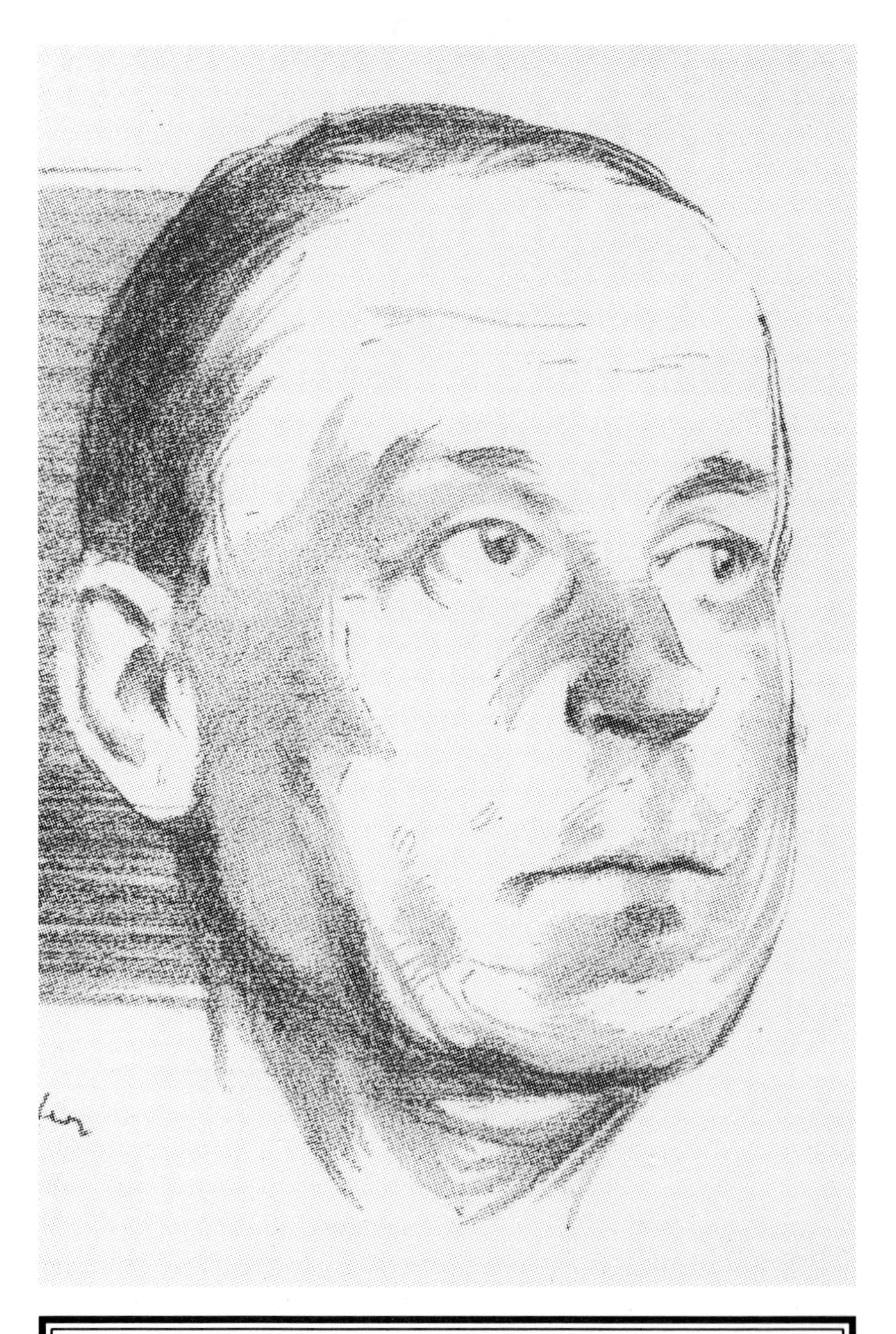

Peter Kürten - "the vampire" - sketched three days before his execution.

PROLOGUE

On the 24th of May, 1930, a police officer advanced with a revolver on a tallish, well set-up man as he came towards the Rochus Church and arrested him.

This was the end for the terrified inhabitants of Düsseldorf of a Reign of Terror that had begun with an encounter on a lonely suburban street in the city at 9 o'clock on the third of February, 1929: "Good evening."

The accosted woman, Fran Kühn, turned and as she did so her assailant grabbed her coat and inflicted eighteen rapid stab wounds on her head, body, and arms.

In the period of sixteen months that lay between these two events there had been perpetrated in the city a series of sexual crimes almost without match in criminal history.

The best police brains of Germany, that is to say, the Crime Police of Alexander Platz, besides the city's own highly effcient police organisation, had been engaged on the task of running to earth the mass murderer, but with no success.

Thirteen thousand letters had poured in on the police; no less than 2,650 clues had been patiently followed up, and such was the public outcry that the claims of clairvoyants and the theories of graphologists and any one else who promised, however remotely, a faint hope of some new line of investigation, had been painstakingly examined.

On the 13th of April, 1931 Peter Kürten entered the dock of Düsseldorf criminal court. He was charged with ten murders and after a trial lasting as many days, was convicted of nine of them.

The crimes with which Kürten was charged and convicted were, however, but a small part of a grand total of sexual murders, murderous assaults, rapes, arson, and larcenies proved against him, not by the astuteness of the police, but mainly by means of information proffered freely by the criminal himself.

Chapter One
The Düsseldorf Atrocities, 1929

In the whole history of crime there is to be found no record comparable in circumstances of frightfulness with the long series of crimes perpetrated in our own time by the Düsseldorf murderer, Peter Kürten.

The epidemic of sexual outrages and murders which took place in the town of Düsseldorf between the months of February and November in the year 1929, caused a wave of horror and indignation to sweep, not only through Düsseldorf, but through all Germany and, it may be said without exaggeration, throughout the whole world.

As one outrage succeeded another and always in circumstances of grim drama; as one type of crime was followed by yet another, public consternation reached the point of stupefaction.

Kürten, however, has been judged; he now belongs to criminal history.

Kürten's crimes were not merely the subject of exhaustive judical examination; justice went deeper in his case and sought to probe the soul of this strange and enigmatic man.

In so doing justice has placed us in a position to understand the nature both of the crimes and of the perpetrator of them. Here is truly absorbing material for study, for Kürten is a clinical subject who yields, in exchange for a careful analysis, a real enlargement of our knowledge of the abnormal operating in the sphere of crime.

I have arranged the extensive material in the following pages in the following way. I shall first deal with and describe, from the medico-legal standpoint, the events which took place in Düsseldorf in 1929. I shall then proceed to deal with the crimes as they were described to me by the criminal himself, and, last, I shall attempt an analytical estimate of the criminal and the nature of his crimes in the light of our knowledge of sadism.

I propose first to describe the state of affairs disclosed by my investigations, later I shall offer an interpretation of them in the light of knowledge later acquired of the perpetrator.

THE THREE FEBRUARY CASES

Case 46. The Murder of the Ohliger Child.

On the 9th of February, 1929, about 9 o'clock in the morning, workmen going to work found in the vicinity of the building upon which they were employed in the Kettwiger-strasse, in the Flingern district, the body of an eight-year-old girl lying under a hedge. The ground at that point sloped slightly towards the hedge, and as the hedge faced a wide open space, it was only by chance that the body was discovered.

The body was completely clothed and clad in a cloak. The clothing, however, was partially burnt and the underclothing still smouldered. The body, which smelled strongly of petroleum, was not in any sort of disorder, for even the openings of the dress and the knickers were not disarranged. A closer examination of the clothing revealed bloodstains from multiple wounds in the breast, wounds made, quite obviously, through the clothing. On the inner part of the knickers near the external genitalia were two small bloodstains. Microscopic examination revealed the presence hereabouts of seminal fluid.

The autopsy showed that the burning had affected practically only the clothing, injuring the skin surface nowhere but on the upper part of the thighs, the neck and chin, over which area the skin was blackened and discoloured, while the hair of the head was a black, charred mass, here and there completely burnt off. On the the left breast were grouped over thirteen wounds, the face was bloated and livid. The stabs about the left breast were grouped over an area rather smaller than a hand. Five of the wounds had penetrated the heart, three had pierced the left and right pleurae; three had penetrated the liver. In the pleural cavities I found 750cc. of blood. Death must have been swift through internal haemorrhage.

The scene of the crime was without trace of blood. The criminal had attempted to burn the clothing of the body only. There were no traces to suggest that soot had been inhaled, and the burning was without vital reaction.

In the stomach was found a mass of chyme, partially digested white cabbage, and remains of meat.

The essential factors to be considered, from the medico-legal standpoint, for a diagnosis of the cause of death and for a theory as to the time of it, as well as for the motive of the murderer, were the characteristic stabs, the congestion of blood which was found in the head, the exact nature of the wounds and the condition of the contents of the stomach, and, last, the injury to the genitalia. So far as the congestion of blood in the head is concerned, one can only suggest that it indicated a forcible strangulation.

The judical autopsy of the Ohliger child established the time of death, the contents of the stomach assisting to that end.

Death must have occurred very quickly through the heart wounds. There were no visible marks where the strangling grip had been applied, but some manner of strangulation must have initiated the attack though leaving no traces on the skin of the neck. No calls for help were heard in the rather populous neighbourhood where the crime was committed.

The mother deposed that the murdered child had eaten sauerkraut about 2 p.m. and had then set out to visit a friend. At 6 o'clock the friend had advised the child to hurry home before dark. There was a public footpath which she could take and which offered her a short cut.

Bearing in mind the fact that in six hours the stomach could normally complete the work of digestion, then the scarcely digested food found in the stomach indicates that death took place between 6 and 7 o'clock in the evening. The autopsy indicated that the child had been waylaid while on her homeward way.

The condition of the genitals revealed an injury of little consequence. Only slight traces of seminal fluid were found on the child's underclothing. It was clear that an ejaculation could not have taken place into the vagina.

From these considerations I arrived at the conclusion that the criminal's objective had not been coitus, but that he must have inserted a finger smeared with semen under the unopened knickers of the child and thus inserted it into the vagina. This must have been done with force, for there was also a trace of bruising of the pelvis.

The stabs in the skin of the breast were all together and parallel. Some of these showed that the knife had been held with the cutting edge of the blade upwards. I concluded from the position of these wounds that that the criminal had done the stabbing in the breast as the child lay unconscious on the ground, delivering the blows in swift succession. Otherwise one would have expected that the stabbings inflicted on a person still conscious would have been placed irregulary. In addition one would expect to find defensive wounds on the hands.

That my conclusions were correct is borne out by the attack which took place on an elderly woman and of which I learned only later. This attack took place five days before the murder of Rosa Ohliger. I attributed it immediately to the same criminal, an assumption which was to be confirmed by later events.

Case 45. Frau Kühn.

At 9 p.m. on the 3rd of February, 1929, Frau Kühn was waylaid at dusk on a lonely road in the Flingern district. The man overtook her, bid her "Good evening," gripped her by the lapels of her coat with the words:"No row!Don't scream!" With the other hand he stabbed her. The woman fell back and screamed for help. The criminal made off.

I found in the case of Frau Kühn twenty-four flesh wounds - on the head, the trunk, and the arms. The victim said that the criminal had stabbed her in rapid succession.

In the case of the third victim (Case 47) there were the same numerous stabs, characteristic of the same criminal. Only five days after the murder of Rosa Ohliger there was found on the Hellweg, on the outskirts of the town, and once again in the Flingern district, the body of a man, by the name Scheer, of about forty-five years of age. He had sustained twenty knife wounds, of which sixteen were over a small area of the neck. Except for one stab, all were horizontal.

Only one stab in the neck and three in the back were vertical. Three stabs had proved fatal: a stab in the temple had caused severe haemorrhage into the brain cavity, the stab in the neck had caused bleeding into the spinal cord, and the stab in the back had resulted in a pneumo-thorax. From the absence of defensive wounds, and from the distribution of the stabs, I drew the conclusion that the criminal had attacked his victim from behind and stabbed him.

Scheer had left a beer-house in the evening in a drunken state. He must have been attacked between 11 o'clock and midnight, but not until the next morning about 8 o'clock was the body found. Despite a temperature of 62 F. the body was still warm, *rigor mortis* just setting in. The combination of stabs, alcohol and low temperature explains the slow death.

At the time when these three attacks took place, all within the short space of ten days, there was no clue whatever to the criminal. The only positive data were given by the findings of the medico-legal experts as follows; a comparison of the three cases revealing them as having the following characteristics in common:

(1) Sudden attack in isolated parts of Flingern.

(2) The choice of dusk; numerous stabs of the same character, among which always one stab in the temple, and all executed in rapid succession.

(3) The employment of the same sort of stabbing instrument.

(4) Absence of a common motive-robbery, etc.

All these factors, taken together, make inevitable the conclusion that the same criminal committed the three crimes and, furthermore, the abnormal character of the criminal.

It was fatal for the detection of this criminal that exactly six weeks later an imbecile named Stausberg appeared on the scene with two attacks on women which had some similarity to the crimes described above and thus confused the issue. I cite them here although they have nothing to do with Kurten himself. Again, there were similar circumstances: dusk, a lonely place on the outskirts of the town, a silent assault, an attempt to kill.

The Stausberg Cases

The sixteen-year-old Erna Penning was on her way home on the evening of the 2nd of April 1929, when she suddenly heard steps behind her. Thinking it was her friend, she put up her coat collar in a spirit of fun in order to render herself unrecognisable, holding it close with both hands. That action saved her life, for at that moment a noose was thrown over her head.

I now quote her own words as to what followed: "I had my hands under the cord and with all my strength I tried to prevent the man from tightning the noose. I saw that he was very excited and that he was making great efforts to tighten the noose. I stumbled into the ditch towards the bank. The man held the noose together with one hand while with the other he throttled me. He threw me on to my back, fell to his knees beside me and kept on strangling me. I caught hold of his nose and pinched the nostrils together. In a last effort I succeeded in getting up. The man stepped back and took the rope off. He didn't speak a word. I ran away."

Twenty-four hours later came the second attack upon Frau Flake. Here is her account of it.

"On the 3rd of April, 1929, I was walking from the place where I used to work in the north part of the town by an ill-lit street. I heard steps behind me and saw a man coming. I walked more slowly in order to let him pass. The man must have jumped at me very quickly because suddenly something was flung over my head and I was jerked violently backwards. I was pulled from the road into the field. I could not shout, for the man had tried to push a handkerchief into my mouth. I clenched my teeth. He said, half aloud: "Open your mouth." He tightened the loop still more. Then he listened to see whether I still breathed and held his hand in front of my mouth. He then hauled me another ten metres. I heard steps approaching and tried to shout, but I couldn't. I struggled with my legs. It was then that I was released and the man turned away and ran across the fields. I loosened the loop and dragged myself towards some people who were standing in the road."

From this witness's statement it was clear that a dangerous attack had taken place. The attack had been witnessed by a man from a distance. He deposed as follows:

"When I approached I saw that a man was dragging a woman behind him across the fields. She was not on all-fours, but was literally dragged along the ground."

The medical report, made the following day, revealed the serious nature of this assault. Frau Flake was not able to swallow properly. On her neck she had a large, very red swelling, on the left a painful reddish mark. The skin of the whole face was covered with contusions in size from a pin point to a pea. The conjunctivae of both eyes were partly congested. In the mucous membrane of the mouth were numerous abrasions.

The criminal had been seen running away from the assaulted woman, and he was very soon identified. He was the twenty-year-old Stausberg, the imbecile son of a family lodging in a common lodging-house. It was difficult to interrogate Stausberg because, having an impediment in his speech, he spoke in broken sentences.

I reproduce his account of the two attacks mainly in his own words. First his comments on the Penning assault:

"The girl was a head taller than I am. She had put up the collar of her coat - a fur coat. Therefore, I wasn't able to tighten the rope. I had the rope with me. At one end I made a noose, and at the other a loop for my hand. When I saw the girl I took the noose from my pocket and threw it over her head. She struggled and kicked and cried out for help. I, too, was on the ground."

Of the attack on Frau Flake, he said: "I saw her going along. I was furious. I had got the rope all ready and threw it from behind over her head. I took my hankerchief, said: "Open your mouth." I did not pull her along by the cord. It was under her armpits. I only attacked her because I had a grievance."

Stausberg must be regarded as proved guilty by his suprisingly accurate account of minute details of the two attacks, on the one side, and the objective data on the other.

Naturally, nothing was more simple than to accuse Stausberg of the three February attacks. His comments upon them were, indeed, startling. He knew so many details that he could not have known from the newspapers, being an illiterate. So it came about that he was suspected of having commited these crimes, and this despite certain grave doubts.

The attack on Frau Kühn he described as follows: "I had gone to Gerresheim to look for work. Then I walked. A woman was walking in front of me. It was dark. I gripped her on the breast and stabbed the woman first in her head, then i went on stabbing. Blood came immediately after the first stab. She fell down. I stabbed into her heart. She shouted for help. I ran away. I couldn't help it."

The death of Rosa Ohliger he describes, but with discrepancies when compared with the facts of my medical report.

"The child came towards me. I said: 'You come with me.' The child didn't say anything. She went with me up to the church. It was dark. I did not see any people. I took out my knife and stabbed. First in the head [*indicating the right temple*], then I held the child and stabbed her [*with his left hand he grips the coat of the investigating police officer near the neck and with his right hand he executes rapid stabbing movements towards the left breast*]. Then I kept stabbing. Then the child fell down and was dead immediately. I hadn't stabbed more than three times.

"When the child was lying on the ground I didn't stab any more. That is quite certain. That is not a lie. Then I listened a bit, whether the child still breathed. And then I left her lying... I went to a shop and asked for a litre of petroleum. I paid twenty pfennig for it. I went back and poured the petroleum over the clothing. But not all of it. Some petroleum remained in the bottle. I set it afire with a match to the coat. The flame was high up to the knee. At home I washed the blood from my coat. My mother asked me where the blood came from. I said from my nose. "

(When the next day the murder had been reported in the papers, Stausberg's mother had asked him whether he was the culprit. He answered "Yes, I certainly did it." His mother told him to "keep his mouth shut.")

"You see that I can also keep my mouth shut."

Last, his description of the murder of Scheer.

"It was late in the evening. I was out with a friend. I wanted to drink beer. When I wanted to pay the tavern-keeper said: 'It's all right.' Outside the inn he said to me: 'You scoundrel.' He swayed. He came towards me. I don't take anything from anybody. He wanted to punch my nose. I don't let anybody punch my nose. I took my knife from my pocket and stabbed him. He was done for. He fell over right away. I always hit on the head and then that does the job. He wanted to give me a shove. I caught hold of him from behind. I don't let any fellow talk to me. I don't stand anything from a girl either. He fell on his face. He felt in his pocket and found a knife which I took from him. I think I left it lying there. The others say I am a little devil. I don't stand for anything, and then I see red. I took the knife from him otherwise he would have killed me."

At a later hearing of the case:

"I gave him a stab in the neck, then I kept on stabbing. A stab on the side of the head. Then he fell over. I listened once and then I cleared out. It is the same knife as with the woman and child. Later I lost the knife."

When the real criminal had been detected there was a tendency to reproach the police officials for suspecting Stausberg. But as Stausberg had proved his propensity for homicidal impulsive acts through his two attacks, his accusation of himself was, with reason, regarded as credible. It is valuable addition to our knowledge that an imbecile who is almost a complete idiot can invent so thorough and deceptive a false confession.

Stausberg's prosecution was stopped under Paragraph 51 of the criminal code and he was removed to a lunatic asylum.

In August, however, there were further attacks by a "ripper," despite the elimination of the supposed murderer. These crimes differed entirely from the crimes of the idiot and this circumstance supported the theory that Stausberg was, indeed, guilty of those crimes to which he confessed, even where there was no corroboration. Thus these new atrocities were attributed to some unknown perpetrator or perpetrators.

The Knife Attacks of August 1929

On the 21st of August, 1929, in the western suburb of the town of Lierenfeld, three people were stabbed while walking home at night.

Case 55. In the vicinity of a church square a Frau Mantel was accosted by a stranger. He said: "May I accompany you, Fraulein?" Frau Mantel making no reply was rewarded by a stab in the back.

Case 54. Round about the same time a stranger approached Anna Goldhausen and, without speaking a word, gave her a stab which penetrated between the sixth and seventh ribs, penertrated both liver and stomach and incapacitated her for a long time.

Case 56. Again, about the same hour, and in the same quarter of the town, a man named Heinrich Kornblum was accosted and stabbed in the back.

In this case the knife had, in one instance, cut the victim's braces, a circumstance which resulted in the perfect impression of a knife stab, and, hence, the shape and dimensions of the blade, 15 mm. On these data I came to the conclusion that the knife used in this case was not that used in the case of the Ohliger child or in that of the man Scheer. This seemed to be but one more ground for suspecting some culprit other than Stausberg.

The murder of Gross, which took place between the last-named two crimes, stregthened my belief in the theory that we had to seek more than one culprit.

On the night of the 30th of July, 1929, the thirty-five-year-old prostitute Gross was found naked and strangled on the divan in the house of convenience. She showed no wounds except the characteristic marks of strangulation on the neck.

This case differed but little from the fairly frequent murders of prostitutes common to all large towns; for it happens, often enough, that these woman are killed in the course of their profession.

There was nothing about this case to incline me to the view that it was another committed by the same unknown as in the previous cases under investigation. Indeed, up to this very day the murder of Gross remains an unsolved crime. Incidentally, Kürten had nothing to do with it.

Again, the types of crime which took place at Flehe were of yet another category as will appear. These involved the five-year-old child Gertrude Hamacher and her fourteen-year-old adopted sister Louisa Lenzen.

They had gone to the market place on Saturday evening and had failed to return home. During that night a search was made for them in every public place and thoroughfare between the market-place of Flehe and the lodgings which were not far off, but in vain.

The following Sunday morning at six o'clock their bodies were found on the market garden, only 200 metres from their lodgings. The younger child, Hamacher was found lying amongst some runner beans; the elder, Lenzen, lay some seventeen metres away on a freshly turned vegetable bed. Both bodies were lying almost face down, the clothing being in order, the genitalia unharmed. The finding had in common the facts of strangulation by violence and the two cut throats.

It was obvious that the two children had left the highway and gone to the dark allotments, for the detectives were able to follow the tracks of a man and two children up to the bean patch. The soft earth about the beans showed only traces of the child Lenzen's footmarks and those of the criminal: they led from the bean patch to a place some ten metres further away where the ground was much trampled, after which, for a further seven metres, at which point her body was found, the footprints of the child only were visible.

The time of the deaths can be stated very precisely as a quarter past nine. It was about that time that cries of "Mamma ! Mamma!" were heard from that direction. Despite that, people passed the path close to the bean patch some moments later without noticing the bodies in the dark.

My conclusions were as follows: the true interpretation of the child murders, as the handiwork of a sadist, had to be considered as incontestable. Either they were purely lust murders, sheer killing for the sake of lustful excitement without actual sexual violation of the children; or the murderer had been disturbed and alarmed before he could consummate his purpose.

It is less easy to reconstruct the crimes themselves; though the examination of the wounds by autopsy suggests very strongly that the crimes were the work of one criminal. The absence of defensive wounds on the hands of the children is evidence that they had been unconscious at the time of death. In the case of the younger girl, Hamacher, although the only external signs of injury were the throat wounds, the condition of the lungs, the compressed epiglottis and the haemorrhage into the oesophagus behind the larynx, strongly suggested strangulation. It would have been easy to use the knife in a double stroke upon a victim already unconscious. The criminal, it may be conjectured, gripped the child first and thus silenced her, next flinging her down amongst the runner-beans, while the other girl, now terrified, called from the allotment for her mother. The criminal must then have come up and silenced her by throttling, next cutting her throat in two attempts - the bruising being bisected by the wound suggests as much. The actual cutting of the throat was rendered difficult, it would seem, since the criminal had still to hold up his unconscious victim. Therefore, he stabbed her yet four times more in the back. At that point the girl regained consciousness and attempted to escape; but because of the stab in the aorta, she must have collapsed after a very short run.

This reconstruction of the course of events, based upon the autopsies, tallies with the clues examined upon the scene of the crime, for the footprints of the man return from the place of the struggle to the younger child, Hamacher. It must remain pure conjecture whether it was only at this point that the criminal proceeded to kill the unconscious child by cutting her throat. These child murders aroused public indignation and horror to a high degree; yet clues as to the perpetrator of the crimes were scant; indeed the footprints and the wounds were the only available data.

Case 59 On the evening of the same day - a Sunday - on which the bodies had been found, yet another sexual crime was discovered. The twenty-six-year-old domestic servant, Gertrud Schulte, was accosted in the afternoon in Ober Cassel by an unknown man about thirty-four years of age. Schulte accompanied him and together they visited the outdoor market at Neuss, coming finally to the meadows which flank the Rhine at that part. When they had setted down the stranger, who called himself Baumgart, made immediate and importunate overtures to the girl, suggesting very plainly that there should be sexual intercourse. Using force, he held her down and attempted to remove her knickers. The girl defended herself vigorously. "I would rather die," she protested. At that moment she felt the pain of a wound in her throat and heard the words: "Then you *shall* die!" The unknown continued to stab the girl, ending with a final stab in the back so violent that the blade of the dagger broke. He then desisted, saying: "Now you can die," and made off.

Hearing her cries, a party of young people came running up, found the victim still conscious, and took her at once to hospital.

The Schulte girl had three wounds on her head and neck: on the crown of her head one some 10 cm. in length; on the right ear lobe and on the front of the throat a large diagonal wound which, however, only severed the skin and ended in a spur which suggested not one, but two movements of the blade, two distinct slashes. In addition, ten wounds were found, four of which were in pairs beginning at the left lower jaw.

The case of Schulte was of the greatest importance to the police, for here was a crime in which the criminal's method and, even more important, both man and weapon had been described minutely. Nevertheless, although this case seemed so clear it left a certain perplexity in the mind sinced we had formed the opinion that a sadist who had satisfied his sexual appetite on Saturday by the murder of two children would not have troubled to tackle a victim capable of offering a stout resistence already by the following Sunday. Again, strangulation, a characteristic common to all the other crimes, was here absent. But there remained a broken dagger blade to remind us, inevitably, of the knife wounds of the July victims: those wounds, obviously, might have been caused by just such a dagger.

The Hammer Cases

Case 63. On Sunday, the 29th of September, 1929, the servant girl, Ida Reuter, set forth at 4 p.m. on an excursion to Dusseldorf from the place in Barmen where she was employed. The following day at 7 a.m. she was found dead in the meadows beside the Rhine, near Dusseldorf. The body was lying in a posture typical of sexual outrages, with bare legs parted, the clothing disarranged, the genitals exposed.

From the site where the body was found, there were indications on the ground of its having been dragged seventy metres from a place near the promenade on the banks of the Rhine where, probably, the girl had been first attacked. The criminal had taken the knickers and contents of her bag, the bag itself he had thrown into a garden.

When the murder Commision arrived the body of the girl was already stiff. About the head a circle of bruises was visible. While differing as to size, some having an intricate conformation caused by the succesive blows on the same site, the general character of all was the same.

From other cases we know that if a hammer strikes the skin of the head that particular skin surface will burst in a characteristic manner, resulting in a fissure wound more or less gaping and a depressed fracture.

Again, it may be expected that if the surface is struck by a direct blow, the impression of the hammer face will be left at the point of impact. Of course, the thick hair of a young woman would break the force of the blow and minimise the effects of it. and it is equally obvious that if the skull is round and the blow a glancing one, the impression will be but partial. A point of interest I noted was the change of appearance of these head bruises which took place after the parts had been preserved. For whereas, after removing the blood-clotted hair, I found them indistinct, they showed up very clearly after the process of preservation. Werkgartner mentions, in this connection, the character of wound marks in the epidermis revealed by experimental shot-gun wounds where the weapon was in direct contact with the head.

I came, therefore, to the conclusion that these head wounds, and the bruised areas about them, were the result of repeated heavy hammer blows from a square-faced hammer; for they were all in character and of marginal length of 2 cc.

The later autopsy on the skull itself fully confirmed my first assumptions regarding it.

Case 64 On Saturday, the 12th of October, 1929, at 6.30 a.m. the unemployed servant girl, Dorrier, was found gravely injured and unconscious. Once more the scene of the crime was in the western part of the town, namely, Flingern. As in the Reuter case, the criminal had dragged Dorrier from the scene of the crime behind some bushes.

Dorrier died without ever recovering from the coma in which she was found, on the 13th of October. She had sustained similar, but less serious head wounds than Reuter. Round about the left temple were bruises more or less uniform and from 4 to 5 cc.long. on the right side of the head there was a large single wound; and on the occiput a further wound. At the entrance of the vagina there was a large tear; in the mucous membrane were the imprints of finger nails. Both temporal muscles were lacerated and the adjoining parts of the skull splintered. The skull showed a battering of both temples, the brain was damaged only on the surface, on the left temple there were two nut-sized wounds.

After the comparison of the head wounds I came to the following conclusions: the wounds of Reuter and Dorrier conform to such an extent that is necessary to presume the same criminal and the same instrument of murder in both cases. That the criminal delivered the blows with a hammer which had a convex square face of about 2 cm. The cause of death in both cases was head injuries resulting from hammer blows. It is amazing that Dorrier, whose wounds from an anatomical point of view were much more grave than those of Reuter, survived for so long. The blows on the head of Reuter were more numerous, but the injury to the brain was much less. That Reuter died, nevertheless, so quickly was due to the injuries of the numerous vessels from which she had bled to death. The flow of blood into the lungs further accelerated death. One can sum up as follows: the blows on the head caused Reuter to fall unconscious. She had scarcely a chance to cry out. Compare this with the statement of Frau Meurer. Then there was the great loss of blood and the infiltration of blood into the lungs. Since no considerable pool of blood had been found on the promenade where the murder was committed, the criminal must have dragged Reuter away immediately after he had struck her down. He dragged her seventy metres, as was shown by the blood marks in the grass, and on arrival at that point Reuter must have been dying or already dead. Otherwise, a bigger mass of blood would have been found. In the case of both women proof of sexual violation was fothcoming. The position in which the body of Reuter was found was rather suspicious: on the back, with an uncovered abdomen and widely parted legs is the typical position of the woman who has first been silenced before being sexually assualted.

The classification of the Reuter murder as a sexual crime explains the circumstances that the body was dragged away from the place where she was killed - a promenade which is frequented by lovers after dark - to the greater solitude of the meadows beside the Rhine. There the criminal was able to commit undisturbed the sexual violation of Reuter who, it is probable, was by that time already dead.

On making an autopsy I found, when dissecting the vagina, that I was able to empty almost 2 ccm. of spermatic fluid into a glass. In the microscopic examinations which followed I found numerous spermatozoa, among them a few still moved. These data would establish for us the hour of the crime, provided that the murder and the sexual act were commited at the same time. For this reason, the spermatozoa would have remained motile only for a few hours in the acid secretions of the vagina. The state of the digestive processes, the complete *rigor mortis* when the body was found at seven in the morning, make reasonable the assumption that the murder was commited before midnight.

In the vagina of Dorrier I was not able to establish the presence of spermatozoa, but the organ had been subjected to rough treatment and thus labelled this case, too, as a sexual murder. While it is true that one cannot say with any certainty that the vaginal wound of Dorrier is a simple coitus wound, the condition revealed by the autopsy in this case does suggest the same criminal.

Case 65. On the 25th of October, 1929, Frau Meurer, thirty-four years of age, at about 8 o'clock, was on her way home along the isolated Hellweg in the Flingern district, when she was accosted by a man.

"Aren't you afraid?" he said, "quite a lot of things have happened here already."

Frau Meurer paid no attention to him, but he continued to walk beside her. She cannot remember the blows which followed hard upon these words. An hour later she was brought into the hospital unconscious.

On the forehead and over the right ear the hospital physician found oval wounds of a diameter of 2 cm. with lacerated edges which exposed the bone of the scalp which was not damaged. After two weeks Frau Meurer was discharged as cured. Her wounds might have been caused by hammer blows or blows from some similar blunt instrument. This episode was important because two weeks earlier in that same place Dorrier had been killed by similar wounds.

The same evening Frau Wanders was attacked in the Hofgarten in the heart of Düsseldorf. She was in the habit of soliciting there late at night and thought she had succeeded in picking up a man when she saw a stranger approaching her. After negotiating with him for a little, she recieved a blow on the head which rendered her unconscious. She regained consciousness very soon and went to the police and then to the hospital where four head wounds were found. Later, when I made my examination, I found a square depression fracture over the left ear and two smaller depression fractures on the crown and on the right temple. They were square hammer impressions.

My deduction that the wounds were the result of hammer blows was confirmed later both by the confession of Kürten and by the finding of the hammer. I shall deal later with these points in more detail.

The last two murder cases

Case 67 On the 7th of November, 1929, Gertrud Albermann, aged five years, was seen at 7 o'clock in the evening in the Flingern district. Two days later her body was found in the morning in an isolated place against the wall of a house owned by people named Haniel. The body was lying among stinging nettles beside the footpath and was face downwards, with parted legs. The clothing appeared to be undisturbed, but on removing the coat it was seen that the clothes had been slipped up over the posterior and the knickers torn. The autopsy revealed little post mortem staining and aneamia, congestion of the face, and typical traces of throttling with the thumb imprints on the right. There were two stab wounds in the left side of the head, thirty-four in the breast.

The body of the little Albermann child was found on the 9th of November as stated before. A few hours later the so-called "murder letter" was received: it had been posted already on the 8th of November, in the evening, in Dusseldorf, and addressed to a Communist newspaper. It contained the information that the body of the Albermann child was lying hard by the wall of the Haniels' house. Although the letter arrived too late, it became important because of a reference in it to a second body lying buried on the edge of the wood near Dusseldorf.

Once already, on the 14th of October, 1929, the police had received a peculiar communication describing the interment of a body at the edge of the woods and containing a plan on which the burial place was marked.

On the 15th of November, 1929, digging brought to light a female body which, by the clothing and other marks of identity, was identified as a servant girl, Maria Hahn, who had disappeared on the 11th of August 1929.

On that day, a Sunday, Hahn had had a day off, and had last been seen in a beer-garden with a man near the place where her body was thus later found. The body of this girl, which had been lying buried for three months in the loamy earth, was quite well preserved, desiccation, the formation of adipocere, and the absence of worms had contributed to the preservation. The wounds were as follows: three stabs in the left temple. These penetrated through the skull, that nearest the front piercing also the brain, green at that point. In the skin of the neck there was a group of seven stabs in a small area. These were all superficial. In the breast there were ten wounds, two penetrated the heart, two the pleurae.

My findings were as follows: A comparison of the autopsies of the Albermann child and Maria Hahn show a considerable affinity. Evidence of throttling could not, of course, be proved in the latter case, but the stab wounds were alike in both cases. Each body had stabs in the left temple. In the skull there were the same triangular forms showing a knife with a rather broad back. The largest stab, in the case of Hahn, was in the forehead.

The Albermann child had been last seen at a quarter to 7 p.m. For lunch she had eaten sauerkraut between 12 and 1 o'clock. For tea she had a roll with butter and apple-kraut. Towards 6 o'clock she ate sweets and apples. In the stomach were 300 grammes of chyme, consisting of two masses differing distinctly in their white-yellow and rust-brown colour. The first I identified microscopically as white cabbage and the latter as apples. The food had been badly masticated, the cabbage leaves had been swallowed whole, the pieces of apple were 1-2 cm. thick. Of the bread nothing could be traced in the stomach as it was highly digestive. I came to the conclusion that the stomach of the Albermann child had stopped in the digestive activity owing to the murder, at a time when all the cabbage eaten between 12 and 1 o'clock was still in the stomach, but the roll eaten at 4 o'clock was entirely digested.

It must be borne in mind that sauerkraut is not easily digested, moreover that it had been badly chewed; a roll, on the other hand, even when swallowed in somewhat large pieces - as was the apple - may be fully digested in three hours. Hence: 4 plus 3 = 7 o'clock.

In the bowels we found neither cabbage nor apple. As the apple had been eaten at 6 o'clock and its remains were still completely in the stomach, one can arrive at the conclusion that death took place only a few hours after 6 o'clock (Hahn had less food fragments, but it is impossible to draw any useful conclusions in her case, since we do not know at what time she took her last meal). Assuming that she had a rich dinner within the hour of her death, that event had to be presumed to have occurred about midnight. The place of the death of Hahn can be presumed to have been near the place where her body was found on the edge of the wood; for it is unlikely that the murderer dragged the body very far. The body of the little Albermann was discovered in so typical a position that she must have been killed and sexually violated where she was found. The position, with the knickers torn up behind, arouses the inevitable suspicion that the child had been put in this position in order to rape her from behind. At the place where the body was found only the smallest traces of blood were discovered, for the rain which fell on the 7th and 8th had washed most of it away. Most of the blood had been absorbed by the clothes.

The chemise, the petticoat, the vest, the frock and apron, the vicinity of the breast, the left side and the left upper back, were half drenched with blood, while the right half of the underclothing showed only a few blood spots. It would therefore follow that while the child was bleeding from the stab wounds in the breast, it must have been lying on its back and inclining to the left side. Had it been in an upright position, the blood would have run down to the legs and could not have taken the direction to the back. Upon these considerations I drew my conclusions: the criminal had throttled the Albermann child at that place where the body was found. The child had sunk down unconscious. The criminal had stabbed the child as she lay on her back through her buttoned-up coat. He unbuttoned the coat probably only to gain access to the genitals. Then he changed his mind - was he disturbed by her dying convulsions, or did he not want to put himself in contact with a victim bleeding copiously? The criminal placed the coat over the uncovered abdomen of the child and thus left her lying there.

The Close of 1929 - Analysis of the Findings

With the Albermann case the series of murders and attacks in Düsseldorf ceased. The winter remained quiet. The Düsseldorf Murderer - for such was the name the whole world had given the criminal, or criminals - had not been apprehended, despite the fact that an enormous police machine had been set in motion against him. Because of this failure the press launched an attack against the police, in my opinion, unjustly. It is only necessary to consider the facts as I have related them to appreciate how few were the clues in the hands of the police to assist them in their search for the perpetrator. Indeed, two of the attacks were perpetrated by Stausberg; the murder of Gross was at the hand of an unknown criminal; and, these three crimes apart, there remained an insufficient number of common factors upon which a theory could be constructed pointing unequivocally to a single criminal.

Where a series of crimes are committed, the same technique inevitably suggests the same criminal. That is an old aphorism of criminology. But just this very thing is missing in our cases. Certainly, there were points in common. In five murders the sexual motive was perfectly clear from the condition of the genitals. In the other cases, that of the murdered Scheer or the stabbed Kornblum, or again, in the case of Frau Meurer, it could not be definitely demonstrated.

In a different category was the type of outrage that began with the strangling of the Ohliger child, Hamacher, Lenzen and Albermann. These were cases in which throttling was a common feature; but among the surviving victims, throttling was not employed. Further, the multiplicity of stabs in the one series of victims and the absence of stabbing in the case of the other series, along with the hammer blows, all argued against one and the same criminal. And to these factors was added the view that Stausberg had been responsible for the February attack, an opinion which held good until the November findings on Albermann. It was in particular for a criminal who dealt death with a hammer that we sought. I myself had been confirmed in this error because of my investigations of attacks which had taken place in the town of Eschweiler in the Aix la Chapelle district.

Since 1926 six attacks on women in lonely parts of the town had been reported to the police. In all these cases the criminal had approached the women unawares from behind, and rendered them unconscious with a hammer-blow to the left of the head with the object of attempting subsequent sexual outrage. On the first woman who had been attacked in 1926 I found a square depression fracture over the left ear with the length of three and-a-half cm. which was already healed. The last case - 30th January, 1930 - had in addition lacerated bruises on the left part of the head and two cuts on the forehead and chin. The criminal from Eschweiler, obviously also a sadist, has not been identified up to now. I had presumed at once that this criminal had nothing to do with the hammer cases in Düsseldorf. Nevertheless, his technique showed similarity with one or other of the Düsseldorf cases. Thus in this case we came to the conclusion that as in the Düsseldorf case we had to assume a hammer specialist in addition to the stabber. Another grave error in the search for the principal criminal was a preconceived opinion that he must be a madman, the ghastliness of the murders, and the terror which gripped the whole population, all helped to make this error an easy one into which to fall.

One may refer here to the London killer, "Jack the Ripper", but these crimes were, after all, very different. In a short space of time, a few months, six prostitutes were murdered in Whitechapel, always in the same, their bodies being mutilated. The London crimes stopped suddenly with the suicide of this abnormal criminal.*

So it was that we sought in Düsseldorf, too, for a criminal maniac.

***There is no ground for Professor Berg's statement that the identity of Jack the Ripper was ever established.**

Chapter Two
Kürten's Confessions Bring the Solution

Suddenly all these uncertainties and perplexities were ended by the capture of the criminal and his confession. This totally unforeseen outcome was not due to the efforts of the police, but to a sheer coincidence, coupled with the criminal's lack of caution.

It was the famous Maria Butlies affair which resulted in the discovery. For that reason I propose to describe it here, and do so in Kürten's own words.

"On the 14th of May, 1930, I saw a man accost a young girl at the railway station and go off with her. Out of curiosity I followed the couple along the Graf-Adolf-Strasse, the Karlstrasse, Klosterstrasse, Kolner Strasse, Stoffeler Strasse to the Volksgarten. When the man wanted to go into the dark park with the girl, she resisted him. I seized the opportunity and approached the couple.

"I asked him what he meant to do with the girl. He replies that the girl had no lodging and that he proposed to take her to his sister. At this point the girl asked me whether the Achenbachstrasse was in that neighbourhood - it was there the man's sister was supposed to live. When I assured her very convincingly that the street was in an entirely different neighbourhood, she stepped to my side, and the man made off very quickly. We returned. The girl told me that she was out of work and had nowhere to go. She agreed to come with me to my room in the Mettmanner Strasse 71. Round about 11 o'clock we got to my room which is on the third floor. Then she suddenly said she didn't want any sexual intercourse and asked me whether I couldn't find her some other place to sleep. I agreed. We went by tram to Worringerplatz and on towards the Grafenberger Wald, going along the Wolfschlucht until we came to the last of the houses. Here I seized Butlies with one hand by the neck, pressing her head back very hard and kissing her. I asked her to let me have her. I thought that under the circumstances she would agree, and my opinion was right. Afterwards I asked whether I had hurt her, which she denied. I wanted to take her back to the tram, but I did not accompany her right to it because I was afraid that she might inform the police officer who was standing there. I had no intention of killing Butlies. She had offered no resistance. We had sexual intercourse standing, after I had pulled down her knickers. There was another reason why I could not do anything to her - I had been seen by a friend in the tram. I did not think that Butlies would be able to find her way back again to my apartment in the rather obscure Mettmanner Strasse. So much the more was I surprised when on Wednesday, the 21st of May, I saw Butlies again in my house."

Butlies supplements this statement thus:

On the 14th of May she had come from Cologne to Düsseldorf. There on the railway station she got into contact with a "Frau Bruckner", and made an appointment with her for 8 o'clock in the evening of that day. She had then waited in vain on the railway station for the woman and in the end had been accosted by a man who wanted to put her up.

Her statement corroborates Kürten's. After her adventure Butlies took the tram from the Grafenberger Wald back to the town. Then she walked the streets of Düsseldorf. At last she went to the Gertrudishaus, where she told the Sisters about the attack. On the 17th of May she wrote to her new acquaintance, Frau Brucker, in Dusseldorf-Bilker Allee - a letter in which she hinted that she had fallen into the hands of a murderer. The recipient of the letter, Frau Brugmann, suspected the connection with the Dusseldorf murderer, and took the letter to the criminal police department. The writer of the letter was interrogated and eventually succeeded in finding the house of the unknown man. On her own account she had already made enquiries in different houses in the Mettmanner Strasse for a man of a certain type and, at last, she had heard from the inhabitants of No. 71 that a crying girl had once come in the same way asking for a man of the same description. Her description fitted Peter Kürten, who lodged there. That was on the 21st of May.

Kürten continues his narrative:

"On Wednesday, the 21st of May, I happened to look over the bannisters and saw Butlies and recognised her. She can be recognised easily. She has very fair hair, is slant-eyed and bow-legged. She left the house again. At lunch-time she came back. This time with a police officer. I saw her stand in the entrance door and speak to the landlady. Then in the afternoon she came again to the house, this time coming up to our floor. She entered the flat of the Wimmers and she saw me. She was startled. I think it is likely that she recognised me then. I knew what would happen after that!

"That same evening I fetched my wife from the place where she worked; 'I must get out of the flat' I said. I explained the Butlies case to her. But I only mentioned the attempt at sexual intercourse, saying that as it could be called 'rape' along with my previous convictions, it was enough to get me fifteen years' penal servitude. Therefore I had to get out. I changed. Throughout the night I walked about. On Thursday, the 22nd of May, I saw my wife in the morning in the flat. I fetched my things away in a bag and rented a room in the Adlerstrasse. I slept quietly until Friday morning."

The events of this Friday were described to me by Kürten in writing.

"It was at nine in the morning when I went to my flat. Shortly before I reached No. 71 two men came out of it. I found out afterwards they were detectives. I thought right away that they were that. When I went into the flat my wife was still there. When I asked her why she had not gone to work today she answered: 'I did, but I was taken away from it by two detectives who brought me home'. Both these men had searched the place and a few moments before they had gone down the staircase. Then my wife asked me to leave the house saying she did not want me to be arrested there. I did as she asked and later met her - she had gone back to the place where she was employed. I then asked her to come with me for a little while. Two days before I had told her about the Butlies affair. Today, the 23rd, in the morning, I told my wife that I was also responsible for the Schulte affair, adding my usual remark that it would mean at least ten years' or more separation for us - probably for ever. At that my wife was inconsolable. She spoke of age, unemployment, lack of means and starvation in old age. When the lunch hour approached I had not even then succeeded in calming my wife down. She raved that I should take my life. Then she would do the same, since her future was completely without hope. Then in the late afternoon I told my wife that I could help her. That I could still be something for her. I told her that I was the Düsseldorf murderer. Of course, she didn't think it possible and didn't want to believe it. But then I disclosed everything to her, naming myself the murderer in each case. When she asked me how this could help her, I hinted that a high reward had been offered for the discovery as well as for the capture of the criminal; that she could get hold of that reward, or at lest some part of it, if she would report my confession and denounce me to the police. Of course, it wasn't easy for me to convince her that this ought not to be considered as treason, but that, on the contrary, she was doing a good deed to humanity as well as to justice. It was not until late in the evening that she promised me to carry out my request, and also that she would not commit suicide. I then accompanied her almost to the door. It was 11 o'clock when we separated. Back in my lodging I went to bed and fell asleep at once. What happened the next morning, the 24th of May, is known.

"First a bath, then several times around the neighbourhood of the Kortzingens' flat (Kürten had planned a robbery here). Lunch, a hair-cut, and then, at 3 o'clock I met my wife according to the arrangement and there the arrest took place. As a matter of fact, my wife had carried out my order a bit too quickly for me. I want to point out again that I never collapsed on the 23rd or 24th of May, but kept steadily before me my purpose to the very end."

Thus Kürten, I now contrast his statement with that of his wife:

"In the morning, after the detectives had brought me from the place where I work, my husband came to the flat. 'You must have done something awful!' I said. 'Yes' he replied. 'I did it. I did everything.' Then, with that he left the flat. We then met my arrangement at 11.30 in the morning in the Hofgarten. We had dinner in a restaurant in the Duisburger Strasse. I could not eat anything, but he ate up the lot, my portion, too."*

"At 2 o'clock we were walking over the Rhine Bridge back and forwards. In the late afternoon I asked him what he meant with his words 'I have done everything.' 'If you promise solemnly that you won't give me away I'll tell you something,' he said. I promised. 'I have done everything that has happened here in Düsseldorf!' 'What do you mean by that?' I asked. 'Everything-the murders and the attacks.' 'What, those innocent children, too?' I asked. 'Yes' he said. 'Why did you do that?' I asked him. 'I don't know myself,' he replied, 'it just came over me.'

"Then all the big cases were talked over, including that of Mulheim. When I got terribly excited about it all, he said, 'I've done something very silly. I ought not to have told you.' That afternoon Kürten was very depressed and in a way I had never seen before. He told me that he had not cried once in his whole life, but yesterday evening, when he was alone, he had cried bitterly. In the afternoon while we spoke only about the fact that the detectives were after him, he was quiet and self-possessed. But towards the evening when I wanted to go home he was as I have never seen him in his life before. He was very cast down. He could not look into my eyes. All the indifference had disappeared. He burst out with it all, telling of the murders and the attacks as if some power forced him to it. I thought he had gone crazy. Nothing had been said about any reward."

Who could not understand Frau Kürten - who would reproach her that she was not able to carry alone the weight of this ghastly secret - but that she gave it away to the police when pressed by them?

She had a last meeting with her husband near the Rochus Church, for the following day, the 24th. That, too, the woman, who was quite distraught, reported to the police. The church square was quietly surrounded and Kürten was arrested as he walked towards his wife. He was quite composed. Subsequently, he often told me how he

***(Kürten's appetite never failed. Even at his last meal, at his own request, he had Wienerschnitzel with baked potatoes and a bottle of wine. He enjoyed it so much that he asked for it again in the course of the evening.)**

smilingly calmed the detective who advanced excitedly towards him, the revolver levelled at him.

When Kürten was questioned by the police he not only told of the attacks of 1929, but he gave also an account of a long chain of crimes without being questioned. For reasons to which I will return presently he lengthened this chain with some imaginary links, but he soon brought it back again to the facts.

THE SEQUENCE OF THE CRIMES

According to Kürten's own statement

Born in 1883 in Koln-Mulheim. Passed his childhood there. Left for Dusseldorf 1894; 1897 apprenticed as a moulder. In 1899 first convicted for theft.

Table of Offences

Nov 1899 Attempted strangulation 18 year old girl unknown.
From 1900 to 1904 in prison

1904	Arson	Barn after harvest
1904	Arson	Hay loft
1904	Arson	Two hay-ricks
1905 to 1913 in prison		
1913	Attempted strangulation	Margarete Schafer
1913	Murder by strangulation and throat-cutting	Christine Klein, Mulheim
1913	Axe blow	Unknown man
1913	Axe blow	Unknown woman
1913	Axe blow attempt	Hermes, sleeping girl
1913	Strangulation	Gertrud Franken
1913	Arson	Hay-rick and hay wagon

1913 to 1921 in prison

1921	Strangulation	War widow
1925	Strangulation	Tiede
1925	Strangulation	Mech
1925	Strangulation	Kiefer
1926	Strangulation	Wack
1927	Arson	Three hay-ricks
1927	Arson	Shock of sheaves
1927	Arson	Two barns
1927	Attempted strangulation	Anni Ist
1927	Arson	Two barns
1927	Arson	Plantation
1928	Arson	Barn
1928	Arson	Farmyard
1928	Arson	Shock of sheaves (x 2)
1928	Arson	Hay-rick
1928	Arson	Hay wagon
1928	Arson	House
1928	Arson	House
1928	Arson	Shed
1928	Arson	Forest fire
1928	Arson	Haystacks
1928	Arson	Sheds
1929	Arson	Stacks
1929	Arson	Barns, sheds, stack(ten cases)
1929		
Feb 3	Attack with scissors	Frau Kühn
Feb 13	Stabbed and killed	Rudolf Scheer

Mar 8	Strangled and stabbed after death	Child-Rose Ohliger
March	Attempted strangulation	Edith Boukorn
July	Attempted strangulation	Maria Witt
July	Attempted strangulation	Maria Mass
July	Attempted strangulation	Unknown domestic servant
August	Strangled and stabbed to death	Maria Hahn
August	Strangled and drowned	"Anni" - a housemaid
August	Stabbed with dagger	Anna Goldhausen
August	Stabbed with dagger	Frau Mantel
August	Stabbed with dagger	Kornblum
August	Strangled and throat cut	Child - Hamacher
August	Strangled and stabbed	Child - Lenzen
August	Stabbed with dagger	Gertrud Schulte
August	Attempted strangulation and thrown into river	Heer
Sept	Blow with tool	Ruckl
Sept	Attempted strangulation	Maria Rad
Sept	Killed by hammer blows	Ida Reuter
October	Killed by hammer blows	Elisabeth Dorrier
October	Attack with hammer	Frau Meurer
October	Attack with hammer	Frau Wanders
November	Strangled and stabbed with scissors	Child - Albermann

1930		
Feb	Attempted strangulation	Hilde
March	Attempted strangulation	Maria del Sant
March	Attempted strangulation	Irma
April	Attempted strangulation	Sibille
April	Attempted strangulation	Unknown girl from Herne
April	Attempted strangulation	Young woman, Hau
April	Attacks	Several girls
April	Attack with hammer	Charlotte Ulrich
May	Attempted strangulation	Maria Butlies
May	Attempted murder	Gertrud Bell

The way in which Kürten enumerated all his offences, tabulated here in a sequence chronologically accurate, and the way in which he dictated it with every detail, is quite extraordinary. He was not accused of these crimes one by one, but reeled off on his own account, beginning with No. 1 and ending with No. 79, every single case, dictating them, in fact, to the stenographer and even showing enjoyment at the horrified faces of the many police officers who listened to his recital, day by day.

Kürten was examined very closely by the Criminal Investigation Department and by the judge. Even so, I got him to describe to me personally the precise details of all the cases. A comparison of my shorthand note with the protocol of the police and judge shows a close similarity on all main points of fact. His statements show his character, his intelligence, his instinctual life, so clearly that from it every reader educated in criminal psychology can obtain an absolutely clear picture of the personality of the criminal. Therefore I propose to record not only his talk concerning the cases of 1929 which are, of course, of great interest, but also these other cases. From his recital of the facts it transpires that my original deductions set forth earlier in this work were correct.

The following is the original form of Kürten's statement. As I propose to deal with the motives, as he gave them to me, in a later chapter, I shall not touch upon them at the moment. I might mention here the fact that Kürten, when interrogated by the police officers, suppressed facts, or misrepresented them in order not to disclose the motive that actuated him. In the following cases the numbers are those of the above table:

CASE 1 The First Murder

Kürten gave the following statement:

"In November 1899 I picked up an eighteen-year old girl in the Alleestrasse. I went with her to the Hofgarten, past the Zoo, to the Grafenberger Walk as far as Rolandsburg. On the way home amid lovely country I throttled her. I left her lying there, supposing her to be dead and heard no more from her."

Nothing could be discovered concerning this case which went back thirty years. Note how exactly Kürten remembers all the details of his work.

CASE 6 Margaret Schafer

This case is interesting because the statement of Kürten can be compared with the statement of the throttled victim.

Kürten thus describes the affair:

"In June 1913 I picked up a girl on the Brehmstrasse and took her out on several subsequent occasions. One Sunday we went to a dance at Gerresheim. On the way home I throttled the girl several times. When she was scared I said 'That's what love's like. I won't kill you, though'. After that she put up with it. We had sexual connection on a bench."

To the jury Margaret described her adventure with Kürten as follows:

"We walked in the woods the whole night. Kürten would not let me go home. He had my bag with the keys in it. He wanted to kiss me and he knocked me about, afterwards becoming friendly again. Then he threw me on to a bench and tried to have sexual intercourse with me. In the struggle my dress got torn and I cried, and then he became kinder again. I looked simply awful and in that state could not have taken the tram. We sat on a bench. Kürten threw his coat about us both and we fell asleep. Dawn came and I woke him up.

Then he started again as before, tore off my ear-rings, bit me, half strangled me, pulling my hair out in handfuls. He looked like the very devil himself. I begged him to calm down for otherwise he would end in hell. My words had some effect and he did calm down. He made me swear that I would not tell anything to anybody we might meet. We came eventually to the Rolandsburg. Kürten had breakfast there. I went to the waiters who were sitting in another room and told them of the jam I was in."

CASE 7 Murder of the child Klein

It was about the same time, in the summer of 1913, that there took place a strangling case that was not equalled in ghastliness until the year 1929. It was Kürten's first murder.

Kürten thus describes it:

"In the summer of 1913 I committed many thefts. It was my speciality to frequent at such times houses where the ground floors were utilised as business premises, in particular, inns, where the proprietor and his family lived above.

"It was easy to search such premises without fear of discovery. For this purpose I have even left Düsseldorf and gone to other towns. I went to Cologne, and, in particular, to Koln-Mulheim, the town which is, by the way, the town of my birth.

"One Sunday evening - it was a Feast day-I searched for a suitable house and came at length to the Wolfstrasse. I broke into a house in this street, an inn owned by Klein. I went up to the first floor. This was about 10 or 11 o'clock. I opened different doors but found nothing worth stealing. In a room facing the stairs there was a bed in the left corner near the window where I entered. It was a large bed in which adults could sleep. In the room were also a cupboard and a table.

"So much light came through the window from the street that I could see clearly everything in the room. In the bed I saw a sleeping girl of about ten, covered with a thick feather bed. She was lying with her head towards the window. I seized her by the neck with my hands and throttled her for one or two minutes. The child woke up, struggled to free herself, scratched my hand then became unconscious and still.

"Her arms were thrown up above her head. I then drew her head over the edge of the bed and threw the feather bed to the foot of it. With one or two fingers I penetrated the genitals. With a small but sharp pocket knife I made a deep cut in the throat of the child. I started on the left side of the throat, drawing the knife to the right with the right hand. I heard the blood gurgle up and drip on the mat. It spattered my hand. The whole business did not take more than three minutes. I then left the room and made off."

How very clearly, after seventeen years, Kürten remembered every detail of the place and of the crime, a comparison with the photograph of this room in the Public Prosecutor's Department at Dusseldorf shows.

(Kürten, who so often combined a reckless audacity with extreme caution, here, apparently, committed his crime in a room the door of which he had not even troubled to lock.)

The autopsy revealed the following:

The 111 cm. long corpse was pallid. There was hardly any post mortem staining. On the face there were regular blue-red ecchymoses. The tongue was bitten.

On the throat there were two wounds separated from each other, the one shallow, only 1 to 2 mm. deep, the other deep, 9 cm. in length. The upper wound edge suggested a single stroke, the lower wound had been made by four movements.

Certain discrepancies in the autopsy show that the memory of Kürten, otherwise extremely good, becomes unreliable at the climax of the sadistic gratification (i.e. four knife wounds instead of one, the different position of the body).

After the murder in Mulheim there followed those incendiary crimes which are rather regularly distributed throughout the career of Kürten. Kürten also alleges that he attacked two people with an axe from behind about that time. But as these alleged crimes were committed seventeen years ago it was impossible to trace them. Nevertheless, I mention them here because of the circumstantial account of them given by Kürten.

CASE 8

"One Saturday evening in June, 1913, I left home at 8 o'clock and set out for Gerresheim. From a cellar under the Holy Trinity Church I took a chopper. At about 11 o'clock I saw an unaccompanied girl enter a house. In the passage I gave her a sharp and heavy blow on the head so that she crumpled up without a murmur. The girl about 1.68 m. tall, slim, and between eighteen and twenty years of age."

CASE 9

"In July 1913 I went with a chopper to Gerresheim about 9 o'clock in the evening. After a long search I saw a man sitting on a bench in the park. I crept up to him and hit him on the head and he collapsed without a sound. On my way back I set fire to a cart laden with hay."

With the following attempt the short chopper period is finished.

CASE 10

"In July 1913 I went up to the first floor of the house on the corner of the Munster and Ulmenstrasse. I had a chopper with me. I had been to the house once already to steal. I was just about to cleave through the head of the sixteen-year-old girl when a man jumped out of bed. I ran away, throwing the chopper on the bed as I ran."

(Witnesses corroborate this statement. When the householder came home after chasing Kürten in vain, he found the chopper on the blanket of his child's bed.)

Here I want to observe that Kürten dared to approach men on three occasions only. In one case the man had fallen asleep, and in the other two they were, or appeared to be, drunk. These were cases 9,47 and 56. Kürten's precautions were so great that he even desisted from his attack upon a woman victim if she only had firmness enough to offer a courageous resistance.

CASE 11 Gertrud Franken

"At about 9 o'clock in the evening on a Saturday in July 1913, I set out for the house of the Loscheckes. I had a skeleton key with me and with it gained entrance to the first floor. I went into a room and up to the bed and strangled one of the children lying in it for some time. I left the room and went home again. There were three beds in the room. The girl I throttled was, I reckon, sixteen or seventeen years old. She did not scream or shout." (To enter a bedroom in which there were three occupied beds, and to make a murderous assault upon an adolescent in one of them, is an inexplicable proceeding and departure from Kürten's habit of cautiousness.)

The strangled girl was born in 1896 - thus Kürten had estimated her age correctly. A big interval now follows in the sequence of the crimes, due to a long term of penal servitude followed by Kürten's marriage in Altenburg. Then, once more, in the environs of Dusseldorf, a place well known to him, Kürten renewed his criminal activities.

CASE 14

In 1925 Kürten started to have relations with two servant girls, Tiede and Mech. This is how Kürten tells of it:

"I met Tiede and had sexual relations with her in her room where she was employed in the Bodinusstrasse. I got something god to eat there, too, and I could do with it, for I had at that time to work pretty hard. A week after meeting Tiede, I became acquainted with Mech, a housemaid in a situation on the Bergischen Landstrasse. There, too, I got something to eat. I often grabbed Tiede by the throat and seized hold of her. When she got angry with me I used to try and pacify her. 'That's what love means,' I told her. She let herself be calmed down. I had not told her my real name and I had pretended to be younger by ten years, and that I had a better job than I really had. Then my wife came along and Tiede realised that I was married and gave me away to the police. I got two months' imprisonment for attempted seduction. During the trial I defended myself vigorously against the charge. But I got the two months and did it, in 1927.

"Then Mech and Tiede met and Mech cut up rough and charged me with rape, but I was acquitted. Then she charged me with using threats and insulting behaviour. For that I got eight months' imprisonment. I served six months, two being remitted on my undertaking to leave Düsseldorf. That wasn't so easy, so I wrote to the Ministry with the result that the condition was cancelled."

Next follow several cases of strangling.

CASE 16 Maria Kiefer

"In the summer of 1925 I picked up Maria Kiefer in the Parkstrasse. We made an appointment for the following evening. I went to her place as agreed upon and there Kiefer waited for me at the front door. That was about 10 o'clock. She took me with her into the washhouse in the cellar where we had sexual intercourse, but not without her consent. Then I seized her by the throat and strangled her, but Kiefer managed to escape from the grip of my hands and cried out. So I left the house quickly."

(Here, according to Kürten's statement, sadistic impulse and act came after, and not before, the sexual act.)

Investigations revealed that Kiefer was born in 1889 and died in 1929, but to a witness she had told how she had been accosted by a man who she learnt later was married.

CASE 17 Maria Wack

"In the spring of 1926 I picked up Maria Wack in the Duisburgerstrasse. We went into the Hofgarten and talked about our personal affairs.

"We met frequently after that and one Sunday we went to the Grafenberger Wald. There I attempted to force her backwards on a bench while I seized her throat. As she put up a resistance I abandoned the attempt and left her on the bench. I never saw her again."

Wack comments upon this as follows:

"In June 1926 I became acquainted with a man who called himself Fritz Ketteler. I was cleaning the doorstep when he accosted me. We made an appointment and inside three weeks we had been out five times. Ketteler was am employee of the railway and behaved decently in every way. One Sunday he suggested that we should go to the Graftenberg. Dusk had fallen in the woods and we were passing a bench when he suddenly seized me, flung me on it and groped with his hand under my skirt. I defended myself. Apparently, passers-by frightened him, for he desisted. I jumped up, grabbed his hat, and ran away. He called after me, asking for his hat. He then exchanged his hat for mine and made the remark that I ought to be human. There he left me standing, and made off."

CASE 22 Annie Ist

"In the summer of 1927 I picked up a girl named Annie Ist on the Brehmstrasse. From then on I saw her frequently. On a Saturday evening we went into the Grafenberger Wald. We had sexual intercourse on a bench. I then seized Ist's neck and strangled her. But she was a robust girl and managed to free herself. She ran away screaming. Her dress had been torn at the neck.

Ist comments as follows:

"Kürten's statement is correct. He called himself Ketteler, Mettmanner Strasse 71. We met each other several times. On one occasion it ended with sexual intercourse. At the end of July 1927, we went to a fair at Rath and returned through the Grafenberger Wald. It was there that we had sexual relations, but when Kürten wanted intercourse a second time I demurred, but at last gave in. After intercourse, he strangled me without any reason, bashed my face and tore my dress from my neck. Nevertheless, I asked him to take me home, which he did. We met each other several times again, but there were no more sexual relations. I got some information about him and discovered that his name was not Ketteler, and that he was a married man, so I broke off our relationship. When I saw in the newspapers the photograph of the Düsseldorf murderer, I recognised him instantly, but I did not denounce him to the police."

Now I come to the cases of 1929.

CASE 45 Frau Kühn - 3.2.29.

Kürten states as follows :

"On a Sunday evening I strolled about the neighbourhood of the Hellweg in search of a victim. I had pocketed a pair of scissors for this purpose. Towards 6 o'clock I saw a woman, going along the Bertastrasse. I went up to her and shouted "Stop!" and then "No noise!" Then with the scissors I stabbed her blindly. I left her lying unconscious. I heard cries for help and made my way quickly down the Hellweg. When I was cleaning the scissors at home I noticed that from one blade the pointed part had broken off about 8 to 10 mm. I had thought that the stabs were much deeper." (By X-ray photograph I was able to determine the fact that the point of the scissors was impacted in the bone. When Frau Kühn was confronted by Kürten she failed to recognise him because of the darkness at the time of the attack.)

CASE 46 The Murder of the Ohliger child

Kürten's account:

"On the 8th of February, 1929, I left home at about 6 o'clock at night. I went towards St Vincent's Church where I met a girl between eight and ten years of age. I asked her where she wanted to go. She said 'Home.' I asked, 'Where do you live?' She said: 'In the Langerstrassse.' I said: 'Come, then, I'll take you home.' I took her by the hand led her along the Kettwiger Strasse as far as a hoarding. Here I seized the child's throat, strangled her and put her on her back. With my right hand I drew scissors out and stabbed the child in the left temple and in different places about the heart. The child seemed to be dead. I went back to my flat and searched myself for blood stains. I also cleaned the scissors. There were no blood stains on my clothing. Then I went to the movies as I still had a free ticket, and then home again. I filled a beer bottle with petroleum - we have a petroleum lamp - and then went to the scene of the crime with the object of pouring it over the body and setting fire to it. But there were too many people about. I therefore leant the bottle against the hoarding and went home. The next morning, at 6 o'clock, I got up and told my wife I had to go to the WC. I ran quickly to the scene of the crime, poured the petroleum over the body and set it on fire. There and back did not take me more than five or six minutes. I felt no sexual excitement and did not touch the girl. My motives was only to cause excitement and indignation. I wanted to increase the general indignation by setting light to the victim.

"I did not masturbate on the corpse, nor did I even touch the child sexually. The place where I first throttled and stabbed the child is only one or two metres from where I put her down. When I strangled her she was standing. I took two or three places with her towards the hoarding. I had both hands on her neck and dragged her with her feet on the ground."

(When the child was dragged one of her shoes slipped off and was later found at that place.)

CASE 47 Scheer

"On the 12th of February, 1929 I left home about 8 o'clock in the evening and for three hours I searched in vain for a victim. My wife, I knew, would be returning home about 1 o'clock. Then in the Hellweg I ran into a man. He seemed to be drunk and noisy. He shoved me. 'What do you want?' he asked. I looked at his hands to see whether he was armed. Then with the flat of my hand I struck him in the neck. He went over backwards and fell flat on his face. I took the scissors and gave him a heavy stab with them. He grabbed for my legs and half lying, half kneeling, in front of me, clung to me. I next stabbed him in the right temple and again in the neck. At one stab in the back my scissors stuck and I could hardly get them out again. After another stab in the back I heard the blood spouting. Scheer collapsed. He relaxed his hold on my leg and lay face downwards. Even in the dark I could see the large pool of blood. I grabbed his feet and dragged him towards the ditch and shoved him until he rolled down. After that I wanted to go home, but after taking thirty steps or so I turned back and cleaned the uppers of Scheer's boots to obliterate the traces of my finger prints. The whole thing didn't take me more than eight minutes, one of which I spent standing over Scheer before I dragged him to the ditch. Next day, at 8 o'clock, I returned to the scene of the crime. On my way back I met a detective and opened a conversation with him. He, too, probably was going to the place where the murder had been committed, for detectives were already standing there. The detective looked at me suspiciously. How had I come to know of the crime? he enquired. I told him I had heard of it by telephone. Meanwhile we had come to the cordon and I was stopped." (This fantastic episode was later confirmed during the hearing by the detective in question. I wonder what would have been the result had the detective been as clever and quick in sizing up the situation as was Kürten.)

The following cases, 48 to 51 and 53, are again cases of strangling.

CASE 49 Maria Witt

The tragi-comedy of the 11th of July, 1929, Kürten described as follows at the police station investigation:

"During the first half of July, 1929, I picked up a servant girl named Maria Witt on the Grunerstrasse. We chatted pleasantly and made an appointment. Several times we met in the Heinrichstrasse. One Sunday I fetched her to go to Kaiserswerth. Suddenly on the Graf-Recke-Strasse my wife came up from behind us with the words: 'Ha, ha! So you've got yourself a new wife, have you?' With a rose that Maria had brought me from the garden of her employer, I gave my wife a smack on the cheek. Then, without a single word, I turned and left both the women standing there. The scissors I had put in my pocket.

Maria Witt confirms this statement: Kürten had introduced himself as Ketteler, a locksmith, entitled to a pension, being in the employment of a gas company. She had a good impression of him and had on one occasion actually sent roses to his suppositious address on the Ackerstrasse.

"His wife came up to us with the words 'Oh, how nice!' and struck me in the face with her hand."

CASE 50 Maria Maas - 21 July 1929

"That Sunday after I had left my wife and Maria Witt, I picked up another girl and asked her to come with me to the Heerdter Festival. We remained there for some time. I bought some peaches and then we strolled towards the Rhine. We sat there and talked, meanwhile dusk had fallen. Suddenly, I gripped her neck and strangled her violently, but she freed herself and ran into a tent nearby."

Maas, who was born in 1904, made this statement;

"When the man accosted me and introduced himself, I only

caught his Christian name - Fritz - and that he was a Post Office official. He behaved in every way like a gentleman. We went to the Festival and there he bought peaches. We also went to a beer garden, and afterwards we strolled towards the Rhine. He asked me repeatedly for a kiss, but when it darkened I wanted to go home. On that he gripped my neck and without a word compressed it. I freed myself and ran towards a little tent. For days five impressions of the nails of his hand were visible on my neck."

The girl, by the way, did not report to the police voluntarily, she had to be searched for.

CASE 53 Anni

"On the same evening I picked up a girl on the Oberkasseler Brucke who called herself Anni. We went to a beer garden. Anni said that she came from Westphalia. When darkness fell I strangled her throat until I thought she was dead. Then I dragged her along the bank and threw her into the Rhine."

This case could not be traced or cleared up. No girl had been reported missing and as it is a very rare thing that a body thrown in the Rhine does not come up again, the police doubt the truth of Kürten's statement.

CASE 51

The girl in the Freitagstrasse Kürten alleges he met between the 21st and 28th of August 1929. He did not know the name. He had taken her for a walk along the banks of the Rhine to see the firework display. Then when he attempted to throttle her she had run away screaming. This case could not be traced.

CASE 52 The Hahn case

No other crime is more significant for an understanding of the personality of Kürten than this. Kürten himself has told about it in all its details, and even confessed to the examining magistrate the sexual motive. Here is his statement:

"On the 8th of August, 1929, I was strolling in the Zoo district. I hadn't any intention of committing any offence on a girl at the time. On the Hansaplatz a girl was sitting on a bench. She accosted me.

I sat down beside her and we talked pleasantly together and made a date for an excursion to the Neanderthal the next Sunday. On Sunday, punctually at 1.30 in the afternoon, I found myself in the Hansaplatz where the girl was already waiting. We went to the Neanderthal, visited a beer garden and then on to the Stinter mill. We stayed there for three hours, drank a glass of red wine each. There also I bought her a slab of chocolate. Towards 7 o'clock we went to Erkrath where we had supper with beer. We then strolled past the house of the Morps, and along by the river. Here we decided to have sexual intercourse. After sexual intercourse we left the bank of the river and went into the meadow. Here I decided to kill her. I led Hahn to a big bush near a ditch and there we settled down. It was half-past nine. Suddenly I strangled her until she became unconscious, but she came to herself quickly again. Again I strangled her. After a bit I stabbed her in the throat with the scissors. She lost a lot of blood but regained consciousness, repeatedly asking me in a feeble voice to spare her life. I stabbed her in the breast a blow that probably pierced the heart. I then gave her repeated stabs in the breast and head. The process of dying probably took an hour. I let the body roll into the ditch and threw branches over it. Then I crossed the meadow and came to the road that runs from Morp-Papendell highway. I had taken the handbag of Hahn with me. From it I took the watch of the dead girl. I made a gift of it to somebody later on. The bag with the keys I threw into an oatfield.

"When I got home my wife was already in bed. Next morning we had a row, because she was suspicious about the night before. She became so excited about it that I made up my mind that I would have to find some way of seeing that the body of Hahn wasn't discovered, otherwise my wife would connect the blood stains on my clothes with it. So I went again on Monday after finishing work to the scene of the crime and pondered where I could bury the body. I went back to the flat and fetched a shovel, inventing an excuse to give my wife. Near the scene of the crime, in the corner of the wood, I dug a deep hole in a fallow field, and carried the body along the footpath, avoiding the oatfield. By the hole I put the body down. I got into the hole and dragged the body down to me. Here I laid it on its back as one buries a body. A shoe had slipped off when the body was dragged down and I laid it beside it. Then I filled the hole. During the whole of this funeral ceremony a sentimental feeling possessed me. I caressed the hair and the first shovelful of earth I strewed thinly and gently on the body. I stamped the earth down and smoothed the soil as it was before. As my shirt had become bloody in carrying the body I took it off and washed it in the river and put it on again still wet. I hid the shovel near the river, then I went home and arrived there about 6 o'clock. My wife began reproaching me and asked me where I had been wandering all the night. I had cleaned my shoes thoroughly in the grass, using a cleaning rag which I always carried with me. I think I drank coffee and went to work in the same clothes. After I had put the body of Hahn in the grave I removed her wrist-watch. Four weeks later I gave the watch to Kate W... W... lives in the same house where I live. She often came into my room and we repeatedly had sexual intercourse."

(The witness W ... vehemently denied this assertion. I found, as a matter of fact, that she was a virgin with enlarged introitus of the vagina.)

The shovel was in fact found at the place indicated. Frau Kürten confirms the hour at which her husband left her on the 12th of August, namely, about 11 o'clock pm, when he gave as explanation that he was on night work. Between 5 and 6 o'clock he had come back with dirty shoes and blood on his clothes. Later Kürten admitted that he had not given the wrist-watch to the witness W... The first assertion that he had done so was an act of vengeance for the trouble she had given him and the part she had taken in bring about his capture. Because he had seen her the day before his arrest with Butlies, he drew this conclusion.

Now Kürten changed the instrument of murder and used a dagger instead of scissors.

CASES 54, 55 and 56

CASE 54

"On the day of the Coronation Ball, at the Lierenfelder Festival, I worked overtime until 10 pm. I went to the Schutzenplatz on the Erkrather Strasse in search of a victim. I watched the young girls, how they went him in different directions. I followed two and presently they stopped before a street door. I passed them thinking that one would probably go on. I crossed to the other side of the street and saw that one girl had gone on. I went back again to the other side of the street, keeping my dagger in readiness. I stabbed the girl in the left breast. It was the girl Goldhausen. She collapsed without a sound. I then went off with the dagger unsheathed. I heard cries for help."

CASE 55

"When I went down the Erkrather Strasse I saw a woman coming along. I offered her my company. The woman did not answer, but crossed the road. I followed her and stabbed her twice in the back from behind."

CASE 56

"I then went across the field path. I saw a man lying in a ditch and just about to crawl up the bank. I gave him a stab in the back. I sheathed the dagger and hid it near the Erkrather Strasse. I watched how the physician and ambulance arrived and how a crowd of curious people gathered round. I pictured to myself the indignation of the population, and then went home. It was half past two."

Three days later followed the murders of the children in Flehe: 24th August, 1929.

CASE 57

"On the 24th of August I went out about 8 o'clock and took the dagger with me. I had heard that the Festival was on in Flehe. Until 10 o'clock I was on the look-out for a victim on the streets of Flehe. I saw two girls. They went down a field path. I followed them and told the bigger girl to fetch me from a kiosk four cigarettes for twenty pfennig. She ran off and I stayed behind with the smaller girl. I seized her by the throat, took her over my arm and carried her across the field to another small field path, where beans grew.

"Here I put down the Hamacher child, who was now unconscious, drew my dagger from my pocket and slit her throat. I stood over the body of the child with my legs apart and cut from my left to the right. I returned the dagger to the sheath. Put the sheath into my hip pocket."

CASE 58

"I went back to the place where Lenzen, the bigger girl, has left us. She gave me the cigarettes. I seized her by the throat and strangled her. With my left arm I seized her round the body and carried her, still throttling her, down the path, round the bean patch to the garden, so that I was hidden by the beans. I loosened my right hand. Lenzen slumped down. I realised that she was not quite unconscious. She moved about and began to scream. I then seized her throat with my left hand and holding her down like that, I drew the dagger from my pocket with my right hand and in that position I stabbed her in the breast and side. I then relaxed my grip. Lenzen sank to the ground. Then I made off and at half past eleven I was home again. My wife was still awake. We talked quite naturally. There were no blood stains on me. Neither were my hands bloody. On the way home I had cleaned my dagger with a rag I found. If Lenzen was found in some other position, then she must have moved of her own volition. I left her lying on her back. On the way to the scene of the crime she defended herself vigorously, lashing out with hands and feet. On the following Sunday, the 25th of August, I went once more to Flehe to savour the effect of my crime. I listened to the various accounts given by the inhabitants, going from group to group of excited people, listening to them. It gave me pleasure that the lovely bright Sunday in Düsseldorf had been shattered as by a lightning stroke."

CASE 59

Twenty-four hours after the murder of the children, the attack on Schulte took place. This case is extremely important, because it enables us to compare Kürten's confession with the statement of the witness.

Kürten said "Just about that time my obsession was rather strong upon me. Feeling fairly sure that I would be successful in finding a victim on that day, I had pocketed my dagger. I crossed the Rhine bridge to Oberkassel and there accosted a young girl. Together we went to Neuss where the fair was in progress. I suggested that we should take the path across the Rhine meadow son the homeward way. As we went along we repeatedly embraced and kissed each other. We sat down near the Rhine and I caressed her, but she refused me sexual intercourse. I knelt beside her, caressed with my left hand her hair, then I seized my dagger with my right hand attempted to cut her throat. She shouted out loudly and struggled hard. Then blindly I went on stabbing her. Her shouts, however, attracted people, who called out, 'What's the matter?'

"I went off, but remained standing in a ditch near by, and so saw how Schulte was found by some people. I went quietly over the dam to the Rhine bridge. I could still hear them calling: 'Quick! Police!' At the last stab I had noticed that my dagger was broken, therefore I threw it away. In Oberkassel I took Schulte's bag from my breast pocket, took out the watch and a picture and threw the bag in a garden. Sitting on a bench I awaited the arrival of the police. I was curious to know how much time would elapse before they arrived. Some twenty minutes passed and the thought of the police busy with my victim relieved my tension. I thought that certainly Schulte would die of her wounds. Under the bright light of the street lamp, I examined my clothes for blood, and then I went home. There was no blood on me."

The twenty-seven-year-old Gertrud Schulte said, contradicting him:

"Kürten had been decent to the very end. There was no talk of kissing until after we had settled down. Then he tried to pull off my knickers and threw me backwards. This tussle did not last more than two minutes. He suddenly released me, held me by one hand and said: 'Come! See if you can feel it. I've only a small tail.' Then he threw himself on top of me and knelt between my legs. I threatened to scream. He said 'You can shout here as much as you like. Nobody will hear you.' Obviously, Kürten had not noticed a tent nearby. He laughed when I said 'Let me die!' 'Then you *shall* die!' he replied. I felt a cut on my throat and shrieked. I felt another painful stab in my back and then became unconscious."

Between these dagger attacks and the hammer attacks which began soon afterwards, three minor attacks were perpetrated.

CASE 60 Lina Her

"It was on a Saturday, and I picked up a girl on the railway station. We went to Schumachers and drank a glass of beer, and then walked in the Hofgarten until one o'clock in the morning. Lina seemed prepared to go home with me. As the last train had gone we went along the banks of the Düssel, through Flingern to the Ostpark. There I seized Lina's throat and strangled her. She defended herself stoutly, at which I released her again. But I strangled her again and at last pushed her into the Düssel."

On that Lina comments:

"I met a man who promised to find some 'digs' for me. On the banks of the Düssel he tried to rape me. When he did not succeed he pushed me in the Düssel. I only just managed to save myself."

CASE 61 Sofie Ruck

"In the autumn of 1929, I met a couple in the Rosstrasse. I wanted to interfere, so I hit the man over the head with a chisel. The man ran away. Then I hit the girl several times with the chisel. She fell down. I went off."

Sofie Ruck, in contradiction, said:

"I was cycling on the Rosstrasse. From a side street a man rushed out, dragged me off my bicycle and hit me on the head. For a short while I was unconscious. Then people came. It was on the 31st of August, 1929, at 10 o'clock. I was most certainly alone."

CASE 62 Maria Rad - 26 September 1929

Kürten said: "Towards the end of September, 1929, at 8 o'clock in the evening, I waited for a victim on the Dreherstrasse, but not until about midnight did I see a woman approaching. I walked towards her, seized her throat and strangled her. We both fell down the bank into the field. I felt for the woman's sexual parts through her clothing. She shouted loudly for help. So I cleared out. I was chased. It was the only time I was ever pursued."

Rad, who was born in 1901, said: "Kürten seized my sexual parts and wrenched them round, so that they were swollen. Otherwise his evidence was true."

The hammer-blow cases Kürten described as follows:

CASE 63 The Murder of Ida Reuter - 30.9.29.

"One Sunday I left home at 6 o'clock in the evening. I had pocketed a hammer. At the railway station I saw a young girl, accosted her and proposed a walk. We had a beer at Schumacher's and walked through the Hofgarten and over the Rhine bridge to the poplar wood. During this walk, night had fallen. Reuter hesitated to go any further. Therefore we turned back. midway between the top of the wood and the playground, having made sure that nobody was around, I pulled the hammer from my hip pocket and hit girl on the right temple. For that purpose I had moved to the right side of Reuter. Without a sound she collapsed. People were approaching from the wood. I dragged Reuter from the dam down to the meadows. Here I waited until the people had passed. Meanwhile she had regained consciousness. She said: 'Let me alone.' Then I dragged her a good deal further. I gave her other hammer-blows on the head, and misused her. I pulled off her knickers to wash my hands with them in the Rhine. I left Reuter and went back to the Hansaallee, taking her little case with me. From it I took a ring for some future girl acquaintance.

"After I got to the Rhine bridge I returned to the scene of the crime, in order to drag Reuter down to the Rhine. I thought she was dead. I seized her legs and dragged her towards the river bank. But I noticed a man with a dog, so I cleared off again."

CASE 64 The Murder of Dorrier - 11.10.29.

"I left home on a week-day, about 9 o'clock in the evening, putting the hammer in my hip pocket. By the Residenz theatre I met a young, slim girl, who later told me her name was Dorrier. I asked her to come for a walk. At first she did not want to. In the end she went with me to Schumacher's. We went by tram to Grafenberg and walked along the banks of the Düssel. Dorrier was on my left. Suddenly I gave her a violent blow on the right temple. In order to do so I stepped back. Without a sound Dorrier collapsed. I grabbed her wrist and dragged her several metres from the path. I then used her sexually, after having pulled off her knickers from one leg. I then gave her more heavy blows with a hammer on the head. After the first blow she didn't say anything more, but only groaned. I took off her cloak and also the hat which was very bloody. I hid these things in the bushes."

Later on these articles were found. The sleeves had been torn out of the cloak. With regard to this circumstance, Kürten made the following comment: "You can see from that how excited I was."

CASE 65 Meurer - 25.10.29.

"I left home at 8 o'clock in the evening. The hammer I used on Reuter and Dorrier I had hidden outside. I fetched it and pocketed it. In the Bruchstrasse I noticed a woman going down the dark Hellweg. I followed her and overtook her near the first new building. I started a conversation about the Egyptian darkness of the Hellweg and about the general unsafety. We arrived at the railway arch. As I knew these surroundings pretty well I had by that time made up my mind to commit the crime there. I stepped to the right side of Frau Meurer, took a step back and gave her a heavy blow with the hammer on the right temple. I don't know whether I actually hit the temple. The woman collapsed without a sound. I gave her more hammer blows as she lay on the ground. I took her attache case and went back down the Hellweg. Later on I threw away the case."

CASE 66 Frau Wanders - 25.10.29

"After the Meurer attack I did not go home but to the Hofgarten. I was accosted by a woman smoking a cigarette, who asked me to go with her. I went with her to the Ananasburg, where the path was concealed by bushes. Here Wanders stopped in order to have sexual intercourse with me. I turned her round, meanwhile taking the hammer from my hip pocket and struck her on the right temple.

Without a sound Wanders collapsed and fell over the low railings. I then gave her several further blows on the head. In doing that the handle of the hammer broke and the head flew off into the bushes. I left Wanders lying where she was and went on. Wanders was repulsive to me, for I knew she was a professional prostitute and I never accost that kind of girl. After a quarter of an hour I returned to the place and searched in vain for the hammer."

CASE 67 The Murder of the Child Albermann - 27.11.29

"On the 27th of November, 1929, I set out with a pair of scissors about 5 o'clock at night. I met a little girl at the Ackerstrasse. I talked to her, and asked her quietly if she would come with me. We went into the open across some allotments as far as the wall of the Haniel's place. The child went with me quite willingly and did not cry. I seized the child's throat and strangled it. I stabbed it in the left temple. The child collapsed without a sound. With my left hand I held fast to her throat, knelt down and stabbed the child's breast with my scissors. With the right hand I felt the vagina, after having removed the knickers. Then I carried the body a few metres towards the Lenaustrasse and put it into the stinging nettles. I cleaned my hands on the wet grass. It was raining. There were no blood stains on me."

In February, 1930, the strangling crimes were resumed.

CASE 68 Hildegard Eid - 23.2.30

"I met a girl in the Schadowstrasse. We went to Schumacher's and then to Grafenberg. We spoke about sexual relations on a bench. She was very nervous. Suddenly at midnight I seized her by the throat and strangled her. She defended herself vigorously. I had sexual intercourse with her lying on the bench. I then accompanied her to her flat in the Cranachstrasse. She promised she would not say anything about the strangling. On the following Sunday, the 2nd of March, I went again to the Cranachstrasse to make sure that Hildegard had not reported the matter to anyone. She was already leaning out of the window waiting for me. Together we visited several beer gardens. Then we went to my flat, undressed and went to bed. Before we had had sexual intercourse my wife returned unexpectedly. She remained quite quiet, merely asking the girl to dress herself, after which she took her back to the Cranachstrasse."

CASE 69 Marianne dal S

"In the middle of March, 1930, I offered to treat a girl to beer at Schumacher's. She told me she was not averse from perversions. We decided to practise some of these and for that purpose went to the Grafenberger Wald. There I suddenly strangled her. She defended herself: I could have anything I liked from her! I answered: 'I don't want anything from you,' and strangled her again. But she managed to free herself and ran off."

S commented as follows:

"Kürten introduced himself to me as a well-to-do bachelor. He said I could sleep very nicely in his villa out of town. In the woods I wanted to turn back. He then suddenly seized me from behind by the neck and threw me to the ground and strangled me. I tried to appease him, but like lightning he seized me again. I fell to the ground. He stood over me with his legs spread. I kicked at him with my feet. I managed to release myself. I ran away and hid in the bushes. There I crouched from 10 o'clock till 6 in the morning. For hours I heard people passing the bushes, but I didn't see anybody."

CASE 70 Irma Becker

"In March, 1930, I set out with the scissors. At the railway station a girl accosted me. I took her with me to Schumacher's and went with her to the Grafenberger Wald. She called herself 'Irma' and I reckon she was between twenty-two and twenty-fours years old, and about 168 cm. high. Near the Hirschburg I seized her by the throat and throttled her violently. She defended herself vigorously and screamed. I pushed her down the bank to the Wolf ravine and cleared out."

Becker, who was born in 1907, deposed:

"I arrived in Düsseldorf from Cologne and was accosted by a gentleman. We wanted to go to his flat. While in the woods I still believe that we were on the way to his flat. Kürten then said that he had only enticed me there and tried to pull me down on to a bench, pulled my dress up, tore my knickers down and seized my sexual parts. I defended myself and rearranged my clothes. He then wanted to lead me further on by the arm. After a few steps he pushed me forcibly down the slope. I called for help and rolled over and over several times until I reached the bottom. I had broken my umbrella beating Kürten when he tried to rape me."

CASE 71 Syvilla Wil

"On the 30th of March, 1930, I picked up a girl in the Konigsallee. We chatted together on a bench in the Hofgarten; then we agreed to take a walk together on Sunday in the woods.

"During this walk we had sexual intercourse on a bench and I strangled her. As there were passers-by I cleared off."

Wil, who was born in 1901, described Kürten as having behaved fairly decently. The sexual intercourse on the bench was scarcely completed because she was too frightened and pressed him back. She had not been throttled and Kürten had done no harm to her. He had accompanied her to Rath.

CASE 72 The Girl from Herne

"At the station I accosted a graceful girl about twenty years old and 165 cm. in height. We went to a cafe and from there to Obercassel. In a deserted place I suddenly strangled her. She cried out loudly for help. I released her and made my way back to the station. When I alighted I saw that the girl was alighting, too. The following Sunday I saw her again in the Graf Adolf Strasse. I turned up Steinstrasse. Suddenly somebody seized my by the arm. 'You come along with me to a policeman!' I recognised the girl instantly and said: 'What about you coming with me to the policeman, too, to tell him about my purse which you stole with thirty marks in it?' With that I threw her off."

This girl could not be traced.

CASE 73 Hau - 13.4.30

"One Friday I became acquainted with a girl of thirty years of age in the Konigsallee. I went with her into a cafe and then to the Hofgarten. We sat there until 11 o'clock. Suddenly I gripped her under her clothes. She smacked me in the face. I smacked her back."

Hau returned home on a Saturday with a scratched nose and reported that she had been beaten and throttled by a man in the Hofgarten.

In her examination on the 14th of June, 1930, she stated: 'I became acquainted with a nice man, a builder's assistant, named Franz Becker. In the Hofgarten he made love to me. He drew me towards him and tried to feel under my skirt. With my clenched fist I punched his eye. His punched back with his fist, so that my mouth bled. He said: 'Is that what I get for treating you in the case?' I gave him three marks and he gave me back two marks fifteen pfennig. He kissed the blood from my mouth. He wanted to detain me longer, but I ran away. He shouted after me: 'Consider yourself lucky that we are not alone in the Hofgarten!'"

There followed three attempted attacks in which Kürten was disturbed. These were followed by the three final attacks.

CASE 77 Charlotte Ulrich - 30.4.30

"At 9 o'clock I picked up a girl in the street and went with her to Schumacher's and afterwards to the Grafenberger Wald. I lulled her suspicions by saying that there were always couples there. Where there is a broad view I gave her a blow with the hammer on the right temple. She collapsed, screaming loudly. I left her lying there. I saw this girl several times after that; the last time on the Wednesday before my arrest. The hammer I used was similar to the one I had used before. I struck with it several times and I saw the blood flow."

I had occasion to examine Charlotte Ulrich in prison. She told me that on the 1st of May, towards midnight, Kürten accosted her on Graf Adolf Strasse and invited her to have a beer with him. In this way she missed the last train to Duisberg and was unable to return home that night. As it was raining heavily, she accepted his invitation; but she did not wish to go with him to his flat. Kürten then proposed a nice night cafe. It was because she was a stranger in the place that she became frightened in the Grafenberger Wald, but Kürten reassured her: 'Do you think, maybe, that I am the Düsseldorf murderer?' he asked at a point where the lights of the adjacent cafe were still visible. So they went on until Kürten tried to throw her on to a bench, when she defended herself. While the struggle was proceeding, she saw how he unbuttoned his coat and trust his hand into his pocket. A little later she received a blow on the side of the head, and she felt the blood pouring down her face as from a tap. She then felt a second blow over the right temple and then she lost consciousness.

When she came to herself again her hands were covered with blood and her bag gone. She ripped up her petticoat and staunched the blood and made her way towards the light and eventually reached the railway station. There she asked a man for the first-aid station, but he advised her to go to the police. This she did not want to do, for she was wanted by the police. In the end this man took her to friends of his and these people cared for her for a fortnight. Later, in fact, she spent three months in prison for persistent stealing.

Ulrich also stated that her hands had been swollen and black, and that the nail from the ring finger was missing. She had raised her hand to her head to protect it from the hammer blows. On both sides of her head Ulrich had fresh, pink scars, angular in shape. Beneath them could be felt the fracture in the cranium. It is amazing that this woman did not ask for medical aid with such grievous wounds, and it is equally remarkable that she was up and about again at the end of a fortnight. This case provides a striking instance of the power of the will to accelerate recovery.

CASE 79 Gertrud Bell - 16.5.30 The Last Assault

"In the Schadowstrasse I became acquainted with a girl and we made an appointment for the following evening in the Rhine Park. We attempted to have sexual intercourse there on a bench, but there were too many people about. We therefore made an appointment for the following Sunday at Nordfriedhof. There a sudden thunderstorm came on, so Gertrud took me to her room. We had relations on her bed, but her mistress came knocking at the door, asking all kinds of questions. We then agreed on a meeting in her room for the 24th of May ... Meanwhile I was arrested."

Gertrud Bell: "Kürten called himself Franz Weidlich from the tramway depot. After we had sexual intercourse Weidlich was very nervous. I asked him to spend the night with me, but unsuccessfully. On the following Thursday I met him at the Worringerplatz. There he said that I was far too good for him, that, after all, I didn't know him at all, and that he was a bad man."

Such is the notorious "great" confession which Kürten made after his arrest. Before the examining magistrate he varied it only in a few particulars. With me, too, he adhered to all his salient statements. As I have already remarked, the fullness of Kürten's confession awoke at first doubts as to his veracity.

After he was lodged in prison and I had begun my observations of him, I referred in talk with him to these doubts. I propose to set forth these conversations here.

Kürten: "It is very easy to describe crimes one has not committed. Take, for example, the case of Gross, with which I had nothing to do at all. There I could have said, for instance, that on such and such a date I met a girl at the station I had to pass on my way home. She accosted me and took me with her to her room on Kurfurstenstrasse- and so on."

Kürten next described the girl's room, the strangling and the actual circumstances.

Kürten: 'I left the electric light burning. One could scarcely credit it that such a confession could be founded on the very full newspaper reports and yet be simply an invention. To that extent, I quite understand your doubts, Professor."

I then asked Kürten why he had confessed fully in all the cases. He replied: "Professor, why don't you understand that I am fond of my wife - that I am still fond of her? I have done her many wrongs; have been unfaithful over and over again. Yet, though my wife knew this quite well, she never let me know. My wife has never done any wrong. Even when she heard of the many sentences of imprisonment I have served, she said; 'I won't let you down, otherwise you will be lost altogether.' Professor, you know the big reward that was offered for my capture? At the police station we reckoned altogether twenty thousand marks, the arson rewards, together with the Government reward. It was then that I said to myself: If you confess only the case of the girl Schulte, which can be easily proved against you, you'll get at least fifteen years' imprisonment because of the bad prison record. I am forty-seven. After my release I would have been sixty-two. What could I make of my life at sixty-two? Life wouldn't mean anything at all, then. I had already finished with my life when I first knew the police were on my track. I wanted to fix up for my wife a carefree old age, for she is entitled to at least a part of the reward. That is why I entered a plea of guilty to all the crimes. But I could see that I might not be believed because of Stausberg."

Before the examining magistrate Kürten adopted another attitude with regard to his crimes. Whereas at the opening he adhered to his confession as set forth above, he made an unexpected change of front when confronted by his wife. On the 24th of June, 1930, he surprised the examining magistrate with the dramatic declaration: "I am not the Düsseldorf murderer." He had, he said, confessed to these crimes on the first occasion only to secure the reward for his wife. He then asserted that he had obtained all the details which he had given on his examination from the newspapers to which he had added his own free inventions. As Kürten was persistent, the examining magistrate had no choice, and had to make the best of a bad job and to put on the record all these cases which Kürten alleged he had concocted from newspaper reports. Only one case, that of Hahn, did not fit into this fabric of lies, for no word of it had been published in the press. At last, thanks to the skill of the examining magistrate who succeeded in breaking him down, Kürten, after two months, reverted to his full confession.

Kürten: "Mr Examining Magistrate, you can take it as so, but believe me, that if I tell you the whole, you will hear a lot of horrible things from me."

Kürten then amplified his confession in many ways, yet without revealing any new material of importance. His motive he kept as before; he wanted to revenge himself on society for the wrongs he had suffered in prison. In answer to the judge's question as to whether he had no conscience, Kürten replied: "I have none. Never have I felt any misgiving in my soul; never did I think to myself that what I did was bad, even though human society condemns it. As I have figured it out, when I am executed, my blood and the blood of my victims will be on the heads of my torturers, that is if there is such as thing as a Higher Justice. I have thought of the law of cause and effect, and on the law of the sufficient motive. There must be a Higher Being who gave in the first place the first vital spark to life. That Higher Being would also deem my actions good since I revenged injustice. The punishments I have suffered have destroyed all my feelings as a human being. That was why I had no pity for my victims."

But on another occasion, when alone with the examining magistrate, Kürten said: "I said before that I had no conscience. But I have got one. I felt it often. Even in these last years. It was when I committed adultery. Then I often thought how wrong it was of me with so hard-working a wife."

I had Kürten under observation for the whole period of his imprisonment from June, 1930 until June, 1931. The most important of the discussions we had, I will set down in the following chapter. In this chapter the reader will hear Kürten speaking his own words, in much the same way as he did in the confession set out in part above. I have changed his actual words very little, though here and there the subject matter has been assigned to the appropriate chapter.

Chapter Three
Fate and Personality of Kürten

On its surface the life of Kürten differs but little from that of a criminal psychopath. Born on the 26th of May, 1883, in Koln-Mulheim, he grew up in a bad environment. He was a good pupil in the primary school, learned the trade of his father, a moulder, and offended against the law for the first time at the age of sixteen. Four further sentences followed in quick succession. They were mostly for theft until 1904. During a short period of freedom Kürten confessed to four arsons in 1904.

Then followed the long sentences of penal servitude - 1905 to 1913. This last sentence is only separated by a brief span of freedom in 1913 from the last sentence of seven years. Yet even this short interval is crowded by seven major crimes. In 1921, on being released from the penitentiary in Brieg, he went to his sister in Altenburg and settled down. There he found permanent work in a factory and married. There are four years of peace and decency. In 1925 his evil spirit lured him back to Düsseldorf and here he began his crimes with arsons and rapes which, in 1929, culminated in the monstrous offenses.

I will now go into details:

(a) Descent

The family history of Kürten was investigated by the examining magistrate. His father, now seventy-one, was a sand moulder and an efficient workman. Be he was a drunkard and an uncontrolled, egotistic type. He always earned enough to keep his numerous children, though much of his money went on alcohol. The examining magistrate described him as a man who scarcely knew any moral restraints, yet demanded for himself every sort of respect, nor did he suffer contradiction or any challenge to his will. Even today, he impressed the examining magistrate by his self-possession. His observations sometimes revealed humour and irony, coupled with an intense irascibility.

His manner of speech at his examination was abrupt and self-possessed. To sum up, he was formerly a heavy drinker, irascible and violent, and on that account seven times in prison. Sexually uncontrolled, he had been imprisoned for incest with the eldest daughter, a sentence of eighteen months' penal servitude in 1897. Kürten's father had nine brothers and sisters, two of whom are supposed to have been drunkards. The grandfather was a railway worker. He was a hard-working man of peasant stock, but he drank and was a poacher. He was ultimately dismissed for theft and later sent to penal servitude.

The grandmother, on the paternal side, Elizabeth Kürten, died at seventy years of age; and she, too, was reputed to have been an alcoholic subject. Eight of the children of this couple reached ripe ages. Some of them had bad reputations for violence and drunkenness. The mother of Peter Kürten came of a respectable family. Her father was a hack proprietor. There were five brothers and sisters, all described as sane, physically and mentally, and who all lived to a ripe age. Mrs Kürten secured a separation from her husband following his attempted incest and imprisonment. In 1911 she married a joiner. She died in 1927.

The father of Kürten married for the second time in 1919 a working girl from whom he separated in the following year. Of the ten brothers and sisters of Kürten, two died young, one fell in the War. One of the sisters, Elizabeth, married young and became a good housewife. The other married sisters were described by Kürten as being very over-sexed. Two of the brothers served long prison sentences.

(b) Kürten's Youth and Prison Sentences

Kürten: "In 1895 my parents moved to Düsseldorf Grafenberg and there I attended school. I passed easily and was a good scholar. Then I became an apprentice to a moulder. Father was a good workman, but also a hard drinker, hopelessly addicted to alcohol. It was customary in the foundry for people to drink hard, though it isn't so nowadays. The whole family suffered through his drinking, for when he was in drink, my father was terrible. Windows were smashed, things were all broken up. I, being the eldest, had to suffer most. Often have I hidden away from his rage, either in the woods or in the school buildings. For weeks I would not return home. At those times I was a real vagabond. I used to steal money from women and children out shopping. Once I was caught at it and should certainly have been sent to the reformatory but for the interference of my parents. As you may well imagine, we suffered terrible poverty, all because the wages went on drink. We all lived in one room. You will appreciate what effect that had on me sexually. Then poverty developed into bitter destitution when, in 1897, my father was sentenced to eighteen months' imprisonment for the crime of incest with his eldest daughter. When he came out of prison my father got his job back. I worked in the same foundry as an apprentice. There was never a Sunday for us, for on Sunday my father did all the odd jobs and I had to help him with them. He had installed a little foundry for making small aluminium articles in the cellar. Mother was good, decent, and respectable.

"When I look back and think of the married life of my parents today I really think that had they not been married one would have had to think of it as rape.

"Father was not orthodox and wanted nothing to do with the Catholic religion. In short, my youth was a martyrdom. I was not even sixteen when I stole money from the factory and ran away.

"I never went back home after that. I don't want to omit describing my prison experiences because I am convinced that in the light of them my whole subsequent life can be explained. Once I had to do two days in prison. When I came out I was received by a police official who fettered me and led me through the whole town to the Berger Gateway. You can imagine what I felt like! I then came to know what it means to be without a roof to one's head.

"The crimes I began to commit then can be explained by sheer want. I stole to eat; got good food under false pretences. In 1909 I got a week in prison, in 1910 six weeks, six months, three days, and so on, to the extent of three-quarters of the year. Then came a long sentence - until 1914. It was then that I became acquainted with disciplinary punishment in prison, and of the severest kinds. It was terrible what I suffered under it. I would describe it all as barbarous and I suppose most men would do so today. Apart from the fact that hunger in adolescence is real torture, I suppose there was some ground for these sentences (for theft). I do not condemn those sentences in themselves, but I do condemn the way they are carried out on young people. The prison officials then were quite different from those of today. Fettering was a common form of punishment. Once I was fettered for three weeks. At that time we had a lieutenant staying at the prison to be educated as a prison inspector, and he had a lot of visitors to whom he used to show the prison. I was taken out of the dark cell and exhibited. The lieutenant made a little speech about me, saying what difficult prisoner I was. Once a clergyman came. He fell on his knees and kissed my fetters.

"All that had a very bad effect on me, so that I can tell of these things in full justification. Nothing is worse than the spiritual suffering of one who is tortured through the infliction of pain. For some of the things I did in prison I have no other explanation than that I was not quite myself - a sort of psychosis. Sometimes what I did was senseless. I had cell madness. That resulted in my not being able to think logically.

"I served all my sentences until 1903 in Düsseldorf. The treatment of the prisoners was harder then than it is now. I don't want to claim that all the punishments I got were all inflicted unjustly. My anger and resentment were really directed against the prison officials who got me into trouble by their exaggerated reports on me.

"I dare say that frequently I did not do my work properly. From 1905 to 1912, I spent much of my time spinning in my cell in Münster prison. My rages in my cell, which occurred periodically, were the result of harsh treatment. In Münster I had a sort of prison psychosis. One day I rolled myself up in silk under a table.

"In April 1921, I was released from Brieg. Seven months of that sentence had been remitted because I carried a wounded official from the firing line on the occasion of a mutiny. On the other hand, I myself took part in another mutiny."

Very enlightening is the report of the head warder of the Brieg penitentiary. "Kürten," he said, "appreciated every situation at once, and when the favourable moment arrived, used it adroitly for his own advantage. He had no consideration for his fellow prisoners. He tried to hoodwink the prison officials by extreme sycophancy. For example, when the man who usually said prayers before the convicts fell ill, Kürten volunteered at once. It was astonishing with how much piety he recited the evening prayers. Once he threw a box of felt slippers at an overseer. 'You seem to think I am your messenger boy' he said. He also tried to win the favour of the officials by betraying to them plans for attacks on them or of mutiny."

Here are the observations upon Kürten by the prison doctor "On the 16th of January, 1907, Kürten lacerated the skin over the main artery with a knife and spoke a great deal of incoherent nonsense. This incident he pretends to have forgotten. In November, 1911, there is a note in his dossier describing a state of excitement observed by the physician in which Kürten spoke of suicide. I may add that Kürten's conduct in the prison was faultless in 1928."

Regarding this period a fellow prisoner says of Kürten: "Kürten was amiable and sly, he liked to hob-nob with the officials. He was also capable of being brutal. He talked a lot about his sexual adventures; he told how once he had bitten a woman's genitals until the blood came. He said, 'That's the greatest enjoyment one can get.' He then demonstrated how he would behave in doing it. He used to ask all the criminal sexual perverts questions and gave them advice, and told them how to conduct themselves on trial."

Of this statement, Kürten asserts that it is pure invention. On the contrary, he said, he had always restrained himself and never given himself away to a fellow prisoner.

Nevertheless, we find this same prisoner coming to the police with his suspicions of Kürten after the murder of Hahn in November, 1929.

Kürten was never so indiscreet in his talk again, though to another subsequent witness he dropped hints. This witness, Klauth, said: "Kürten thought a lot of his wife, but he also said, 'I like veal best, something I can really tease in the dark in quiet places.' I asked: 'Are you a pervert?' He answered 'Even old goats like to eat a green leaf now and then. A change is nice.'"

(c) Marriage

Kürten's wife was born in 1880 in Schlesien. She was the daughter of a tailor who was also a house-owner. As a domestic servant she went to Berlin in 1896, got into bad company and was on that account brought home in 1897. There she earned her living as a factory worker.

In 1903 she began to have intimate relations with a gardener, a relationship which lasted for eight years. Although this man, to whom she became engaged, had promised to marry her, he jilted her in 1911. For this she shot him and was sentenced to five years' penal servitude.

Released in 1915, she remained in Leipzig until 1920, working as a dressmaker, and then took over a sweet shop in Altenburtg. There she became acquainted with a sister of Kürten, and on the 12th of May, 1921, with Kürten himself. He was unsympathetic to her because he used to go about with other women. But as he threatened that he would push something between her ribs if she would not have sexual relations with him, she gave herself to him. As Kürten had a permanent job in 1923, they married. Frau Kürten also knew that her husband had involved himself with a certain girl named Oehler and that this girl threatened to bring a charge of rape against him. It was Frau Kürten who persuaded her not to take this course.

Frau Kürten describes her husband as otherwise good. He had sent her money regularly from Düsseldorf. When she rejoined him after separation he confessed at once that he had been twice unfaithful, with girls Tiede and Mech. Yet despite her annoyance, he had gone off the following night with Tiede. Frau Kürten explained to Tiede that Kürten was a married man; but the Mech affair lasted until 1927, when Kürten was arrested.

As to their conjugal life, Frau Kürten said:

"Kürten was very excitable and then he bullied and shouted. But when I remained quiet, he, too, soon calmed down. For my part, I have taken all things as a punishment for my own old life. The Altenburg period was by far the best. There he was home-loving and took part in club life. It was in Altenburg that Kürten left the Catholic Church, but only because of the tax. Not until we came to Dusseldorf were we married in church. That was on the advice of the prison priest. But Kürten never wanted to hear about going to church or about God, either. In 1928 he wrote from prison that he had changed altogether, but when he was released he forgot all about that.

"Once, when I mentioned the murders and said that I was frightened, he wanted to see me home in the evening from the place where I worked. I never saw any trace of his crimes. He frequently had sexual intercourse with me, even against my will. In the last two years he was extremely keen on it. During this period he used to ask me to lie down naked."

In short, the marriage of Kürten had to withstand a good many strains. When the wife found her husband in bed with a strange girl, and when she saw him walking in the street with another girl, she forgave, so that one cannot help admiring the forbearance of this woman.

But she knew well that with Kürten reproaches would be wasted. He would threaten suicide or lament that he had so little in life and yet that little was begrudged him by his wife.

On the other hand, Kürten always spoke in a very nice way of his wife. He said the examining magistrate,: "My relations with my wife were always good. I did not love her in the sensual way, but because of my admiration for her fine character."

This seems odd, for, on the whole, Kürten spoke badly about women. He went even so far as to hint that his own sister desired to have sexual relations with him; a conclusion he drew from her tenderness, her kisses and embraces.

Chapter Four
Kürten the Sadist

Inevitably the question of the prisoner's sanity, and, hence, his legal responsibility, became a major issue of the trial, since Kürten did not deny his guilt, and the acquittal on the tenth capital charge was a formal verdict returned for lack of corroboration of admissions made by the accused.

Were not the monstrous character of Kürten's crimes and their ghastly total evidence of insanity? At the time there were some who felt this very strongly: but they were a very small minority. The majority cried aloud for revenge upon the fiend who had massacred little children, young girls, men, and women for no other end than the gratification of an abnormal sexual appetite. For this quiet, nice-looking man who faced his judge with carefully brushed hair, and smoothly shaven cheeks, was no other than the so-called "Düsseldorf Monster" whose crimes had horrified the world.

But that was not the problem the four eminent medico-legal responsibility as defined by Section 51 of the German Pental Code where it is thus defined: "A state of consciousness or a diseased disturbance of mental activity which impedes the operation of free will, absolves a criminal from responsibility for his actions".

All four medico-legal experts who assisted the Court had to deal with. They were concerned only with the question of legal and psychiatrical-legal experts came to identical conclusions, namely, that Kürten was suffering from no organic mental disease or from any functional mental disease; and that he was, therfore, responsible in law for his crimes.

The work which went before these findings was done with remarkable thoroughness which not only disposed convincingly of the theory of epilepsy, but considered also the nature of the crimes themselves and their motivation for evidence of loss of consciousness, or a disease destructive of mental activity.

Kürten once under arrest, spoke with remarkable frankness, particularly with Professor Berg, who was eminently successful in winning his confidence. Those conversations, over a long period, make it quite clear that Kürten well knew the nature of his acts. His accounts of these crimes, wherever checked independently (and that was wherever it was possible to check them) were found to be exact and this was quite a remarkable feature of the evidence of such victims as escaped death at his hands and lived to testify against him. They bore out Kürten's own account in every detail.

Let us take first Kürten's memory. It functioned with extraordinary clarity where his crimes were his subject matter. This is significant because the vividness with which Kürten preserved in his memory the minutest details of each crime, and his emotional state during its perpertration, gives us the measure of his pleasure in the deed and in retrospective contemplation of it.

Where Kürten dealt with past matters that had little or no emotional value for him, his memory was not particularly remarkable, indeed, it was sometimes defective.

His most intense experience, then, were his crimes and the lucidity of his memory of them is the first indication of his sanity in the legal sense.

We come next to the motive, and here again it is the criminal himself who supplies the material for scientific interrogators. In so far as he had any true insight into his own psychological state Kurten was compeletely self-revelatory. He was truthful and his contradictions, rightly viewed, are the index of Kürten's attempt at objective truth. But since there are few acts that arise from simple psychological processes and many that come from complex ones, the subconscious plays always its deceiving part, for it is there that a true motive may hide an unflattering moral ugliness.

To take the simple case of the judge who never errs on mercy'sside: the degree of his severity provides the measure of his masked sadism, and in so far as he becomes a factor in the manufacture of antisocial individuals, he may be said to represent the failure of an attempted sublimation of an abnormal psychological component, namely, sadism.

Kürten admitted to a feeling of tension before the crime and of relief after its commission. It was the recurrence of this condition that convinced the experts of the definitely sexual character of the motive: and Kürten, who emerged under examination as a remarkably truthful man, admitted this.

Of this aspect of Kürten's psychopathological pattern, Professor Sioli, one of the expert witnesses at the trial, remarks that Kürten planned and carried out his crimes in order to achieve sexual satisfaction which he could obtain to the extent demanded by him only by acts of violence.

The idea of expiation which Kürten evolved as a concept sprang from his desire ro be rid of every inhibition which might stand between him and the commission of his next crime. "His megalomania," Professor Sioli observed, "and imaginative fantasies brought about a state of emotional fixation with regard to the whole process." Kürten's sexual urge was a perverted urge.

The question which had to be answered at the trial was whether this perverted urge was of such a psychopathological nature as to render Kürten incapable of exercising free will. The circumstance that Kürten always behaved himself and kept his lust on leash where he was known and where there was danger of discovery, seems to answer this question, when, with it, we have make-weight evidence of the cunning and the awareness and self-possession exhibited by him when disturbed in the commission of a crime.

Of his arsons Kürten said: "I committed my acts of arson for the same reasons - my sadistic propensity. I got pleasure from the glow of the fire, the cries for help. It gave me so much pleasure that I got sexual satisfaction in those cases."

And again of the so-called "murder letters" sent by him to the police, he observed: "I expected that the influence of these letters and the excitement they would cause would have a sexual effect upon me, and it was for that I wrote the letters and the reactions came as expected."

Kürten, under examination, had submitted as motive the expia-

tion idea, and it had to be tested by clinical methods whether this was a delusion or merely an idea abnormally inflated. He, himself, describes the idea as "designed to fit in with the idea of compensatory justice." It was in his mind when he wrote the first "murder letter", after the murder of the little Klein girl in Koln-Mulheim in 1913. He declared it as his belief that the innocent blood of his victim would be visited on his tormentors.

Such ideas came to Kürten, however, only after the commission of his crimes and may reasonably be considered as a rationalisation that masks the true sadistic nature of the motive and is, no doubt, in this way to be psychologically explained.

There remains the problem of the genesis of Kürten's sadistic perversions, perversions difficult to parallel quantitively in the literature of psychopathology. One may advance the heredity factor, a bad environment, the encounters and mischances of childhood and youth, the process of spiritual deterioration inevitable with long prison sentences, the sadistic fixation of the libido, the sensitiveness to adverse criticism and the megalomania, and yet be without a convincing explanation, a satisfying answer to the psychological riddle he presents.

The explanation comes only when into the account is taken the exaggerated and arrogant claim made by Kürten for the satisfaction of his sexual urges at all costs. It is, fundamentally, the repudiation of the rights of others as against the rights of Peter Kürten. It is the operation of a monstrous and unique egotism.

The forensic investigations into Kürten's psychological state extended over a long period, and it is probably true to say that no great criminal has ever been the subject of so thorough psychological analysis. Nor can there be much doubt that had Kürten stood his trial in an English court, the rule in Macnaughton's Case would have meant his conviction.

Macnaughton's Case (1843) lays it down that for a man to be insane in the eyes of the law:

"It must be clearly proved that, at the time of the committing of the act, the party accused was labouring under such defect of reason,

from disease of the mind, as not to know the nature and quality of the act he was doing, or if he did know it, that he did not know he was doing wrong."

Nevertheless, since the terms of reference imposed by the law on the scientific experts were legal rather than scientific, the question settled by verdict does not finally dispose of the question which Kürten poses in his sinister and enigmatic personality for the psychopathologist and medico-legal expert.

Kürten was found to be suffering from no mental disease and the autopsy made after his execution revealed him as phsysically normal, save for a persistent thymus gland. There was no other abnormality.

Kürten received a trial that may stand as a pattern of judicial method and temper: it was painstaking, fair, conducted despite the inevitable and healthy high feeling running against the prisoner, without prejudice or emotion. It was, further, noteworthy for the large and important part played by the medico-legal experts, not only as witnesses during the trial, but before and after in the investigation of the prisoner's psychology.

A word about Kürten the man. In personal appearance Peter Kürten was a well-built man of medium height, neither good-looking nor unprepossessing. He was clean-shaven and fresh-complexioned, and he took inordinate trouble to make the most of his looks, even to the extent of using make-up and hair pomades. In all his personal habits he was meticulous, never showing himself save in a well-brushed suit with carefully creased trousers, his hair sleeked, his shoes brightly polished. To preserve the shine on his shoes he carried always a cloth in his pocket. This meticulousness or narcissistic tendency truly reflected the complacency and self-satisfaction of the inner man. Kürten dearly loved himself and it was the kernel of his tragedy, perhaps, that he was unable truly to love any other human being. He seems to have suffered from what might be termed a "spiritual deficiency" disease.

Women were attracted to him at once and so easy were his conquests that he came to have a deep contempt for all women. As a seducer, he was past-master in the art of the honeyed word and able always to pose in some role warranted to impress each particular victim. He learned how brutally direct a man may be with a woman. He was, in short, a man with a remarkable technique of seduction.

In the populous Mettmannerstrasse, where he occupied with his wife a small top-floor flat, he was regarded as "a nice man". When his neighbours learned that Peter Kürten was the Düsseldorf murderer, they were incredulous, believing that the police had blundered.

(a) The motives of Kürten's crimes as revealed by medico-legal examination.

If one considers that, apart from the thefts which were dealt with by the courts, most of Kürten's crimes remained undiscovered, then one can understand that Kürten appeared to his acquaintances as a quite harmless being.

Like every other worker in the factory, he did his work quietly, was seldom unemployed, was moderate and economical, did nothing to annoy his fellow workers. Yet, save for his wife, he had no human being who was dear to him, no friend, no comrade. His fellow workers considered him vain. One witness described how Kürten always changed his clothes thoughtfully and carefully, standing before the mirror for a long time; how he used hair pomade and eau de cologne, and how sleek he then made himself look.

In fact, even in prison, Kürten always paid great attention to his appearance; he was slim and, comparatively, a good-looking man, with thick yellow hair always parted carefully, clever-looking blue eyes, and, on the right cheek, a small scar the result of a quarrel in 1904, though this was not very noticeable. In 1922 Kürten sustained a head wound through a blow from a falling piece of iron. It left a scar of a finger-length on the skin of the scalp, and years afterwards Kürten complained of headache. Otherwise, there were no physical abnormalities.

As far as his psyche is considered, I always found Kürten of a pattern. That was already the case in 1928. As a prisoner awaiting trial he was generally amenable and quite frank with me - even confidential. Even when he was relating to me his experiences in the other prisons he remained calm, becoming only ironic. He was also always ready for the many enquiries and interrogations, and even after sittings which lasted hours, he showed no sign of fatigue or irritability.

To the police Kürten denied a sexual motive for his crimes. He did not wish to be known as a lust-murderer. So, too, before the examining magistrate, he made the admission that there was a sexual motive only towards the end of the enquiry, and then, in a very roundabout way.

During my talks with him in prison, I soon succeeded in winning his confidence. I explained to him that so far as his trial was concerned what he revealed to the court was his own affair, but that what he revealed to me as the prison physician was protected as a professional secret.

After turning matters over in his mind for some time, and not before he had asked of the examining magistrate the effect of Paragraph 300 of the Penal Code Manual, Kürten opened up to me in quite a different way about his motives. Of course, it was his intention that I should make use of these confidences, but only in such a way as to assist rather than damage his defence. But he gave me a completely free hand to make use of his statements for the purpose of science.

The ice having been broken, Kürten communicated to the psychologists his secrets - those secrets so carefully guarded at the time. They are of the utmost significance for an understanding of his psychological make-up.

In setting down Kürten's statements I merely directed his attention to its subject matter by interjected questions. I began with a question as to the motive for his crimes. In the beginning he denied to me, also, the sexual significance of these and invited me to believe his old motives, namely, vengeance on human society. But I explained to him that he was giving himself away by starting each confession with the same formula "I went out to search for a victim," and so, too, with the termination-expiation for the wrongs done him.

To that objection Kürten replied: "So far as the motives of my crimes are concerned, as I have so far described them, I took everything I said about my excitability and inner tension from books, namely, Lombroso. The statement of motive I made was the result of the trend of the Criminal Director's questions - he was so preoccupied with the psychological aspects of the case. Even so, I am bound to say that I did have a constant desire - you will call it the urge to kill - and the more the better. Yes, if I had had the means I would have killed masses. I would have caused catastrophes. Every evening, when my wife was working late, I scoured the town for a victim. But it was not so easy to find one."

In this way the "nice" man of the Mettmannerstrasse became the "monster" who stalked the streets of Düsseldorf stabbing and slaying, the while dreaming in his dark soul (which, however, perserves with crystal-clarity the minutest detail of each crime) of how he will one day deliver Düsseldorf from "the monster", be acclaimed the city's saviour, and appointed Chief Police Commissioner. And, alongside this fantasy of fame, he weaves his megalomaniac's fantasy of gigantic catastrophes, the annihilation of whole communities by fire and dynamite.

Midnight passed, Kürten returns, red-handed - in hard fact - gorged with the blood of his victim. By the time his wife comes back, he has wiped or washed away every trace of blood. Then, as the tired woman prepares for bed, Kürten chats pleasantly to her of the daily round, their neighbours, and, undressing, sleeps soundly at the side of one women for whom he seems to have entertained some sort of decent sentiment. And no evil dreams disturb the sleep of this man, who, like the vampire of legend, first sates himself on the blood of his victim, and then returns to silence and oblivion.

"The sexual urge was strongly developed in me, particularly in the last years and it was stimulated even more by the crimes themselves. For that reason I was always driven to find a new victim. Sometimes even when I seized my victim's throat, I had an orgasm; sometimes not, but then the orgasm came as I stabbed the victim. It was not my intention to get satisfaction by normal sexual intercourse, buy by killing. When the victim struggled she merely stimulated my lust. For example, I would like to quote the case of Ohliger for which Stausberg was wrongly accused. I didn't have sexual intercourse with the child. It wasn't necessary because I had already ejaculated. The reaction had already set in while I was throttling Ohliger, but not ejaculation. It was only while I was stabbing her that the excitement ended in ejaculation. I had my member out and ejaculated without erection, which is much nicer; that happened, too, with Hahn, and gave me a shudder down the whole back. I was to explain to you also, Professor, about your conclusions as to the sexual parts of the child Ohliger. When I was throttling the child, I inserted my middle finger into the vagina. I had pulled down the little knickers a bit and later on rearranged them. But I did not feel anything - only when I took the scissors and stabbed I had an ejaculation. In handling the child I might have introduced some seminal fluid with my finger - which you found later on - that was the first case. At midnight I went back to the body. I wanted to touch it. I won't deny that I did it to get fresh sexual excitement, but there was no more ejaculation. Another thing, I only fingered her over her clothing. I could not stay long because my wife was bound to come home."

I now directed Kürten's attention to the burning. "That, of course, I did not do to destroy the body by fire. I got sexual excitement in doing it but no ejaculation. The following morning at 9 o'clock I returned once more, when she had been found. I then saw the officials and the crowd of people and I nearly had an ejaculation, but not quite. That I wasn't out for normal sexual enjoyment you can tell from the Scheer case. That was a man.

"I was scouring the Hellweg for a victim. I saw a man coming along. I thought 'That's a suitable subject.' Not a soul to be seen anywhere! The man was staggering. He bumped into me. He was drunk. I stabbed him with the scissors. At the first stab in the temple he fell down. That at once I got sexual excitement, and the more I stabbed the more intense it became. I gave him a severe stab in the neck and I heard distinctly the faint gushing of his blood. That was the climax. Then came the ejaculation. I stopped stabbing and just rolled the body over the bank.

"The following morning, when I went back, the Murder Commission was there. Then I enjoyed another ejaculation despite the intense cold. As you know, it was horribly cold at that time. Yet I was not conscious of it, though I had on only a very thin coat. When I am in that condition I am not even conscious of fatigue. During my long night prowlings, when I covered long distances, I was so intent upon my purpose that I never noticed any fatigue at all. And that despite the fact that I had been at work throughout the day.

"You have asked me when I first detected in myself a tendency to cruelty. Well, that goes back decades. When I was a child I did not torture animals, at least, not more than other boys do. Of course, we went birds-nesting and caught frogs. But I was prematurely developed sexually and at the age of fifteen or sixteen I was already like that, then I used to stab sheep, for instance, that were grazing on the Grafenberger meadows. When I did that I realised that it gave me an agreeable feeling, but without any ejaculation. That was the start of it all, and the first time that I became conscious of the connection between cruelty and the sexual urge. I had also at that time cut off the head of a dog. Then I realised that there was something nice in it. You can imagine that, Professor, and you must try it for yourself sometime - how the blood rushes absolutely silently when you cut off the head of a goose.The origin of this feeling goes back a long way. When we lived in Koln-Mulheim a dog-catcher lived in the same house. At that time there was one in every town. The dogs were captured, slaughtered and eaten. The lard was sold as a specific, being used to fix cobwebs over wounds. This dog-catcher used to torture the dogs he caught. For instance, he used to prick them with a needle or break off their tails, saying that he wanted to see whether the animals were healthy. I watched this frequently and enjoyed it. I was then nine years old. This dog-catcher also showed me how you make the dogs attached to you, taught me how to play with the dog's genitals until it ejaculated. An animal like that can't be beaten away. Later, when I was thirteen, I often thought about that dog-catcher while I was taking young buzzards and owls from their nests with other boys, or when I caught squirrels or martens. Those we sold to the dealer Otten on the market - I suppose you know it. And we made a nice bit of pocket money in that way. I still have a scar on my finger where a squirrel once fastened his teeth on me. I had to compress his neck to make him let go. In handling it like that I had an ejaculation, although only a boy of fourteen. Later, by reading and through talk, I learned about this sort of thing. Seeing blood gave me a pleasant feeling. At that time the slaughter of pigs in people's homes was more frequent than it is now, and I always like to watch it. Already, as a schoolboy, I loved to see fires. The shouting and the excitement were fun to me. Whether my youthful onanism had anything to do with it, I don't know. That was not very important, it was only temporary. By the time I was thirteen I knew all about sexual matters, and in my own home I saw my parents have sexual relations. Of course, I soon decided that I would try for myself. I began first with a schoolgirl and got as far as contact with the naked body, but not to proper intercourse, as the girl resisted and moved about too much. In this way it occurred to me to try it with animals. There were goats in the stables and also a good many sheep used to be kept penned. For this purpose I went to neighbouring stables where it was easy for me to get in. I actually did have intercourse with female animals; I did actually force my member into the animal. Then later I thought no more of it. It was only a temporary thing about the age of thirteen.

"Soon after that I became aware of the pleasure of the sight of blood. To-day it is not clear to me why I went to the stables beyond the Hirschburg. The house is still standing there. I stabbed a pig in the back, it bled terribly and squealed. Then I was seen and recognised because the son of the house and I were schoolfellows. There was a terrible row about it at home.

"It was in my thirteenth year that for the first time I secured a complete orgasm by wounding. I attempted sexual intercourse with a sheep; whether it succeeded or the sheep would not keep still, I forget. I stabbed the sheep and at that moment ejaculated. I repeated that frequently for two or three years. After that I only had connection with females. That was at Coblenz.

"It was after that that I ran away with embezzled money and was accosted on the street by a girl of about eighteen years of age. We lived together until the embezzled money was all gone. The sexual intercourse we had then was quite normal. Yet, even then, I pinched the girl, for wounding was not yet the essential condition for success in the intercourse. In Coblenz at that time I was not very strongly drawn towards the girl; in three or four weeks we had relations only a few times. That seems rather strange for a young man.

"Then came the first imprisonment. Even at that time I had thoughts about wounding, but they were not insistent. When I came out of prison I became acquainted by chance with a woman and her daughter of sixteen. It was the woman who attracted me, but I paid no attentions to the daughter. That seems rather strange. The intercourse with the woman succeeded only when I ill-treated her. In the beginning she put up with it, but when it became worse and I threatened to kill her, she gave me away to the police and I was punished for using threats and failing to keep the domestic peace. I got one week.

"During my first long sentence for theft, one of eight months, I was separated from this woman. Then I met her again in 1904 and started up with the daughter. I ill-treated her and threatened her with a revolver. It was an out-of-date old thing that would not have been capable of hurting her. I had great fun as they ran away and I sent shots after them. While I was doing that I ejaculated.

"Another shooting occurred at that time. While I was in prison I had figured out how I would shoot a girl I knew in Grafenberg. At that mere thought I felt sexual excitement. I had known this girl at school. I studied the place where she lived and actually waited for days in order to kill her. One morning I watched her from their courtyard how she got out of bed and then I shot at her. After a while, when things quietened down again, I fired again that evening through the window. Then I fled to the Grafenberger Wald, was chased and arrested and found with the weapon. I confessed and got a year's imprisonment.

I directed Kürten's attention to the throttling cases:

"I told you already that throttling in itself was a pleasure to me, even without any intention to kill. Take, for example, the Schafer case in 1913 (compare Case 7). I had taken this girl out frequently and at last we spent the whole night in the Grafenberger Wald. I then throttled her several times and she did not mind. I just calmed her down: 'This is all part of love,' I said, 'I don't want to kill you.' It was only the beginning, when I inserted my member in her vagina on the bench; it was in the wood that I had an ejaculation, and then without sexual connection at all.

"It was just the same in the case of Franken in 1913. (Case 11). There, too, I throttled the girl for some time and saw how the blood spouted from her mouth and in that way got my ejaculation. In other cases I did not achieve my end by throttling; for instance, Maas, (Case 50) I throttled her violently, too, but she freed herself and ran away."

When I asked Kürten whether he had ever throttled any of his victims to death, he replied that he thought he had done so in the case of the Ohliger child because she did not move after the throttling. He said, also, that in August, 1929 (Case 53), he had throttled Annie for so long that he thought she was dead and he had then thrown the body into the Rhine in order to conceal traces of his crime.

Kürten then spoke of the effect of imprisonment upon him: "The long sentences I served when still quite young had a very bad effect on me. Other prisoners think of naked women and masturbate. This I did very seldom. I got no pleasure from it. I got my climax of enjoyment when I imagined something horrible in my cell in the evenings. For instance, slitting up somebody's stomach, and how the public would be horrified. The thought of wounding was my peculiar lust and it was in that way that I got my ejaculations. I can remember exactly how it happened in 1905 in the prison at Metz. There, for the first time, I got an ejaculation by thinking of grievous woundings and the actual killing of people. That went on for years. If I hadn't had that I would have hanged myself. There is really nothing astonishing about the fact that, having got out of prison, well used to such imaginings, I was urged to do the things. You remind me, Professor, of the Mulheim crime. It is certain that just then I had seven years in Münster behind me. Actually, I had gone out to steal and the murder was incidental. But you are quite wrong, Professor, if you think that this crime stands as a single case in those years. No, one thing and another happened, but there were no big jobs. But when the decision came, it came suddenly because of the opportunity - in contrast to the last years when the urge has dominated me continuously. The child Klein (Case 6) lay in her bed asleep. I seized her throat, and at once my sexual excitement began. During the throttling I grasped the child's vagina with my fingers in order to tear it open, but it was not enough for my lust: I cut the throat. It is the blood that is decisive in most of the case, throttling alone is insufficient to produce ejaculation. There is, for instance, the case of the Italian. I only know her Christian name, Marianne. She could satisfy herself by sucking, but I got no pleasure out of that, so I throttled her for about ten minutes, but without success, for she did not scream, but defended herself vigorously (Case 69). Then, again, the case of Anna Ist, I treated her so badly that she was black and blue. Yet even after that she went out with me again. Some women are funny!

"I can't say, Professor, that there were periods when my urge was stronger or weaker. Only during the period of hunger in Brieg prison I became a walking corpse and had no desire for sex. That is why nothing had happened at Altenburg. I only ill-treated women in order to get an ejaculation, but without complete sexual intercourse. It was only when I came to Dusseldorf and began to have relations with Tiede that I indulged more frequently in cruelty. In the beginning Tiede put up with it. Then, when she learned that I was married, she charged me with it. Besides her I had Mech and Kiefer in the Parkstrasse at the same time. When there seem to be long gaps in the list of my crimes I confess it is due to the terms of imprisonment, or to the fact that I failed in some projected assault. There are smaller attempts in between which I do not remember clearly myself and therefore have either not confessed or divulged. It was during this period that I committed arson on many occasions. I did not reveal all of the arsons during the investigation by the police. I then gave another reason for these crimes, but that was because it was more or less suggested to me and out of egotism I did not contradict them. It is not true that I wanted to kill the vagabonds sleeping in the haystacks I fired. It is the fact that I had no such thought. In my imagination arson played the same role as other mass accidents; when the people dashed about screaming I enjoyed it immensely. The bright glow of the fire at night was exciting, but one thing is certain, the frequency of the cases in these last years was due to the injustice of the sentences I served. When in 1926 I was sent to the remand prison I was absolutely mad. I had the feeling that I was innocent. To that feeling there were added imaginings of a sexual kind. Therefore, after my release in 1927 many more arsons took place than are mentioned on the list here. Besides, in addition to the case of Ist, there were minor cases of attempted throttling. In 1927 I was sentenced again for false pretences, which wasn't false pretences at all. Tiede had sworn falsely. In 1928 I again suffered an unjust prison sentence for alleged threats and insults. I was absolutely innocent. I resent that even to this day. You will now realise, Professor, why there were frequent arsons from 1927 onwards.

"I must answer your question whether I was suspected by anyone with a 'No.' I revealed everything after my arrest and without being asked. I don't want to pretend to you, Professor, that a desire to boast had not something to do with that confession - it was a bit of Kürten senior coming out in me. You must try to put yourself in my place. The highest police officers were hemming me in. They all marvelled at me as a miracle. That is why I took on me more than was really true.

"For instance, the murders in Altenburg, the details of which are fresh in my memory from gossip. They often marvelled at my memory. Things that happened twenty or thirty years ago I can describe to you with every detail. I can recall the day and the hour of every arson I committed. But the statements which I made previously about wanting to kill the down-and-outs sleeping in the haystacks by firing them are true only in so far as I had no original intention of killing people in that way. During the fire itself the thought that human beings might be burnt added to the sensations that I experienced. I always watched the fires, usually from near at hand, so near in fact that I have been asked to give a helping hand. Otherwise I was among the spectators of the street ... The shouting of the people and the glare of the fire pleased me. During big fires I always come to an ejaculation. If you see in the list sometimes several arsons in one evening, then I had had no success with the first or the second. I also ejaculated when I fired the woods. It was a lovely sight when one pine after another was consumed in the flames fanned by the sharp East wind ... that was wonderful.

"At the arson in the Wolfsaap I had no success in the beginning, so I left it and made my way to the Stutzhof farm and set a barn alight. But as the barn was some distance and is isolated, there were few people about, for the people were all at the Wolfsaap. So I went back again to the barn. Meanwhile some excitement had started up. Fire engines came up, rumbling; the tiles of the roof cracked with the heat and the reports of them bursting resounded to the borders of the woods. The owls then hooted and I ejaculated. Again, when I fired the peat belonging to the Heumieten (Case 29), there was not enough noise. A policeman had to come and arouse the people and even then they didn't get up. That is why that same evening I set fire to the Hohenzollern colony. That was another matter altogether. The whole colony crowded together and I ejaculated. I tried to set fire to the Dusseldorf Orphanage several times, but the fire always petered out again. I probably ought not to have done it because of the orphans.

"The three arsons of January 1929 that took place on the same evening (Cases 42-44) also came about because it was too quiet at the first fire at the Papendell haystack. The second fire at the barn in the field did not catch and only at the third fire, when the stack was blazing and there was a great commotion, did I have success."

I led the talk once more back to his sexual acts:

"You ask me how it is possible for me to have normal sexual intercourse at all. Well, if I don't ill-treat the woman during the intercourse, then I get no orgasm. Even with my wife, I had to use a sort of fantasy, otherwise I was impotent. It was usually my wife who took the initiative for intercourse. After we had been married six months she used to say: 'Are we married or aren't we?' She has always had to help me to get an erection and even then, in order to succeed, I had to conjure up all kinds of fantasies and then it took a long time. So, too, with my victims, I never succeeded without brutalities, not even with Hahn. She believed that I had had complete intercourse with her, but I did not ejaculate. Without violence with her, but I did not ejaculate. Without violence my member slackens quickly in the vagina. It was so with Butlies and the others with whom I was supposed to have had complete connection."

I next spoke to Kürten about the single cases that took place, one after the other, for so far he had mentioned them. The statement he made was as follows:

"I have told you already that the main thing with me was to see blood. Here I must tell you of another recent case. Whenever I happened to be near a serious accident in the street I felt sexually excited. A short time before I was arrested I saw a brakesman fall from the freight wagon of a street car on Erkrather Strasse, and go under its wheels. The blood gushed out and I pretended to assist the victim. I then had an orgasm. Such cases happen frequently, even with animals. Thus, once on the corner of Mintropstrasse I saw a horse that bled to death. By chance I saw it all and ejaculated.

"Whether I took a knife or a pair of scissors or a hammer in order to see blood was a matter of indifference to me or mere chance. Often after the hammer blows the bleeding victims moved and struggled, just as they did when they were throttled. I never got an orgasm at the start of these proceedings and for that reason I had to continue them. For instance, the Albermann case (Case 67), I felt nothing while actually throttling. That was why I repeated what I did in the Mulheim case, putting my fingers into the child's vagina. On that erection took place at once, and I then introduced my member into the vagina of the child. That was only an attempt, for my member relaxed again and I had to stab. Then only ejaculation took place. I can hear the bleeding, even when the stabbing is through the clothing, into the heart.

"It was thus as I lay on the Albermann child, my member still in the child's vagina, while I continued to stab her breast. It was similar, too with Hahn. There, too, I had no satisfaction during the sexual act, only later on during the throttling I became stiff again and when, as I stabbed her throat, the blood gushed from the wound, I drank the blood from the wound and ejaculated. I probably drank too much blood because I vomited. The Hahn girl was still alive, despite the terrible loss of blood. Finally, to kill her, I stabbed her in the breast and again I heard the gushing of blood. My return twice to this girl's body was for purposes of security: the body could not be left in the stream. As I carried the body to the grave which I had dug I thought about crucifying her. I had taken strong staples with me and wanted to nail the body to a tree with outspread arms. But I had not time. That, of course, was warranted to stir up some excitement. I then stood in her grave and drew the body down to me. In fingering it and holding it firmly - the under part was naked - I became once more sexually excited and had an orgasm. It struck me that the body was not stiff, but quite flaccid. She hung limp over my shoulder when I carried her. What cause prevented rigor mortis from developing?

"I must now answer your question whether simple stabbing was sufficient to satisfy my sexual desire and I must answer 'yes'. For example, when I was going after Anna Goldhausen I got sexual excitement on turning the corner and going towards her as she came towards me. I had an erection as I stabbed her, but no orgasm; therefore I went on stabbing. I had no satisfaction when I stabbed Frau Mantel because the woman shouted so terribly that I had to run away as fast as I could. Only in the third case of stabbing did I have an orgasm - that of Kornblum - but without complete erection. Afterwards my wife discovered the spots on my clothes in the same way as she discovered it in the case of Hahn and reproached me with it.

"Also with Frau Kühn I had an orgasm despite the fact that it was bitterly cold and that the whole attack took but seconds. With the Flehe children the throttling and struggling of the little Hamacher had an exciting effect and the sound of the blood when I cut her throat made me ejaculate. With the older child, Lenzen, it was the resistance that excited me and finally the stabbing which brought the climax, but without erection.

"That evening I was already in a state of strong sexual excitement. Again, the day after the crime, when I visited Flehe and saw the tremendous excitement of the people, I ejaculated."

(All this Kürten told me the summer of 1930. When, in February, 1931, I referred again to the murder of the children, Kürten was doubtful if he had ejaculated twice within such a short period as he has stated above. But I am of the opinion that his first account is correct as the sound of the gushing blood had been always an infallible means with him.)

"The Schulte case (Case 59) on the following day, did not differ from the others. My sexual lust was appeased because of what had happened the day before, and it was only in the dark, during the shouting, cutting and stabbing that I had an orgasm.

"In the case of Reuter, too, I ejaculated. (Case 63) The girl had collapsed after the first hammer blow and then when I had dragged her away from the path she regained consciousness and bit and struggled. It was through that that I became excited even without the shedding of blood. Even so, I had to continue striking with the hammer, for I had had no ejaculation when I had connection with her. It was much the same with Dorrier when she was lying unconscious after the first hammer blow. I had already exposed myself, had an erection, and had already penetrated her, but even then I had to keep on striking with the hammer until I ejaculated. I also gripped her neck with my left hand."

Here, too, I want to mention that Kürten gave a totally different account of the Dorrier affair in February, 1931. He then denied the coitus altogether and said that he did not even penetrate and that he had only attempted to do so. He said that in uncovering her he had seen her bloodstained linen and concluded that she was at her period and therefore checked himself from any further advance. This alternative account is noteworthy, since it does not explain the vaginal injury of Dorrier.

"In Wanders' case (Case 66), the excitement had no climax because the hammer broke - her head was harder than the hammer." (During one of the last interviews I had with Kürten prior to the jury trial, he himself referred to the blood-drinking). "I have already told you, Professor, of the Hahn case and how I drank the blood from the wound of her neck. As I told you, I stabbed her throat and, lying across her, I drank the blood that gushed out. While I did that I thrust my scissors with my right hand several times into her breast.

"In the case of Ohliger I also sucked blood from the wound on her temple, and from Scheer from the stab in the neck. From the girl Schulte I only licked the blood from her hands. It was the same with the swan in the Hofgarten. I used to stroll at night through the Hofgarten very often, and in the spring of 1930 I noticed a swan sleeping at the edge of the lake. I cut its throat. The blood spurted up and I drank from the stump and ejaculated.

"Your question too, Professor, whether the recollection of my deeds make me feel ashamed, I will tell you.

"Thinking back to all the details is not at all unpleasant. I rather enjoy it. To be sure, I pity the victims, but in conjuring up the memories in my imagination I even succeed in getting sexual satisfaction. These explanations, Professor, are only intended for you as a scientist, for I have told you with complete frankness my innermost feelings.

"So far as my own fate is concerned, I am tranquil. It is because of that that I am able thus quietly to answer your question whether I am not sorry for my confession with 'No'. It is better that I made an end of it. I would not have stopped my attacks. I was impelled over and over again. But I also want to point out that I was able to master my urge. Therein lies my guilt - that I did not do it in the murder cases. I know quite well that there I am guilty. Therefore I want to shoulder my punishment. After having spent twenty-four years in such institutions I prefer death to pardon. Though prison is different today from what it was in earlier times I see the contempt on the faces of the prison officials and the other prisoners. Those men, Professor, don't understand, as usual. But, after all, people are right when they say: 'The beast! The wild animal!"'

It was on this occasion that Kürten asked me particularly about the execution in detail - whether, his head chopped off, he would still hear the gushing of blood. That would be for him, he said, the pleasure of all pleasures.

It was while he was awaiting trial that Kürten changed this attitude towards death. The frequent interviews with physicians and lawyers probably had something to do with this change. Shortly after the jury-trial I once more asked of him what verdict he anticipated; and whether he would prefer a life sentence to death. He answered: 'That depends, Professor, on whether the court finds for murder or manslaughter. From the legal standpoint murder presupposes deliberation. This I certainly deny in the Mulheim case; that was a spontaneous act done quite blindly. Such a deed is no premeditated murder.

"As to the later cases I shan't have any such luck with that plea. It will be difficult for them to consider those cases as manslaughter. It is difficult, Professor, to answer your question about the death sentence. When a man has been sobered up after the event, as I have been, he lets things go their own way. If the Ministry confirm the death sentence, well, then I shall be executed; but if there is the slightest ground for the view of legal irrcsponsibility, then there might be some chance for a petition for pardon.

"After all, an execution does not achieve much. It is doubtful whether they can wash off with my blood the blood I have shed. It boils down in the end to an act of vengeance which the people have asked for. When I myself think about my deeds, and in particular about the children, then I abhor myself so much that I am impatient for my execution. That's the way you feel when you sober up. On the other hand, capital punishment itself is criticised even by the legal experts, so that one says to oneself; 'What, chop off a man's head simply because the people shout for it?'"

Now there is revealed to us a Kürten utterly different from the man interrogated by police and judge. These crimes, hitherto incomprehensible, become comprehensible, the wrong-doings of an abnormally directed sexual urge. The criminal becomes the sadist but nothing fundamentally new for sexual pathology is opened up by Kürten's crimes. Qualitatively, he does not differ from other sadistic criminals; only quantitatively, but quantitatively he stands out as a man unique in recent criminal history. Indeed, to an extent that justifies a more detailed examination of the man's sadism.

(b) Analysis of Kürten's sadism and of his motivation

Of the sexual perversions sadism alone is of outstanding importance in forensic medicine, for with sadism sexual intercourse itself is either complicated with acts of violence or acts of violence lead to the stimulation of sexual lust in place of the normal sexual act. The medico-legal expert encounters sadism in many degrees from the acts which accompany coitus itself, such as a wild gripping and pressing with the fingers into the flesh of the woman, to the biting and violation, the killing and dismemberment. It is common to all sadists that they cannot achieve orgasm without violence. They differ merely in the types of these acts of violence, most of them adhering to a single method which they use repeatedly. In this category come the hair-cutters, the clothes-destroyers, the knife-stabbers. Among the most dangerous sadists are the actual lust murderers and these, one finds, usually proceed according to a prescribed method. This was, at all events, the case with those lust murderers whom I had under observation. I need only recall the case of Tripp, well known through the press. The characteristic of the professional criminal sadist enunciated by Heindl is true also of the sadistic criminal. He commits his deeds always by the same method. Nothing avails to deflect the professional criminal from his habitual modus operandi, even when he knows that to follow it involves his ruin. Again and again, as though under compulsion, he reverts to his specific method.

Heindl's judgement is right in principle and applies to Kurten's case, with this proviso: Kürten differed from the average sadist in that he pursued different methods of violence alternatively.

But this seems an exception from the rule. The changes in method of procedure in Kürten's case spring from his general criminal nature and are the result of his preoccupation with protecting himself against discovery. He has said himself that in this way he would be able to create the impression that several men had been active in the Dusseldorf crimes. Furthermore, his change of weapon was the natural consequence of the breaking of his dagger and his hammer, neither of which could be replaced without grave risk of discovery. He was even at pains to hide his daggers and hammers in the open and to take back to his lodgings only the innocuous household scissors.

Kürten's sadistic tendencies are revealed quite early in his childhood in his love and enjoyment of the spectacle of animal slaughter. For he claims to have first experienced lust under such circumstances. Thus his next step was determined, namely, to attack animals himself. In this period - the thirteenth to the fourteenth years of his life - comes the episode of bestiality which lasted, however, so short a time that he was unable to say which sexual stimulus was the first. It seems certain that he soon abandoned his attempts at coitus with sheep and goats in favour of sexual stimulation by means of the sight of blood. He himself says that already at the onset of puberty he was familiar with the process of augmenting his lust by stabbing the animals with which he committed bestiality, but that in course of time he had abandoned bestiality altogether.

The sight of the gushing blood, and the hearing of the noise made by it, remained his peak point of enjoyment to the last. As Kürten reports, shortly and very vividly, in Case 13: "The drunk man sat on the bench. I approached him from behind and struck him with the sharp edge of the axe. He fell over. I took cover and saw how he bled. I then ejaculated."

Note well that it was not the ruthless blow with the axe, but the sight of the blood that produced the effect. That was the infallible means of exaltation with him, even when other often-tried means, such as throttling, hammer blows, etc., failed to produce any effect, or did not produce an effect quickly enough.

Thus with the sixteen-year-old Franken he says: "I throttled her several times. I saw blood come from her mouth and I then had an orgasm."

So, too, in the cases of Ohliger, Albermann, and Hahn. This was the stimulating factor that produced the second surge of lust almost before the first had exhausted itself - Hamacher and Lenzen - and was so quick, indeed, that he did not even have an erection.

Kurten does not wish to be regarded as a child or animal torturer in the ordinary sense of the word. The cruelty to animals, as he describes it, was, however, already sadistically directed. Very soon he used violence against the big animals as well. Thus he confirms established experience that the early tormenting of animals is a sure sign of future criminality. Just as monstrous as his torturing of animals in youth had been, so his crimes were to become at a later period. Very soon Kürten became familiar also with the lust-producing effect of the glare of fire, a fact which explains his frequent arsons. But this effect was not conditioned only by the flames, at least not later on in his life when in order to achieve the highest climax of lust he had to have in addition the spectacle of the anguish of the victim of his crime.

This brings us to the second component of Kürten's sadism: the cruelty. We know that sexual lust and cruelty are neighbours in the Empire of Feeling. The infliction of some degree of pain during coitus is frequent with the man. But it is not the essential pre-requisite for the success of the sexual act: it remains ancillary.

It is very different with the sadist Kürten, for with him the more violent the struggle with the victim the more certain his success. He frequently ascribes the ejaculation to the struggles and resistance of the children. To the investigating magistrate Kürten said "When I strangled my victim first it was because of my tender heart. I did not want it to appear that I had tortured my victim."

This self-praise can be regarded merely as an attempt to buttress up his suggested motive of revenge. He did not advance such excuses to me or to the other physicians.

According to his confession to the police, Kürten must have appeared as a murderer whose objective it was deliberately to destroy his victims. And the motive of vengeance he advanced, and his alleged desire to excite horror in the public mind, fitted the facts, apparently. But as an expression of sadism these crimes underwent a complete change of character. They were committed solely in order to satisfy his sexual urge. The orgasm being achieved, the interest of Kurten in his victims was usually extinguished. Where he occupied himself further with them it was either to cover up traces of his crime or to search for new lust stimuli, after an interval.

In illustration of the first case I may cite that of Heer (Case 60). At the hearing before the police Kürten said:

"I throttled Lina - she freed herself and I throttled her again, and again did not succeed. I then pushed her into the Düssel."

From these words, of course, the logical inference is that it was a plain lust murder. But to me Kürten said that the second throttling had been crowned with success, that is, he achieved an orgasm and thereafter had but one objective - to be rid of Heer. ("The bitch" was how he once referred to her.) It must have been quite clear to so crafty a criminal that she would not be drowned in the shallow Düsselbach.

(As examples of the recurrent lust excitement note the cases of Ohliger, Hahn and the return of Kürten to the graves of his victims.)

All the various cruelties which Kürten practised served only the single purpose of achieving an orgasm. Let us examine thc series of crimes in this light. The throttling cases are straightforward. He throttles the girls until ejaculation, he then releases them. In order to mask his perversion from the woman, and to conceal the real significance of the proceedings, he sometimes feigned coitus. But it is only *intromissio sine ejaculatione* as in Case 7. The girl Schafer, of course, had her own interpretation of the throttling attempts. She says: "In order to make me submissive he throttled me." But Kürten explained the affair differently:

"What happened on the bench was only the beginning. I was in her, but I did not achieve my aim. Only after repeated throttling did I do so."

Thus, too, in Case 17, the coitus with Kiefer in the laundry was but a preparatory action. Here, too, his confession is as follows:

"I throttled her during intercourse with the intention of killing her. I did not succeed."

Kürten expressly drew my attention to the fact that the addition made in his confession to the police - "I had a revolver with me" - was a lie. He said: "I did not even possess one. I only said that out of bravado."

In several cases of throttling, Kürten found that things did not turn out as he had reckoned. For instance, in Case 17 Wack, Case 22 Ist, Case 50 Maas, and Case 72 (the girl from Herne), as these young women were able to free themselves from his throttling grip and to cry out. In other cases Kürten claims that he achieved his purpose by throttling alone. Thus, in Case 52, in the Freitagstrasse: "I throttled her a long time until I came, then I released her because there were people about."

In Case 62 (Radusch) Kürten had throttled the victim and bruised the vulva: "The orgasm took place without erection." Here the stout defence of the woman and the rough treatment of the vulva and the infliction of pain achieved the end. Here, too, the tragi-comic meeting with Hau comes in. (Case 73). When Kürten, seated on the bench in the Hofgarten, felt under the girl's skirts, she slapped his face. He retaliated and made her bleed. He then kissed the blood from her mouth and ejaculated. Kürten keeps silent as to the comic end of the scene, in which he made the girl pay for the coffee which he had bought her.

In Case 68 (Eidam), the girl apparently submitted to the throttling attempts because, despite them, she was drawn to Kürten. Kürten himself says that during the coitus on the bench he had an orgasm - "because I throttled her during the act."

In Case 69, it was again the violent defence put up by Santo which brought Kürten to the sexual climax. It was much the same in Case 70 (Becker). During the struggle in the wood, when the attacked girl smashed her umbrella over Kürten's head, Kürten achieved satisfaction, and having achieved his climax he cared no more for Becker, pushed her away from him and down the slope, just as he had dealt with Heer previously.

Actually, these abrupt dismissals of the girls were far from being part of Kürten's sadistic programme-that was completed with the orgasm. If, after that, the throttled girls remained comparatively friendly, Kürten, too, became the polite gentleman he was before. The last rape, that of Butlies, is the best illustration of this. When he throttled the girl he had his orgasm. The connection while he was standing was merely a feigned manoeuvre. Butlies herself says:

"I hardly felt anything. Kürten finished very quickly and showed me the way out of the wood." And Butlies was an expert in lechery.

Again, the deposition of Wilbertz: "The intercourse on the bench scarcely succeeded, for I became frightened and thrust him away. He did me no harm. He accompanied me to Rath."

Despite the small degree of violence used, Kürten claims to have achieved his purpose in this case, too. It was not always so easy, for sometimes the throttling was not sufficient to induce orgasm, then it was that Kurten proceeded to the all-too-certain method of shedding blood. To that end he resorted to stabbing with dagger or scissors, or to hammer blows on the head of his victim.

In the account of the crime which Kürten gave to the police, he uses the following words: "It came to sexual intercourse." Several witnesses confirm this. Kurten, in fact, used two methods to achieve sexual gratification. Either he abandoned from the start the idea of actual intercourse, and this was in the greater number of cases, the arsons and the simple throttlings, or he resorted to an attack on the genitals of the victim by gripping under her skirt or by rough handling of her vulva. As had been remarked, the coitus was often merely a sham manoeuvre of Kürten's, but in some cases he did achieve coitus by violence as he confessed and as was proved. For example, with Reuter and Albermann. The explanation here, we may believe, was desire for change; *variatio delectat.* Kürten was unable to suggest to me a convincing motive. Reuter and Hahn were, as he put it, women who were out for marriage. But the child Albermann? Even so, in those cases where Kürten began coitus he only succeeded in penetration, while ejaculation was possible for him only when accompanied by violence. With Reuter this was by successive blows on the head; with Albermann by countess stabs in the breast.

The return to the scenes of his crimes was also a plain sexual urge. Kürten rejects this idea for he does not desire it to be believed that it was his sexual lust that impelled him to it, and as a motive suggests his atonement idea. But when one makes him talk freely about it, then he reveals himself as to his sadistic excitation: "I went, over and over again, to the graves of the victims, returned repeatedly to Mulheim to the grave of Klein and to the Stoffeler cemetery. When I fingered the earth of the grave with my hand I sometimes became sexually excited, and when I recalled in memory the vents, I could stay for hours by the grave of Hahn. But when I had an orgasm on the graves it was without any act on my part. The great thing was that I was within reach of the achievement of my mission."

It appears to have been the rule that he tried to find new sexual stimulants by looking at the scenes of his crimes:

"The place where I attacked Frau Kühn I visited again that same evening twice, and also later several times. In doing so I sometimes had an orgasm. When that morning I poured petrol over the child Ohliger and set fire to her, I had an orgasm at the height of the fire. The scene of that crime I visited again the same morning at half-past-eight and half-past-nine, and later on, frequently."

I do not want to close this chapter regarding Kürten's sadism without mentioning that Kürten occasionally gave himself up to a desire for pain. He says himself that he irritated and made angry some of the women in order to provoke them to strike him. There might also be a masochistic component in the achievement of an orgasm by the defence of these victims. I have in mind the Santo case where the throttled woman kicked vigorously, and the attacked woman who broke her umbrella over his head.

Chapter Five
Kürten's Character Pattern and Some Aspects of Criminal Psychology

I will begin this chapter with the observation that, following twelve months of observation, Kürten was not in my view mad in the sense of Paragraph 51, St G.B (Criminal Code).

The psychiatral observations of him in the mental institution led me to the same conclusion. Neither can we regard Kürten's crimes as compulsive acts committed in a condition amounting to unconsciousness within the meaning of the Paragraph referred to above.

Our definition of the true compulsive act is such act as proceeds from a conscious motive, but passes from its mental phase to the deed itself without any weighing of the pros and cons. Even were one to assume that the urge in Kürten was abnormally strong, he yet, assuredly, comes short of irresistible compulsion. One must certainly agree that Kürten felt in himself the sexual urge most powerfully, more strongly than another man easily excited. In 1929 already he noted the extraordinary increase of the urge. Once he said to me "I wonder what it was, that urge to go out, that demon which drew me out every evening without exception? It is no merit of mine that it did not happen a lot more. When I wasn't able to go out because my wife was home, I sometimes raged with impatience. I had to go, and to get out even if it came only to visiting the woods where I paced up and down in lonely parts, conjuring up in my mind my old crimes."

Fundamentally, it was no more than a habit, this going out in the evening and on holidays to seek for a suitable victim. If he did not find one, and that was, fortunately, the rule, then he only went home unsatisfied. If there was any hindrance, or any danger of discovery interfered with the execution of his sadistic purpose, then he backed down very quickly from its execution. That much he had admitted himself of the several interrupted attacks. Even at his sexual climax he was extremely alert and ready to run for instant safety. The Schulte case (50) illustrates that point well. Kürten had stabbed this girl in rapid succession, the orgasm was achieved, when the whole neighbourhood woke up and Kürten ran away. The attack on Radusch furnishes another example (62). Kürten ran away so quickly that he ejaculated into his clothing.

The sadism of Kürten is a perversion of the sex impulse in an abnormal psychic constitution. Kürten is a psychopath: the unfortunate biological inheritance from drunken father and grandfather came out in him in all sorts of character deficiencies and in the abnormality of this urge. Thus born in him was the predisposition for the deviation of the sexual urge, the conditioning of the direction of that urge by early experiences, and the abnormal excitation of feeling which produces lust, and by impressions and fantasies which in another would have awakened only feelings of repugnance.

The sadism of Kürten is thus a perversion budded from the total personality, which is psychically abnormal. His sadism is, in part, a symptom of a genuine psychopathy because it is the one single component in his degenerate being which swamps and dominates all the others.

I have already indicated the close link between sadism and cruelty. Kürten himself realised it in the course of his medical examinations by various physicians. Towards the end of these medical observations he told me of another memory of his childhood which I would like to mention.

At the age of nine he often played with other boys on the logs which were tied together as rafts and anchored near the banks of the Rhine near Mulheim. They loved to ride on the floating logs. Once he pushed under his raft a boy who had happened to fall off his log into the shallow water so that he was drowned.

Another time he threw a boy from the extreme edge of the raft into the Rhine. This boy, too, was carried away on the tide and drowned. In doing these things he was well aware that he was doing something wrong, but he had an agreeable feeling while doing them.

Though Kürten was subjected to a rigid discipline by his father, he became criminal very young - at the age of sixteen. Once cast into the ways of crime, he was unable to return. One larceny followed upon another, sentences became longer and longer, until, at last, he was sent to the penitentiary for long terms of penal servitude.

Only in 1921, in his thirty-eighth year, a change came over him. He came under the influence of a woman of great will-power. He began to live a hard-working life. The burglaries stopped. But the sadistic urges remained undiminished and showed themselves in an every-increasing way until the Year of the Terror, in 1929.

The other psychopathic tendencies of Kürten kept themselves within reasonable bounds. His inclination to lie and deceive he cultivated to unheard-of mastery. Otherwise he could not possibly have hidden his crimes from his wife and all the world for so long a time. This historic art of dissimulation was such that his mask of a respectable citizen and of a gallant cavalier was scarcely penetrable.

It gave him the assurance which enabled him to lure his victims away and to keep them quiet until the moment of attack. This bearing of his is backed by a stupendous presence of mind and bluff. In the most complicated of situations he finds his way out. His wife surprises him with a strange girl: by a joking word he saves the situation for himself. Again: the girl Schafer, scared by the repeated attempts to throttle her (Case 7), asks the waitress of the beer garden for protection. Kürten disarms suspicion at once with the words: "She is my bride. If she has her moods, you need not take them seriously."

The girl from Herne, having luckily escaped from being throttled, later recognises him in the street and would have him arrested. Kürten rids himself of her with a very assured gesture. This assurance in his bearing Kürten acquired through the long years of a criminal career. After all, he had been for years a professional burglar, and he had made a speciality, as an expert housebreaker, of entering houses where the householder would be known to be downstairs attending to his business, that of inn-keeper. The cases of Klein and Franken show how cold-bloodedly he worked.

In bizarre contrast to his mendacity there appears sometimes a brutal frankness; it is a sadistic feature, as though he desired to savour the terror of his victim. "Now there will be a horrible end" he said to Schafer. And to Hau, after having kissed the blood from her lips: "You can congratulate yourself that we are not alone in the Hofgarten." The queer mixture of mendacity and frankness in Kürten's make-up does certainly force the observer to approach his confessions with great caution. It was this that drew out the preliminary investigations and caused them to last for more than six months.

The Public Prosecutor noticed that Kürten lied often out of his sadistic impulses, in order to get witnesses into trouble. If possible, he wished to involve them in proceedings for perjury. On the other hand, whoever wins Kürten's confidence, as we physicians did during the investigation, must be astonished at the complete accessibility of this strange man. I am convinced that as far as I am concerned Kürten held nothing back. On the contrary, he had an active desire to reveal himself to me. Of this I will give an example. He spoke of his reactions to the many physicians who had him under observations and finished with the words: "When Professor X was here for the first time, he brought his lady assistant with him, and she had such a lovely white neck that I would have loved to have strangled it. Once, when the Professor left the room, leaving me alone with her, I had to keep myself in hand. This sort of thing came over me suddenly often enough, as, for instance, at Mulheim."

Another outstanding characteristic of Kürten's was his vanity. He set great store by his personal appearance. His fellow-workmen noticed how he cleaned himself up thoroughly, and even made-up before a mirror. When he went for a walk he carried a duster for his shoes. When I had to examine Kürten's clothing for bloodstains the room in my laboratory looked like a tailor's shop, so lavishly was Kürten provided with suits. And every suit was well kept, each pair of trousers carefully creased. Every spot had been removed, so that I could detect blood only in the seams of those trouser pockets in which he had carried his murderous instruments. His smartness, his well-cared-for person, was noticed by all the girls and as he had a slim figure, fresh-complexioned face and plentiful hair, all thought him much younger than his age. The witnesses thought him twenty-five to twenty-eight or thirty. This exterior appearance was the mirror of the man himself, a complacency that can be gauged both by speech and deeds. This complacency played a decisive part in his confession. Already at the time of the arrest in Stausberg he claimed to have been engaged in conjuring up the scene when the moment would come when he would reveal himself to the much-lauded criminal police: I am the criminal! He himself says quite openly that he was urged by megalomania to give the list of his crimes. From the amazed and troubled faces of his auditors he read their growing horror and astonishment as the list proceeded, apparently without end. Even in his braggadocio a perverse sense of humour lay concealed. Finally, the manner in which he described his crimes and motivated them is in itself a demonstration of megalomania.

Kürten's vengeance motive was not a free invention and must therefore be considered in addition to the sexual motive. Disciples of Freud will experience no surprise on hearing that Kürten mentioned frequently his wounded feelings and sense of injustice from the start of his examination. In the opinion of the psychoanalysts the criminal differs from the man who adjusts himself to society and the rule of law in a moral way, in that he fails to sublimate the aggressive primitive urges; or, to use the terminology of Freud himself, that the super ego (that is, the moral conscience) is lacking as a decisive factor to influence the ego. The primitive urges remain in the criminal with undiminished vigour and from this develops the disharmony, the tension, between the instinctual life and the moral social existence. Tensions like this, which are abreacted by the common neurotic by nervous symptoms of disease, force the criminal neurotic to crime. He then motivates his actions by the wounds inflicted upon him by injustice: Society, the Law, has treated me unjustly, therefore I am justified in acting against its norms. Kürten has assured me, over and over again, that he occupied himself with such thoughts in the solitude of the years of his imprisonments. Along with his sadistic fantasies, they were a consolation to him for the long deprivations of his liberty. This feature he has in common with many criminals. One need only refer to those who have used this method in their memoirs, for example, the infamous Manalescu claimed that by his larcenies he had only executed the vengeance of the poor on the rich, that his life and actions had been a moral struggle with human society. Basically, the idea of vengeance and atonement in Kürten's case is rooted in sadism. With him it is merely a mask for the sexual feeling. After the various hearings by legal experts and physicians were completed, I asked him once whether he felt more appeased now.

He said "Yes, I am sobered up. I also see that the idea of vengeance and atonement was wrong. For hours I sat beside the graves of my victims to give myself up to this idea. The sexual side of this remained in the background, yet it came into the picture. For instance, I had, as I have already told you, fingered the earth on the grave of Klein. I could imagine from the picture which was affixed to the grave what the child looked like, with her tresses that hung forward over her shoulders. Thinking of that I ejaculated. It was the same at the grave of Hahn. I went at least eight to twenty times within three months to the Brachfeld. Over and over again I was drawn to it. That sort of thing, of course, you understand as a criminologist - that the criminal always returns to the scene of his crime. Whenever I fingered the graves I always had an orgasm again. I was even drawn there when I went for a walk with my wife who, for her part, wished to go to Grafenberg, while as for me, I was impelled to take the other direction to Papendell, in order to visit Hahn's grave. Again, when I went for a walk with my father, I was drawn to the places where I had met Ohliger and Scheer. And when I visited those spots alone I had an orgasm on recalling the things that had happened there."

In this account the true character of Kürten's revenge motive reveals itself as ninety per cent sadism, ten per cent sense of injustice. Even so, since Kürten came back to it again and again through our discussions, I record it here.

The effect of auto-suggestion is, above all, a remarkable feature with Kürten. The solitude of the prison cell developed in him the power to achieve orgasm purely by indulgence in sadistic fantasies.

"I always got the papers, all of them, and as they were displayed it cost me nothing. In particular I read the murder stories. In doing so I always got sexually excited. Besides that, there were always people about the displayed newspapers in whose faces I saw horror." (In answer to my questiion.) "Yes, sometimes I ejaculated. I have read "*Jack the Ripper*" several times and I also liked to go to the cinema where exciting pictures were displayed showing somebody being gripped by the neck or thrown over a cliff."

In addition to these means, Kürten always kept his sadistic instinctual life going by the stimulation of his waking fantasies. Even now he is able to relieve the tedium of imprisonment by this exuberant fantasy weaving.

On the 31st of October, 1931, Kürten asked that I should visit him. "I want to ask you another question, Professor," he said. "Do you think they are finished with their investigation? I wanted to tell you that I have often heard voices and often I thought I saw great throngs of people from my house and heard music. The Oberburgmeister was making a speech and after him the Police President in honour of the police officer who had captured the Düsseldorf murderer. It was so real that I thought I actually heard the voices. With one ear I actually heard: with the other I dreamed. I was sometimes a man divided into two halves."

Besides these more or less pathological features Kürten had notable qualities of character and talent. The reader will recognise his uncommon mental processes in the statements given above verbatim. One sees how Kürten took advantage of every chance to enlarge his general education; and he has certainly come to amazing depths of knowledge of human nature and adjustment to environment. The foundation for this is to be found in his good memory.

A comparative examination of his statements of dates with the records of the fire departments showed that not only did Kürten give the right date, but the exact minute. If one listens to him describing meticulously the interiors of some of the scenes of his crimes, for example, the Kleins', at Mulheim, which he entered seventeen years ago, and if one then compares his detailed description with the sketch made for the investigating magistrate, one can only marvel at the astounding quality of his memory.

Kürten had very sharp eyes for every minor circumstance. To mention but one: he gauged the monetary status of his victims after knowing them only a short time. In 1913 he broke into the home of the Frankens in the evening, saw the daughter lying in bed and throttled her. Seventeen years later he said that there were three beds in the room and estimated the age of the throttled girl at sixteen or seventeen years. Actually Gertrud Franken was born in 1896 and was thus seventeen years old.

Kürten's swift appreciation of each perilous situation gives the real explanation of his long immunity from arrest. Heindl (*The Professional Criminal*, page 225) draws attention to another reason why murderers remain undetected so frequently. Murderers are usually skilled criminals, old soldiers in a warfare waged perpetually with the police. The professional murderer has usually been first for many years a burglar or criminal of some other kind. Occasionally, in the act of burglary, the criminal comes under the necessity of killing so that no witness should remain of his crime. From that point forward murder comes within the frame of the burglar's calculations from the inception of a fresh crime. He then kills deliberately and as a professional killer.

As, according to Heindl, even the mediocre murderer is superior to the police, how much more must that be the case with an expert assassin like Kürten?

I do not want to omit reference to the fact that during his long imprisonment awaiting trial, Kürten got a different angle on his crimes from that which he had had at the beginning. At the end he showed, if not regret, at least a more serious view. He said to me in January, 1931:

"The preliminary investigation is now over; the trial will probably open in April. I am in favour of a quiet sort of trial. I will ask that the public be excluded, so that youths shall not read the reports in the papers. I know from my own case how such reports of sexual crimes aggravated me. I have heard, too in, the streets how even quite young girls are keen after newspaper reports like these and how they promise chocolate to each other if one of them can secure the latest report in the final editions. Yes, at the Wehrhahn I once heard a pupil - I think from the girls' college - saying: 'I would rather like to go with him once, if I was only sure he wouldn't harm me.' She referred to the Düsseldorf murderer. I need only think of the trials of Krantz, Gutttmann, Husmann, and of the damage done by the newspaper reports, to want to have the public excluded for the sake of my family and my wife."

Kürten never showed actual remorse: "How could I do so? After all, I had to fulfil my mission," he said.

On another occasion he said: "If I was let loose today I couldn't guarantee that I would not immediately do something again. I can't feel remorse, but only regret for the innocent victims. Up to today, I have felt no remorse. I could not act differently."

To the prison chaplain Kürten said in his last days that he could not understand how he had been able to kill the child Albermann. The child had been so sweet to him, and when he carried her, she put her little arms about his neck. In short, she was so trustful.

Kürten thought a lot about himself and got to the point of some sort of self-recognition. He calls himself impetuous to the point of brutality; speaks often of his inclination to brag, of the megalomania which is inherited in his family. He is aware of his fatal sadistic propensity. All this, he explains, is due to heredity and his horrible youth.

"What a man becomes has nothing to do with him. It's just what his parents were and that applies to me, too. Just for the pleasure of being bad no man becomes a criminal, there is always a certain something which comes into it and for which he is not answerable."

It is also of interest that in the last months before his trial, Kürten occupied himself in prison with the question of his legal responsibility.

In February, 1931, he said to me: "I must come back to the question about which we have talked already. Paragraph 51 (of the Criminal Code) does not come into question with me. The reports from you, from Bedburg and of Professor Sioli say as much. I have already explained to you, Professor, how I felt before, during and after the execution of my crimes - well, do you think it impossible that there was a pathological predisposition? The urge was so strong that I could not resist it. And there is another thing that has to do with Paragraph 51, something rather out of the ordinary. Though I take it as it comes now - I mean with regard to the execution and so on - the question whether I really had free will remains open." (Note in these words, taken down verbatim, the clever way of expressing himself that Kürten had acquired during those later months by frequent exchanges with legal experts and physicians.) In this way Kürten wished to suggest that he was impelled to the commission of his sexual crimes, for, quite rightly, he recognised that it was from there that the whole question of legal responsibility derived.

Magnus Hirschfeld has pleaded in speech and writing for a far-reaching exculpation of sexual criminals of the type of Kürten, and has stated his fundamental propositions in his *Sexual Pathology* (2nd Edition).

"All the lust murderers," he wrote, "who have been examined up to the present time by competent experts were psychopaths of a marked degenerate type. Only in a single case was there any question whether the hereditary bias is sufficiently strong to restrain the pathological impulses. In most cases this is to be denied."

Ought one to accept Kürten's statements without critical examination? If so, then one should deny this in his case also, and question his responsibility. But I am of the opinion that the problem cannot be boiled down to so simple a formula as Hirschfeld does. And I think, too the psycho-pathology and, indeed, the entire spiritual personality, and not only the instinctual life, must be taken into account.

Kürten's sadistic urges did not permit pity to stand between him and his victims. Only once there seems to be a glimmer of it - when he said to Bell, when she invited him to repeat the sexual act with her, that she was wasted on him as he was a bad man. One might think that Kürten, when for the last time he was together with his wife (Friday 23.5.1930) broke down under the burden of remorse and that he craved freedom from this burden by a confession in some sort of mood of repentance. His wife shared this belief.

Kürten again and again denied this collapse, described so convincingly by his wife. But his reason for the denial was clear: it was to render convincing his idea of atonement, his mission. A psychic collapse does not fit well into this scheme for the presentation of a cool composed hero who remains constant to the voluntary termination of his mission.

Generally speaking, Kürten is inclined to hide behind ironic remarks certain emotions.

Another one attempting to build up from the published reports of his crimes the manner of man Kürten must have been, imagines him as a cold, crude man, a very beast in human shape. But the reader of a newspaper only hears or reads of the horrible. It is otherwise with one who was occupied more closely with this extraordinary man. Thus one is able to distinguish between the sadist Kürten and the man Kürten, and make the discovery that, aside from his defects, Kürten possessed qualities similar in every way to the ordinary run of men. A kind and accessible chatterer, with a wide general knowledge and with sound judgement, he made one forget that the man who faced us was the Düsseldorf murderer ...

In this there is, after all, nothing very remarkable, for according to Magnus Hirschfeld, the majority of sadists have been weaklings and pampered persons, and often, indeed, even of such kindly disposition that nobody would have believed them capable of such crimes.

If Kürten had anything on his conscience at those moments it was not the murder of the night, but the infidelity which went before it, and this is the fantastic thing: for Kürten, a breach of his marriage vows, of the conventional code of sexual ethics, weighed more heavily than bloody murder. This is a psychological curiosity that suggests a double ego.

After his arrest, Kürten was asked why, having made a full confession to his wife, he later retracted when confronted with her in prison. He replied of an irresistible impulse, that the retractation was out of consideration for the feelings of his wife. When she was no longer before him, he again made a clean breast of all. There is no reason why we need doubt this explanation.

During the trial, when Professor Sioli was giving his evidence, Kürten, dapper in appearance, calmly objective in manner, followed closely the following exchange between the expert witness and his counsel.

Counsel for Kürten: "That is the terrible thing - that the man Kürten is a riddle to me - that I cannot solve it. Haarmann only killed men, Landru only killed women, but Kürten killed men, women, children, and animals - killed anything he found."

Professor Sioli: "And was at the same time a clever man and quite a nice one."

It was Kürten's counsel, not Kürten, who was distressed. And this immunity from normal emotional reaction, this spiritual anaeshesia, was revealed in a striking way on more than one occasion. For example, when, seated opposite his wife in a restaurant he at lastt succeeds in convincing her that he is indeed the Düsseldorf Monster and proceeds to eat, first his own dinner and then the untouched food upon her plate. Throughout the long months of imprisonment, too, Kürten ate well and slept soundly. The experiences that followed his arrest were not, in fact, entirely unpleasant. He had, in a measure, attained one objective: he had achieved a world-wide infamy, a vast egotism was gratified.

A word about Frau Kürten. She was three years older than her husband, the daughter of a small tailor, she went to Berlin as a domestic servant and there, falling into bad hands, she became a prostitute. From this life she was recalled to respectability and a factory workshop by a brother who took her to Altenburg. There she took a lover, a gardener who, having promised her marriage, abandoned her after eight years in 1911.

For this she shot him and received a sentence of four years' im-

prisonment. She first met Kürten at the house of a sister in Altenburg. She did not want to marry him, but his soft-spoken and gallant words changed suddenly to threats of violence when she persisted in her refusal. He threatened, quite bluntly, to kill her unless she married him. This she did, frankly revealing her whole past life with a touching spiritual humility. Kürten heard her out, but he did not reciprocate. It was enough that she believed his story, that of the poor war prisoner returned from Russia. (He was then straight from prison.)

Presently she discovered his perpetual infidelities, even to the final insult of a strange girl in the marriage bed. Yet she made no complaint. Had she not sinned often enough? And, such was her philosophy, she must now suffer and endure. That was her attitude as she later spoke of it - to redeem her past.

That Kürten could evoke in this simple woman whole-hearted love and devotion need no more than fill a moment with wonder; for love does not base its sentiments upon or ask a balanced scale

And how bewilderingly strange was Kürten's attitude towards the woman who was his wife - strange until we remember that she was, apparently, the only woman of his experience who offered him something better than crude sexual gratification - a selfless and self-effacing love.

Why did not Kürten reward with scissors, the hammer, the fingers of steel, this drab woman with her perpetual fear of a penurious old-age, her pathetic preoccupation with her simple concept of redemption?

Was it that, in his fashion, Kürten loved his wife in so far as he was capable of that emotion?

Each day, she fanned to feeble life that spark of a normal affection that was extinguished by night when he set forth to "find a victim" or to meet again the girl who returned twice or thrice to the lover whose fingers left her throat blue with the bruises that were part of that brutality "that belongs to love".

Kürten contrived to maintain a normal marital relationship by indulging in fantasies of cruelty with an imaginary partner during the sex act with his wife. This circumstance suggests again that Kürten could, when he would, control his sadistic urge. He probably spoke quite truthfully when he declared that he only had reations with his wife on her invitation: she, on her side, no doubt extended it from normal womanly pride.

It is an interesting fact that only two women victims who escaped Kürten came forward voluntarily to give evidence against him and a fantastic one that neither was able to obtain a hearing from the police.

While such reticence may have been due in large measure to the shame of confessing publicly an intimacy with such a criminal, it may have been due, too, to sentiment.

The idea that a man so far removed from normal emotional reactions as Kürten could be capable of tender sentiments seems improbable: yet it was so. When the father of Kürten, the aged, alcoholic, brutal old criminal megalomaniac, fell on evil days, it was Peter who sought him out and gave filial assistance to this father whom he hated with an unliquidated reservoir of hate, yet loved as well. Surely, in Peter Kürten, we are face to face with a strange being!

To Professor Berg, Kürten admits without shame that the memory of his crimes gives him almost as much pleasure as their actual commission. "No", he says, "I have no remorse."

And this is no pose on his part, no lie, for as the weeks of his examination pass into months, one central face concerning Kürten begins to strike his examiners: it is his extraordinary truthfulness. Throughout the long sessions of the psychological examination, Kürten made no attempt at all to mitigate his crimes, but sought to justify them. He had a mission to fulfill: he is the avenger in his person, of injustice in the world. Those who inflicted suffering, must suffer in turn, even though vicariously; he wishes to bring about penal reform.

What he was actually doing was to ascribe to himself motives he had chosen as appropriate from his extensive reading.

When the moment came when Kürten offered an untrue explana-

tion to his examiners, it was due to the processes of rationalisation, as, for example, when he gave his account of his treatment of the murdered children. Even Kürten, the sadist, does not care overmuch to recall the little Albermann child, who laid her cheek to his own, who was "so sweet", and whose little body he defiled, mutilated and destroyed. "It was my tender-heartedness, he exclaimed, "I never tortured the children."

Clearly, if one is to get any sort of understanding of Kürten one must first enter, by force of sympathetic understanding, the dark labyrinth of his mind. But it is essential to examine the part played by the parents as a factor in the etiology of Kürten's abnormality; the heredity of the family stock; the environmental background against which the infant developed into the child, the child into the man.

Privatdozent Neustadt investigated the family tree of Kürten and revealed the terrible handicap under which he suffered from the first. The father of Kürten was a moulder. He was an alcoholic, a boastful, violent man of unrestrained sexual appetite. Of his behaviour to the mother, Kürten said that had his parents not been married, the relationship might well have constituted rape.*

In 1897, Kürten senior was sentenced to fifteen months' imprisonment for attempted incest with his young daughter. It was but one of many sentences served by him, for he was a recidivist.

Peter hated this father with a bitter hate that lasted throughout life, and he never tired of laying his great sins at his father's door. And the role of the father in the fate of Peter Kürten could scarcely be underestimated.

In attempting to come to the complex of causes which resulted in the ultimate criminal one should not be overlooked: Kürten's boyhood ambition was to become a draughtsman. In this ambition he was thwarted by his father and forced into the moulder's workshop to do work he hated.

It has been said that after love a child's need is for justice. After justice, it might be added, it needs the joy of work. When Kürten senior forced this boy into the moulder's workshop, he denied for him the third of these three essentials for normal, healthy develop-

*** A post-graduate medical degree without English equivalent.**

ment of character.

Peter Kürten was the third of the thirteen children born of this marriage. He was born in Koln-Mulheim in 1883. Three brothers served sentences of imprisonment for theft. The whole family was noted for violent temper, megalomania, and arrogance. According to Kürten, his sisters were all over-sexed, and one actually made sexual advances to him. With the sister who was the subject of the charge against his father, Kürten himself tried to commit incest. The brothers and sisters of his father were described as alcoholic psychopaths; endogenous mental disease, however, was absent.

The grandfather served sentences of imprisonment for theft, the collaterals reveal delirium tremens, paralysis, and feeble-mindedness, while throughout the family, criminals, alcoholics, and psychopaths abound.

This is the heritage of Kürten on his father's side; it is offset by a normal legacy from the mother's stock, for Frau Kürten was a hard working and decent women of a family of normal working class people.

"This genealogical tree," comments Professor Sioli, "affords a critical commentary on the question of how far such hereditary handicaps exert compelling influences on the decendants."

It is a thought that was in Plutarch's mind when he wrote: There is between the generating being and the generated, a sort of hidden identity, capable of justly committing the second to all the consequences of an action committed by the first."

Throughout his examination, Kürten constantly came back to the miseries of his childhood, speaking of them with the greatest bitterness. He spoke often of what he had suffered as a small boy in that overcrowded "home" where his father not uncommonly smashed windows and furniture and used brutally both wife and children.

That these experiences left deep psychic wounds on Kürten there can be no doubt. And it is a reasonable proposition that had Peter Kürten been a well loved child, subjected to good influences and reared in a good environment, the innate tendency to cruelty in him would have become disciplined to the point of a normal ingredientt in his characterological make-up. But that he had an innate propensity towards sadism seems clear.

Kürten's first direct observation of the sex act involved his parents and the infliction of pain and indignity by his father upon his mother, the nominal love object. It is, of course, commonplace that even the normal act between parents impresses a child as having the character of an act of aggression by the father.

What, then, must have been the effect upon the child when the act involved the degradation and hurt of the woman?

Kürten has said that his mother was a good and respectable woman, and one may believe that he entertained sentiments of affection for her, though he was in no way mother-fixed; indeed, so badly did he behave later in life that his mother sent him away. That he hated his father, however, is certain: but the father whom he hated he loved also. How, then, was this impediment to the normal process of identification to be surmounted? Such identification may be carried over to a better pattern in some parent surrogate: but the vessel of the spirit is by now cracked: the child involved is reconciling the irreconcilable, and the result is psychic weakness.

This evil, which was the portion of Peter Kürten from the very moment of conception, suggests a maglignancy of fate, a predestination for a life of evil. Before he had even reached his teens,

Kürten has had sown in the dark soil of his heart the first seeds of that sadism which was to change him from man to monster under the urge of a perverted sex appetite.

It is not without interest to look at some of the outstanding episodes of Kürten's life and estimate the part played by them in determining the ultimate disaster. Let us take first a very early experience.

There lived in the same house as the Kürten family the town knacker or dog-catcher, and it was this man, a sadist, who initiated the boy, Peter Kürten, into the secrets of dog torture. A normal boy might have reacted with an emotional recoil; but not every boy, and the fact that Kürten responded does little more than suggest a latent propensity towards pleasure from the sufferings of others. But one has to bear in mind the fact that many small children inflict pain on animals and insects. As he himself admitted, he enjoyed the sufferings of these dogs, but above all, he was erotically excited by the sight of their blood. This process of torture as prelude to destruction was accompanied by sexual indignities on the animals. There was, for the boy, an erotic element in these outrages and it was linked up with the sight of blood. The fully developed sadist was later to discover a like pleasure in the sound of the gushing blood of his victims.

It was about this time that young Kürten playing on a raft on the Rhine, drowned two of his playmates by thrusting them into the tide. When this fact was divulged by Kürten, and later came out at his trial, it suggested that there had been, even from early childhood, a criminal propensity. This view, however, was combated by the expert medical witnesses. Such crimes, it was suggested, at first sight apparent good evidence of inherent depravity, were to be segregated from the later murders, death being, for a child, no more than a going, a departure. As Professor Hubner, of Bonn, observed at the trial: "Many children, otherwise nice, do such things."

Even so, Freud is of the opinion that it is during the latency period - from five to puberty - that the individual may be expected to reveal abnormal or criminal trends, and this, Kürten certainly did: the child who murdered children became the man who murdered them.

Later Kürten ran away from the privation and horrors of his home and for a time lived as a boy vagabond, thieving in the streets, robbing chiefly women and girls - a significant choice of victim. He was not then into his teens. At school, both at Cologne and later at Düsseldorf, Kürten was mediocre. His adolescent sexuality was abnormal. He attempted relations with schoolgirls, masturbated excessively, and attempted incest with the sister who had been the object of his father's crime. He turned for fresh stimulation to the tormenting of animals: from his thirteenth to his sixteenth year he practised bestiality with sheep, pigs, and goats: always stabbing the animal.

At sixteen he became an apprentice moulder. and appears to have suffered much ill-treatment. One day he decided that he had had enough of it, stole some hundreds of marks from the workmen and run away.

And now, once more, his evil genius becomes active. In Coblenz, the runaway fell in with a prostitute and lived with her. She submitted to physical abuse from him, but did not invite it.

This episode ended when Kürten was arrested for theft and given the first of the seventeen sentences which were to take up twenty-seven of the forty years of his life.

Released from prison in August 1899, Kürten found his mother divorced from his father and so returned to the vagrant life of the streets, pilfering and snatching. During this phase he fell in with a woman twice his age and lived with her. Whereas the Coblenz prositute had tolerated his sadistic malpractice, the new love demanded them. In short, Kürten's sadistic tendencies, even by then abnormally developed, were further forced along this path by the mischance of contact with a masochistic sex partner.

In November of that year Kürten so misused a girl while having sexual intercourse with her in the Granfenberger Wald, that he left her for dead.

Thereafter he knew that he could attain to the maximum of sexual pleasure by such means. In this case, that known as The Girl from the Altstadt, we have only Kürten's statement for the facts. No body was ever found. In all probability the victim crawled away and kept her terrible secret to herself.

This was really Kürten's first murder, since subjectively he had succeeded in a deliberate killing in order to attain to sexual gratification. From that point onwards we have a man who is prepared to go to the extent of taking life to secure an orgasm: we are face to face with the stupendous egotism of the man.

It is a significant fact that Kürten committed his first murder on his release after serving a two year sentence. It brings us to the part played by prison in the development of Kürten's abnormality. It may one day be seen as the decisive factor in his ultimate complete spiritual collapse. For it was in prison that Kürten developed the sadistic fantasy-weaving which, failing ultimate outlet or sublimation, was acted out at the first opportunity. There must be in every prison men and women who are merely awaiting the hour of release to appease abnormal appetites that have been stimulated by the silence, solitude, and segregation of the prison house. That is why it may be said that prisons today are the insurance of society, not against crime, but against its cure. During sucessive sentences Kürten so perfected his powers of evocation that he was able to secure ejaculation by means of waking sadistic fantasies. To secure the ideal solitude for this indulgence, Kürten committed minor infractions of the prison rules.

In prison Kürten was often subjected to harsh treatment and in this way he obtained the subject matter for an easy later rationalisation: namely, that his crimes were committed in revenge for wrongs suffered by him at he hands of society.

Let him speak for himself:

“"These collisions (with warders) occurred pretty frequently. At this point I must add that the amount of work I did was the minimum. This was because, while I was alone, I had done a lot of weaving of fantasies of different kinds, as usually happens, some build castles in the air, others spend their time in sexual thoughts of a lewd kind about women. I began to do the latter and in order to give them a sexual basis, I occupied myself with things of a more violent nature. This gave me pleasure and at night in bed, whilst my eyes were shut, I thought something like this: If you were to attack somebody and wound him severely so as to inflict serious injury, it would be sexually gratifying. Whilst indulging in these fancies, I used already to get ‘eruptions’. *(Q. What do you mean 'eruptions'? A. seminal discharge.)* This happened in such a way that if I imagined to myself that I had cut somebody’s stomach or injured him seriously in some other way, I could get final and complete satifaction from it. I cannot conceal this from you. Since I have told you about the penal establishment, I shall not conceal this sexual side from you. This really happened. As you will see later, there has been a dark sinister thread running though my life, which has as its basis this strong sexual activity.

"All this was the reason why I did not do much work. for I also occupied myself with such things during the day. I also thought of myself as causing accidents affecting thousands of people and invented a number of crazy fantasies such as smashing bridges and boring though bridge-piers. Of course, I could never have carried out that sort of thing. Yet I have some idea of how it might be done, for I had gone in for water sport until quite recently and had pictured the thing to myself in such a way that it might be possible to work it so that the bridges would break, whilst there were a lot of people on them. Then I spun a number of fantasies with regard to bacilli which I might be able to introduce into drinking water and so cause a great calamity. Further I imagined myself using schools in the country where I could carry out these murders by giving away chocolate samples into which I should have put arsenic, which I could have obtained through housebreaking.

"When I had these visions and formed these images, I was always pleased with myself playing such a part. I derived the sort of pleasure from it that other people would get from thinking about a naked woman. And for this I am to blame, I must admit that myself. I might have fought against it but I didn't. I got more and more pleasure out of it; moreover, there came to be added to it the idea of revenge to a certain extent, and that was more or less like this.

"My ideas ran along these lines: this treatment that I was getting was barbarous and only fit for dogs. So I said to myself in my youthful way 'You just wait, you pack of scoundrels!' That was more or less the kind of retaliation or revenge idea. So I had all kinds of ideas, and so to some extent concentrated about different kinds of acts and got a great deal of pleasure out of it. This continued to develop even in later years at Münster. So I thought to myself: if you do so-and-so in such a way then that must affect your tormentors in such a way. For example, I kill somebody who is innocent and not responsible for the fact that I had been badly treated but if there really is such a thing on this earth as compensating justice, then my tormentors must feel it, then it must be transferred to them, even ifthey do not know that I have done it - that I am the author of the crime. But if this compensating justice is not just nonsense and an empty phrase, then they must feel it."

All that needs to be said about so frank a piece of self-revelation is that it should have been possible in prison between convict and prison psychiatrist. For it makes it quite plain that the trained psychological observer is an indispensable part of any prison system whose aims extend beyound the empiricism of punishment as an end in itself and detention as a piece of crude surgery on a social symptom. It shows us plainly the folly of locking up in a cell an individual whose defects or inadequacies as a social being plainly call for the clinic. Moreover, how can justice, a concept after which man always has sought in all ages, be arrived at untll the last secret chamber of the troubled soul is unlocked and its contents explored in the light?

This calls for a healer who can identify himself with the convict who is patient, or, should one say, patient who happens to be a convict? This is an approach poles apart from the orthodox attitude of those mouthpieces and representatives of society, judge, jury, and gaoler.

It is clear that solitary cells ceased to have any horror for Kürten: he courted punishment in order to secure the silence, the darkness, and the solitude, out of which to conjure up the dark delights of his sadistic perversion.

Thus the punshiment cell became for the prisoner a palace of many sinister delights and in this way, under actual State supervision, Kürten's sadism was given hot-house conditions for a forced and monstrous development. It is, after all, a fairly reasonable proposition that the only criterion of any prison rationale must be the degree of its success with cases primarily neurotic, and only incidentally - and then sometimes for inadequate social reasons - to be considered as criminal.

By 1904 the sheerly sadistic-erotic prison fantasies have been broadened out to include fantasies of revenge on society: he dreams of retaliation and being released, indulges in an orgy of larceny, adding now a new type of offence - arson (four cases). During the investigation Kürten described the sexual pleasure the flames and the cries of the victims afforded him.

In that year, 1904, he was called up to perform his military service, deserted, and got seven years. That sentence he served in Münster prison. It was during this sentence that he had an attack of prison psychosis, rolling himself up in the silk upon which he was doing task work and lying under the table as a cocoon.

Prison must come high in any estimate of the factors which made Kürten what he became. He referred over and over again to the effect of prison upon him, saying that he had suffered so much that all humanity had been knocked out of him. And it is obvious that no better forcing ground for his particular abnormality could have been devised had the objective in view been the State manufacture of a great abnormal; a criticism, of course, equally applicable to Dartmoor and most "modern" long-sentence prisons.

Writing of this fearful disintegration of character under prison conditions, Prince Kropotkin said: "Prisons are nurseries for the most revolting category of breaches of the moral law". In which he is borne out by Dostoyevsky on his own prison experience:

"During so many years I ought to have been able to seize some indication, however fugitive, of regret, of moral suffering. I have perceived positively nothing. Seclusion and excessive work only develop among these people a profound hatred, a thirst for forbidden pleasure or a terrible indifference."

A trained prison psychiatrist would not have been likely to have missed the real significance of Kürten's prison behaviour. But the prisons of even the most enlightened of countries have not yet become clinics for treatment of abnormalities whose roots lie in the subconscious: and there can be no cure of the criminal without an understanding of this subconscious by both physician and patient; and no rational treatment of criminality without reforms so radical as to amount to the abolition of the present prisons of the world.

This is the case for the study of the mind and emotions of the delinquent in prison and it is based, at its lowest, on consideration of the self interest of society. And Kürten's case is an example of the high price paid by the community for its failure to recognise the psychopathic facts concerning a prisoner serving sentences for crimes against property, but whose prison conduct, carefully observed by a staff psychiatrist, would have revealed the potential danger of foreshadowed crimes against the person. A prison diagnosis of sadism would have saved many lives.

For Kürten prison was a forcing house for the emotional factor which found its outlet in the sadistic fantasy-weaving or the attempted murder of fellow prisoners. Prison raised in Kürten the potential of desire and perfected the imaginative processes that took the form of the eroticisation of horror. Freedom was the transfer of fantasy to action; Kürten killed.

In a very real sense, he was a prison product; confinment acted as a stimulant or excitant upon his sadistic propensity. He himself makes this quite clear.

It is significant of the part played by prison on Kürten's perversions that immediately he was released from a seven-years' sentence, he maltreated a servant-girl during sexual intercourse and is soon once more in prison (September 1912) for discharging firearms in a restaurant and for molestation of a woman.

Released in August 1913, Kürten went to his mother, whom had meanwhile divorced his father, but was soon sent packing for rough behaviour. He had now begun to specialise in theft from the first-floor rooms of eating houses and other business premises where he would have prior knowledge of the whereabouts of the proprietor.

On May 25th 1913, Kürten committed the first of his sexual murders in Koln-Mulheim, when he cut the throat of the Klein child whilst she lay in bed, and raped her.

A tragic circumstance of this crime was the suffering it brought to the victim's uncle who was accused and tried for the crime and acquitted only "for lack of evidence". This unfortunate man died on active service with this stigma still attaching to his name.

Next, Kürten, during a burglary, attacked a sleeping girl but was frightened off - an instance of the efficient operation of the self-protective mechanism, even when the sex urge was impelling him to some new atrocity.

It is an interesting circumstance that up to this point in his career, Kürten had never once been arrested for a sexual offence, but only for larcenies and like offences "mala quia prohibita".

Professor Berg ascribes Kürten's long immunity from discovery to his simple but extremely effective technique as a criminal. But while it is true enough thar Kürten was adroit, in some measure his immunity derived from a psycholoical cause: Kürten, unlike many neurotic criminals - unlike Dostoyevsky's Raskolnikov - had no need of punishment - no "punishment appetite". His sleep was untroubled by bad dreams and murder lay lightly on his heart. It is when an unconscious desire for punishment is active that apparent (but only apparent) "oversight" results in arrest.

Here it is interesting to note that Kürten was far less successful as a thief than as a murderer. Again, it is possible that Kürten may have regarded theft as a graver moral offence than murder and have unconsciously desired defeat, and so have done or left undone that one thing that made detection and capture inevitable.

Yet, generally considered, Kürten appears to have been immune from the sense of guilt that is the characteristic of the neurotic criminal: he seems to have had no moral suffering until the final phase. Or was it, perhaps, only an apparent immunity, since, at the end, the religious colouring of infantile mind (R.C.) returned, as might have been foretold, to torment the sinner's last earthly hours with thoughts of hell? At that moment, when absence of hope provides the guarantee of his sincerity, Kürten asks, not for his wife, but for a priest. As Stekel somewhere remarks, every fear is fear of the punishment of God.

Kürten's next sentence was one of six years. This took him through the war period, one of the severest privations in the prison, when the numerous deaths among the half-starved prisoners provided Kürten's abnormality with a new satisfaction: he was assiduous in volunteering for the task of handling the dead. He accused himself with having hoarded morphine and aspirin during this period, until he had enough to kill the patients in the ward of the prison hospitall where he worked as volunteer nurse.

Released in April, 1921, Kürten turned up in Altenburg, in the romantic role of a war prisoner back from Russia and he wooed, as has been described, the woman who became his wife. For two years he worked honestly and even functioned as a normal member of society, becoming active in trade union circles and at a political club.

There were one or two lapses, however, which resulted in charges of ill-treatment on servant girls and showed the persistence of his nocturnal habits. From danger of arrest his wife loyally saved him. This interlude closed in 1925 when Kürten returned to Düsseldorf, having arranged for his wife to follow later.

Why did he leave Altenburg where, it would seem, he had made some effort to master his abnormal propensities? The answer must be that the restrictions of a small town hampered and irked and put too plain a limit upon him at those times when his sadism had the upper hand.

In any case, Kürten left Altenburg and saw Düsseldorf again in the evening light and rejoiced that "the sunset was blood-red on my return," interpreting that chance as a sign and an omen, or symbol of his destiny.

This was the beginning of the Düsseldorf Reign of Terror.

The reader by this time has, no doubt, already put several questions to himself concerning Kürten's psychological make-up. Did he project hatred of the father on to the community? Was he forced by the brutalities of that father into a masochistic attitude against which he secretly revolted?

However these questions may be answered, it can scarcely be doubted that Peter Kürten, as a small child, was already neurotic: later he was to revert to this infantile neurosis: but not as an adult neurotic. The answer to the riddle of Kürten's abnormality lies in the realm of his unconscious - in that limitless dynamic of desires with their infantile nuclei, sadistic or aggressive, and in the primitive perverse sexual impulses.

Goethe remarked that he was capable of every kind of crime, which is true of everbody. The criminality of those of us who contrive to steer clear of prison is in those antisocial urges that are satisfied in our fantasy activity. Who can stand self-acquitted of the "shadow murder" of the imagination? In so far as most men and women, if not all, have willed the death of another, the majority of mankind are "murder-minded" now and then.

The significant role of the fantasy as action substitute can be illustrated from the work of many writers. Edgar Allan Poe, for example, so let his neurotic imagination play about a contemporary New York crime that he succeeded completely in "feeling" himself into the criminal's mind; after which he wrote as fiction what subsequent police investigation established independently to be the true facts of the actual crime. The enormous popularity of crime stories and films is the measure of the latent criminality of so-called "normal" people. Kürten, by the way, claimed that it was through reading of crime (he was a keen student of Lombroso) and, in particular, his partiality for the story of "Jack the Ripper," that did much to stimulate his abnormality. And several writers have noted the effect of low literature on the criminally disposed. If Kürten was irresistibibly attracted to that case, it was for the reason that in "Jack the Ripper" he saw a murderer in his own image. One may doubt the soundness of Kürten's estimate of the importance of that story in his career of murder: that it was even a contributory factor seems a dubious proposition.

In the neuroses it is the morbid wish that comes through in a disguise which makes it acceptable to the censor; it is where the compromise is not affected that the result is criminality, or perversion, or both. Kürten had an emotional problem, a dynamic urge which he was able to resolve in serveral ways, but which he elected to resolve by his crimes. Had he possessed some attractive alternative channel for the discharge of this abnormal appetite, had he been able, like the Marquis de Sade, to live out, in a literary form, from high tension to relief, his sexual fantasies of cruelty or, like Baudelaire, to find relief in macabre poetic expression, he might have escaped his fate. It is, at least, a possibility. Baudelaire, denied the richnesss of his mind, was the potential archcriminal that Kürten became: but his greatest crimes are still-born in the sado-masochistic poems **Les Fleurs de Mal.** *By process of inversion Baudelaire made evil his good; while for Kürten the horrific became his sublime. His Muse saved Baudelaire from the guillotine, that muse which brought him relief from the psychic tension of his sado-masochistic urges, urges rooted in a mother fixation and an ambivalent emotional attitude towards his step-father.*

Art may rid the soul of much perilous stuff. Paul Verlaine, in much the same way, achieved by poetic catharsis the purges that rid his soul of its dark burden, so that when he "embarked for Sodom and Gomorrah" it was with pen and paper. Behind the adult Baudelaire, behind every adult who turns from life, there hides the infant who seeks the safety and comfort of the mother's breast. This emotional retreat has been described as the the quest of a lost childhood; it goes, perhaps, further even than that - to infancy, to the Nirvana of the womb itself.

There is a parallel between the French poet and Kürten that is both interesting and significant in any study of sexual crime, for it is the parallelism of the neuroses and crime, neurotic and criminal are never allied. Whether a criminal impulse is carried over the sphere of action or not appears to depend on the relationship existing between criminal instinct and ego. Where criminal instinct and ego go hand in hand, the criminal act is its expression. As Dr Paul Schilder put it, the riddle of criminology is not why certain individuals become criminals, but why so many do not become criminals, since we all have criminal tendencies and impulses.

In Kürten's case one can weigh heredity, environment and fortuitous mischances and encounters of childhood and youth without uncovering the source of so monstrous an abnormality. Many boys are born and grow up with handicaps as grievous as his without becoming criminals. Kürten's own brothers and sisters became, at worst, rather commomplace lawbreakers.

But to return for a moment to the relationship of the neuroses to criminality.

Baudelaire - our example, and a convenient one since the poet has been the subject of a brilliant analysis by Dr. Rene Laforgue - and Kürten, the criminal, were both socially maladjusted individuals. In Baudelaire's case this maladjustment expressed itself in symptoms. Anxiety, illness, pain, and failure at first relieve remorse, then give actual pleasure. There is truth behind the old music-hall joke about the misanthrope who enjoys his misery. For example, it is revealed in the self-sought syphilis, the instrument of the self-punishment mechanism of Baudelaire that sprang from a sense of guilt for the incestuous mother fixation: while, in the case of Kürten, on his lower cultural level, the maladjustment takes the form of acts. That is, of criminal acts. In both cases the result is the same; it is a sexual end that is attained.

Kürten's phenomenal memory was a cause of wonder to the medical experts who examined him, and the French poet possessed, in the same astonishing degree, the power to evoke, with complete accuracy, past and often long-past events. And, memory being selective, we may learn something by examining the material of the memory content of these two abnormal men. Thus Baudelaire recalls his debauches and abnormal sexual practices in detail almost as vividly as does Kürten the bloody details of his most atrocious crimes. Again, both are obsessed with the idea of blood. Both love the horrible. In Kürten's case the blood obsession is so strong that, faced with the headsman's block, he asks if, for a fleeting moment, he will hear the gushing of his own blood. This suggests a master passion that is stimulated by the presence of death. "Death," wrote Baudelaire, "can be the equivalent of the orgasm," and it is something like that with Kürten.

Baudelaire thinks and writes often enough in terms of vampirism, Kürten walks out of the folklore of the Middle Ages to become the vampire of reality in a modern city.

There are in world literature and folklore many vampire fantasies. They occur in all periods and in all cultures. And it is startling to find how nearly Kürten approximates to this vampire of universal legend. The legendary vampire was a corpse that left the grave to stalk the living in order to secure love or to implement malevolence or carnal desire or to avenge a wrong. But whatever the motive of the return, the method pursued remained invariable: the vampire drank the blood of the victim. This is precisely what the Kürten of fact did.

The vampire is universal in myth because the myth is the product of a universal dream-state experience of mankind:

"And the fear of vampirism
sucks the blood from my veins
and the brain from my head."

Professor Berg does not regard Kürten as having the vampire's necrophiliac love of the dead and he passes over several episodes that suggest the countrary. Yet how otherwise can Kürten's conduct be explained? He murders a young girl, digs her grave, lifts her into it and caresses the dead body, experiencing the tenderest emotions that as a living woman she failed to arouse in him at all. Next day he returns to the grave bringing spikes with him, having the serious intention of crucifying the corpse, a project he abandons only because the inert body proves too heavy for him.

Kürten visited, too, the cemetary where another victim, a child, lay buried, seated himself upon the grave, fingered the earth and in this macabre reverie actually experienced an orgasm. "The fantasy of loving such a being (dead)", says Dr. Ernest Jones, "can therefore make a strong appeal to the sadistic side of the sexual instinct" - "Die toten sind unersattlich."

Baudelaire, the neurotic, thus expresses himself: "As for torture, it is born of the evil part of the heart of man, a part that is athirst for voluptuousness, cruelty, and voluptuousness! Ideal sensations, like extreme heat and cold."

And Kürten: "Brutality belongs to love."

Again, it was Baudelaire who wrote: "I am the vampire to my own heart. I am one of those abandoned people condemned to eternal laughter and who can never smile again."

Given the poet's power, Kürten might have written something of this kind.

For the poet, the sadistic impulse was already appeased when he had reduced his mother to tears. For Kürten, in the end, only murder sufficed to satisfy a sadistic appetite. It is all a matter of refinements of feeling to achieve a given end.

Baudelaire's masochism, quite clearly, had its sadistic component; and with Kürten we find the masochistic component in the sadist. More than once he provokes and incites violence from his nocturnal partners in order to enjoy abuse and blows at their hands.

A man may do bad acts to secure his need - moral suffering - for with this self-inflicted pain he achieves self-forgiveness: this is the psychic mechanism of the sadistic medallion in reverse. The process, however, has a secondary end: the suffering affords sexual pleasure. When the sexual instinct becomes bedevilled and the path to normal satisfaction is barred by a portal whose custodian demands a price, that price is always pain: pain suffered or inflicted.

Man, psychologically, is a pyramid whose apex is represented by his culture. It is as we proceed downwards towards the base of the structure of his being that we come, with pardonable reluctance, to the unflattering truth. For man is the victim of the past, and every human life must be a single combat against the ghostly army of First Men. Sometimes in that unequal contest the collapse of the moral superstructure is complete and it was so in the case of Peter Kürten. And so we say of him that he was atavistic, a throwback to a remote and blood-stained past. Yet, strangely enough, there is no outward and visible sign, no physical stigmata, though an attempt has been made by Professor Willemse to provide Kürten with a type-label, but the classification "athletic" scarcely conveys so much as a meaning.

Fate seems to have been against Kürten from the start; and if he became the victimiser of the innocent, it has to be remembered that he began as an innocent victimised. When one considers his sadism and the appalling crimes into which its indulgence led him, in terms of moral responsibility, it is necessary to put aside legal definitions and to invoke in their place a psychological criterion; it is a long road that leads to the jungle of metaphysics.

If, as Professor Berg assures us, Kürten presents no novel prob-

lem in psychopathology, he does raise in an unmistakeable way urgents problems in penology. For it is impossible to study the product of (among other baleful influences) twenty-five years of prison, without asking what part prison played in making a pervert and psychopath into an arch-criminal and enemy of his kind.

Kürten conforms exactly to Freud's narcissistic type of criminal, and whether such self-love amounts to moral insanity is a question that one day will, no doubt, be answered. Quite clearly whatever the etiological factors that set the stage of life for the bloody tragedy in which Kürten played the leading part, he was unable and unwilling from early childhood to recognise that life imposes on the individual the obligation to surrender desires or to pay in good social coin (responsibility) for their gratification.

Final Remarks

After a hearing lasting ten days the jury of the Düsseldorf Criminal Court found Kürten guilty of murder in nine cases. In addition, he was found guilty of attempted murder in seven cases. Despite Kürten's full confession, every crime was investigated by the calling of witnesses during the trial. Nothing beyond what I have set forth in the foregoing chapters was revealed during the trial.

Kürten behaved quietly and in a dignified way. He did not challenge the death sentence, did not feign remorse - which, in any case, he was quite incapable of feeling - nor did he try to mitigate anything. But he noted every disrepancy in the accounts of the witnesses, and he also protested against the observations of the Public Prosecutor and of the experts when they were not, in his opinion, accurate. Most characteristic of all was his final address at the close of the trial.

Kürten's Final Speech

"As I now see the crimes committed by me, they are so ghastly that I do not want to attempt any sort of excuse for them. Still, I feel some bitterness when I think of the physician and the lady physician in Stuttgart who have stained their hands with human blood to the extent of fifteen hundred murders. (*A reference to the case of certain abortionists*) I do not want to accuse, all I want to do is let you see what passes in my soul. I cannot refrain from reproaching you, Professor Sioli, for saying that the conditions of my home were not the decisive factor. On the contrary, you may well assume that youthful surroundings are decisive for the development of character. With silent longing I have sometimes in my early days glimpsed other families and asked myself why it could not be like that with us.

"I contradict the Chief Public Prosecutor when he asserts that it was out of cowardice that I revoked my confession. The very day that I opened up to my wife I well knew the consequences of the confession; I felt liberated in a certain way and I had the firm intention of sticking to my confession so that I could do a last good turn to my wife. But the real reason was that there arrives for every criminal that moment beyond which he cannot go. And I was in due course subject to this psychic collapse. As I have related already, I followed the reports in the newspapers then, and, of course, later, very thoroughly. I convinced myself that on the whole the newspaper reports had been moderate. I may say that I used to intoxicate myself with the sensational press, it was the poison which must bear part of the responsibility of my poisoned life. By being moderate now, it has done a great deal to prevent the public from being poisoned. I feel urged to make one more statement; some victims made it rather easy for me to overpower them.

"I do not want to forget to mention what I frequently said before - that I detest the crimes and feel deep sorrow for the relatives. I even dare to ask those relatives to forgive me, as far as that may be possible for them. Furthermore, I want to point out emphatically that, contrary to the version of the Chief Public Prosecutor, I never tortured a victim. I do not attempt to excuse my crimes. I have already pointed out that I am prepared to bear the consequences of my misdeeds. I hope that thus I will atone for a large part of what I have done.

"Although I can suffer capital punishment only once, you may rest assured that it is one of the many unknown tortures to endure the time before the execution of the sentence, and dozens of times I have lived through the moment of the execution. And when you consider this and recognise my goodwill to atone for all my crimes, I should think that the terrible desire for revenge and hatred against me cannot endure. And I want to ask you to forgive me."

Kürten did not exercise his right of appeal, but he did put in a petition for pardon and thought that it would be successful, since the Minister of Justice then in office was an opponent of capital punishment. Towards the end of June I still found him full of hope for the pardon. Up to the last he always remained in his habitual mood, as is shown by the photograph which I took on the 18th of June in his cell. He expressed his joy in letters from his wife, and over the fact that four thousand marks of the reward offered for him had been paid to her. During the last month he made some response to the ministrations of the Church and he assured me that the waking fantasies, and the sadistic imagery of former times, had entirely vanished. He claimed that he was transformed into an entirely new being, although people outside might well not believe it.

On the 1st of July he received composedly news of the failure of his petition for pardon. Asked for his last wish, he asked to see his Düsseldorf confessor and for permission to write farewell letters. In the thirteen letters which he wrote to the relatives of his victims, he asked pardon and for their prayers, as he himself would pray for them in heaven.

Quietly and composedly, he went to the block on the 2nd of July, 1931.

Kürten was too great an egoist to admit the pact of mutual abstinence from trespass that is a necessary pre-requisite for even a primitive form of society. As Professor Sioli observed of him:

"Kürten failed to realise the hard fact that the fulfillment of every satisfaction carries with it a sense of incompleteness."

Frustration, experience teaches, marches shoulder to shoulder with desire. In the beginning of life and at the end all is darkness and solitude. For an unhappy few there are both darkness and solitude in the brief space of years between womb and tomb.

When one looks at the features of Peter Kürten one sees the face of a very lonely man, and, considering his history, one may ask whether there can be any happiness without that self-abnegation and self-forgetfulness that comes to fulness as desire for the good of others and blooms as love. For love is the gateway of life, as hate is the way of death; and it was Peter Kürten's tragedy that he died without discovering this eternal truth.

BIBLIOGRAPHY

Rene Laforgue:	*The Defeat of Baudelaire*
Ernest Jones:	*On the Nightmare*
F. Dostoyevsky:	*Crime and Punishment*
George Godwin:	*Cain: or the Future of Crime*
F. Alexander:	*The Criminal and His Judges*
Sigmund Freud:	*Collected Papers*
Margaret Seaton Wagner:	*Life and Trial of Peter Kürten*
Kretschmer:	*Physique and Character*

The Silver Screen Shadows of Weimar

1. *M* (1931)

The ghastly precedents of Haarmann and Kürten, much as they gave notice of the type of alienated misfit who would gain prominence in the late 20th century (the "serial killer"), also helped give birth to a Cinema of Murder. In a distinctly Germanic tradition, however, the films they so grimly inspired are characterised more by a foul, oppressive atmosphere than by any excessive degree of gore.

Fritz Lang, one of the classic neo-expressionist directors of the Weimar Republic, a contemporary of Wiene, Pabst and Dreyer, originally intended his movie based on "the Vampire of Düsseldorf" to be called ***The Murderer is Among Us***. That was until dark rumblings were heard emanating from the Nazi Party, who believed, perish the thought, that the title might just allude to them. The story goes that when Lang went to reassure the head of Staaken, the studio where his film was shot, of its true subject matter, the bigshot gaved a warm smile of relief and held out the studio keys in offer. As he did so, he revealed a small swastika insignia on his lapel. From thereon, Lang knew his days as a native German filmmaker were numbered.

Ironically, Lang's wife and regular script writer, Thea von Harbou, was a less equivocal patriot for the Fatherland, and was then, like much of the country, letting her emotions be manipulated by thc not-yet-in-office Adolf Hitler. The murder film they collaborated on, the classic ***M*** (1931 - sometimes subtitled ***Dein Morder sieht dich An - Your Murderer Looks at You***) has surprisingly subversive undertones for a woman of such political pedigree. The criminal underworld (which, according to the film,seemed almost universally unionised in the 1930's) is depicted in no less a sympathetic light than their counterparts in the police force - in fact, they are shown to be far more efficient. How much of this was due to von Harbou's collaborators (the relative unknowns Paul Falkenberg, Adolf Jansen and Karl Vash) is not known. What is certain is that when her husband was summoned by Goebbels and told that henceforth he would make films for the greater glory of the Third Reich (despite having been born of a Jewish mother), he took a train to Paris, and charted a route to the USA, that very night. The year was 1933 - Lang had made his last German film, ***Das Testament des Dr. Mabuse***, the previous year, and would spend most of the rest of his life as an exile in Hollywood. Von Harbou remained and arranged for an instant divorce.

In '31, ***M***, Lang's crime masterpiece, impressed with its heavy stench of taboo violence (never explictly shown). His expressionist grounding is revealed in the shadows and grey skies of a twilit world, and close-ups of the characters' grimily assorted faces. Atrocities are signified by sinister moments of quiet simplicity. We come to recognise the presence of Peter Lorre's squat, frog-faced child murderer (here called "Hans Beckert") by his whistling of a piece from Grieg's *Peer Gynt* (*In the Hall of the Mountain King*). It seeps absent-mindedly from his lips, as he treats an excited little girl to her selection from a toystore window; as he strokes the flick-knife he carries concealed on him at all times. The child's murder is subtly, but shudderingly, evoked: her rubber ball rolls suddenly to a halt; her doll-shaped balloon entangles itself with telegraph wires, before floating off into the grey ether.

Lorre's Beckert (a truly repulsive, but later strangely pathetic, figure) is ostensibly based on Kürten, but seems rather more of an "everyman" psycho. He is an emobodiment of the psychological sickness that, as we have seen, had its earliest expressions this century in Weimar Germany, but wasted no time in infecting the rest of the industrialised world. Lang was apparently given the opportunity to study several incarcerated killers at firsthand, going so far as to spend eight days in an institution for the criminally insane (those adjudged not responsible for their actions under Paragraph 51). There is, however, no indication that he met the "Düsseldorf monster" himself.

In fact, there is at least one sign that the Beckert killings were intended to represent the "epidemic" of murder that swept Germany before the bureaucratised slaughter of the Holocaust gave an official sanctioned outlet to such impulses. Inspector Lohmann (Otto Wernicke), Lang's archetypal police detective (who also appears in the *Dr. Mabuse* films), is told by an elderly detective: "Without this appearance of, let's say, inoffensiveness in private life, it would be impossible to believe that murderers like Grossman or Haarmann were able to live for years in large, busy blocks of flats without their neighbours suspecting them in the slightest."

Lorre's/Beckert's unhinged mania, later witnessed and much at odds with the calculated way he sets about finding his child victims, seems more redolent of the Hannover "werewolf" than the coldly obsessive Kürten. In fact, at the beginning of the film, the little girls in the courtyard of the tenement block, from which little Elsie Beckmann disappears, chant a rhyme which translates as:

"Just you wait a little while,
The evil man in black will come.
With his little chopper,
He will chop you up."

This is strikingly similar to a macabre nursery rhyme which survives from the time of the Haarmann case:

"Warte, warte nur ein Weilchen	"Wait, wait a little while,
Dann kommt Haarmann auch zu dir	Then Haarmann will come to you
Mit dem kleinen Hack beilchen	with his little axe
Und macht Hackefleisch aus dir."	and make mincemeat of you."

The true subject of ***M***, however, is not Beckert's murderous compulsions, which are dramatically depicted but secondary, nor even the "We, too, should keep a closer watch on our children" warning given at the end of the film. ***M*** is about the suspicion, distrust and hatred which infects a community when it is primarily poisoned by a series of atrocious crimes. One of the earliest post-murder scenes shows an argument between two middle-aged men, where insults such as "Bastard!" and "Swine!" intensify to become

"Murderer!" The crime of one of the men is that he has been seen giving directions to a little girl . The watchful suspicion of the man in the street weighs heaviest on the film's underworld stereotypes. Lang's burly, bull-necked bruisers, weaselly thieves and cigarette-smoking tarts are portrayed sympathetically, even romantically. "You can't imagine how furious everyone is about this guy," says the landlady of an underworld bar raided by Lohmann. "Especially the girls... okay, they walk the streets, but, believe me, each one is a little bit of a mother."

In contrast to the seemingly ineffective efforts of the police, the unofficial investigation by the underworld "union" is coordinated by Schranker (Gustag Gründgens), a respected, leather-coated thug. He's as much enraged by the damage the cops are doing to business, as by their misconceived ideas about finding such a man among the ranks of the everyday "villain": "When I come up against a cop while carrying on my business, he knows the risk he runs... but we are not on the same level as this man they're looking for now."

It's a rationalised expression of the moral superiority felt by every housebreaker and sawed-off gunman who pisses in a prison "nonce's" tea, or kicks him down a metal stairwell. Conventional wisdom would have it that this is a granting of the high moral ground to those who would normally slide on the first muddy foothold - but only a pious, unwordly fool will not accept that there are *degrees* of criminality, and that certain acts will disgust even the lowest lout, whatever his brutishness or lack of comprehension.

Lohmann insists that his detectives continue to trawl the underworld's depths: "Such a person, deeply disturbed, must already have fallen foul of the law. We've got to contact every clinic, every prison, every lunatic asylum." Practical advice, given the lengthy record of Kürten, supposedly the real ***M***. But when he states that, "We'll have to make enquiries about everyone who has been freed as harmless but who has the same pathologicial condition as the killer," the murder-minded viewer may ask exactly what "harmless" "pathological condition" (pretty big contradiction) Lohmann (or Lang, or von Harbou) has in mind. When the Kürtens of the world have been encouraged, albeit unconsciously, to develop their own inner universes of sadistic fulfillment, invisible to the indifferent eyes of their jailers, how well-placed is the workaday lawman's faith in being able to identify a "monster" just by his criminal record?

That said, Lohmann's belief in dogged routine seems about to pay off, when Beckert's wastepaper basket yields up a subtle clue in the process of eliminating suspects. But the underworld is already on the case.

A blind balloon seller (member of the Beggar's Union - another of the shadowy, socialistic organisations which populate the film) is alarmed by the eerie whistling of *Peer Gynt.* The last time he heard that same haunting theme, it was whistled by a man who bought a balloon for a little girl on the day of the last child murder. One of his compadres follows the little murderer, pretending to collide with him in order to print a large chalk mark - **M** - on the shoulder of his coat. Startled, Beckert drops the switchblade he has been using to peel an orange, which the innocent little girl he has enticed along with him dutifully picks up and hands back.

The chalky **M** remains on the murderer's shoulder like some displaced mark of Cain. Too late, he spots its dead-symmetrical mirror reflection, realising he and the little girl are being tracked by vigilante beggars.

After a truly expressionistic sequence, with tight corners and claustrophobic corridors representing his trapped state of mind, Beckert is cornered in the attic of a warehouse. Schranker and his cronies carry the hysterical little man to an abandoned factory. Its cellar becomes a kangaroo court - a court made up of everyday villains and their women, pimps, whores, beggars, and, quietly bewildered, the mothers of some of the murdered children. With a single bulb hanging above his head, the little murderer is unnerved by the blind man's presentation to him of a doll-balloon (justice is blind?), and his identification of him, by voice and handshake, as the killer of little Elsie Beckmann. The intimidating Schranker acts as chief prosecutor, confronting Beckert with photos and press cuttings of murdered and missing children. In total contrast to Kürten's calm self-denunciation, Lorre's little murderer shrieks with fear, chews his fingers, and makes a mad, futile dash for the exit (granted, the real Kürten was at the relatively tender mercy of the law, though ultimately his fate would be little different). Lorre's flesh-creeping performance is extraordinary. Moving us from revulsion to something approaching sympathy, he pulls off the unenviable task of making a blood-thirsty psychotic *human* - something not notably achieved again until by Carl Boehm in Powell's ***Peeping Tom*** (1959), and Anthony Perkins in ***Psycho*** (1960). Made almost pitiful by the vengeful braying of the mob, Schranker grants him a right to some kind of justice, declaring, "We are all law experts here, from six weeks in Tegel, to fifteen years in Brandenburg," (German prisons). He appoints a corrupted lawyer for Beckert's defence, while making no bones about what the outcome will be: "We just want to render you harmless... but you'll only be harmless when you're dead."

Much laughter greets the little murderer's protestation that "If you kill me, it'll be cold-blood murder!", and his demand to be handed over to the police. Schranker sardonically mocks what he sees as Beckert's wish to "invoke Paragraph 51" (which failed, in reality, to save either Kürten or Haarmann), "...and spend the rest of your life in an institution at the state's expense... or else there'd be a pardon and there you are, free as air, protected by the law because of mental illness."

Despite our knowledge of the calculating steps he has taken to entrap little girls, the audience cannot but help detect small grains of truth in his counter-accusation: "What right have you to speak?... Criminals! Perhaps you're even proud of yourselves? Proud of being able to break safes, to climb into buildings or cheat at cards... But I," he emotes with crazed sincerity, "I can't help myself! I haven't any control over this evil thing that's inside me - the fire, the voices, the torment." Cue disomfort among the audience - just as we are aware of the injustice of a mob of hoods setting themselves up as judge and jury, so we are unable to swallow whole the little murderer's defence of himself. "I want to escape from myself!", he insists, arrresting the attention of the less rabid members of the "court". "I am pursued by ghosts. They never leave me... They are there, always... except when I *do it*." Like Kürten, Lorre's little murderer has postponed any attempt to wrestle with the dark portion of his psyche until retribution stares him in the face. Unlike the "Vampire of Düsseldorf", however, Beckert speaks with a voice of stark fear, and his sexual mania is veiled. Obviously, the cinema of the 1930's could not articulate too loud the vile ecstasy of the sexual sadist; but Lorre, in his doomed, breathless attempts to explain himself, in his vivid mime of what it's like to strangle a child, and the rapt closing of his eyes as he speaks of "*ghosts*" and "*doing it*", came as close as anyone then could to portaying the ugly, dark passion of the Monsters of Weimar.

From thereon, until the climactic intervention of the law, the drunken, debarred lawyer acts as spokesman for the social conscience. He argues that the cornered Beckert is a worthier case for medical attention than execution, against the harpie chorus of prostitutes who (quite naturally) scream for vengeance on behalf of the mothers. The lawyer illuminates the absurdity of the trial, annoying Schranker by referring to him as "Our very honourable President... who is, I believe, wanted by the police for three murders." But all his arguments prove merely academic. As the film ends with the little murderer's arrest/salvation by the police, we never truly know whether his claims of helpless compulsion would be believed by the law, or whether, like Haarmann and Kürten, his crimes are too far beyond the pale to win him the protection of Para 51.

Seymour Nebenzal, the head of Nero Films, producers of ***M***, produced an American remake of Lang's classic for Columbia Pictures in 1950. As the film quickly fell into obscurity, and as even Columbia themselves do not seem to possess a print, this writer must reserve judgement. All that is known is that Lang himself declined to direct the remake, saying that he had already made his statement. The film became the directorial debut of Joseph Losey, later better known for archetypal '60's movies *Modesty Blaise* and *Accident*. The production code authorities (an amended version of the restrictive

Hays Code still being in place) agreed to pass its taboo subject of child murder only if it bore clear similarities to the original accepted classic. Despite this, Losey claimed to have made only a single conscious visual reference to one shot from the original.

Closer to the original source material, though even more obscure, is the French movie, ***Le Vampire de Düsseldorf***, (1964). Written by and starring one Robert Hossein, all prints of this uncelebrated feature seem to have long since passed into oblivion. The contemporary reviews which have survived note that Hossein tended to romanticise this most horrible of criminal cases, paying little attention to grim detail (Kürten's crimes are implied but largely unseen), and showing the murderer to be a tragic figure very nearly saved by the love of a good woman. Hossein and his leading lady were certainly more glamorous in appearance than the seemingly-youthful-but-middle-aged Kürten and his aging wife could possibly have been. One critic seems to have been offended by the portrayal of the vampire as a "poetic soul", though this suggests Hossein may have been influenced by the brave analogies drawn between Kürten and the decadent poets in George Godwin's essay.

(Incidentally, the likeable psychopath in the recent Belgian black comedy, ***Man Bites Dog***, makes a dismissive remark about Hossein to the documentary crew that passively follows his every move. Apparently, he too finds the handsome Frenchman's portrayal of a killer a little too silky for belief.)

Beckert, the child murderer (Peter Lorre), cornered in the underworld, in Fritz Lang's classic "M" (1931).

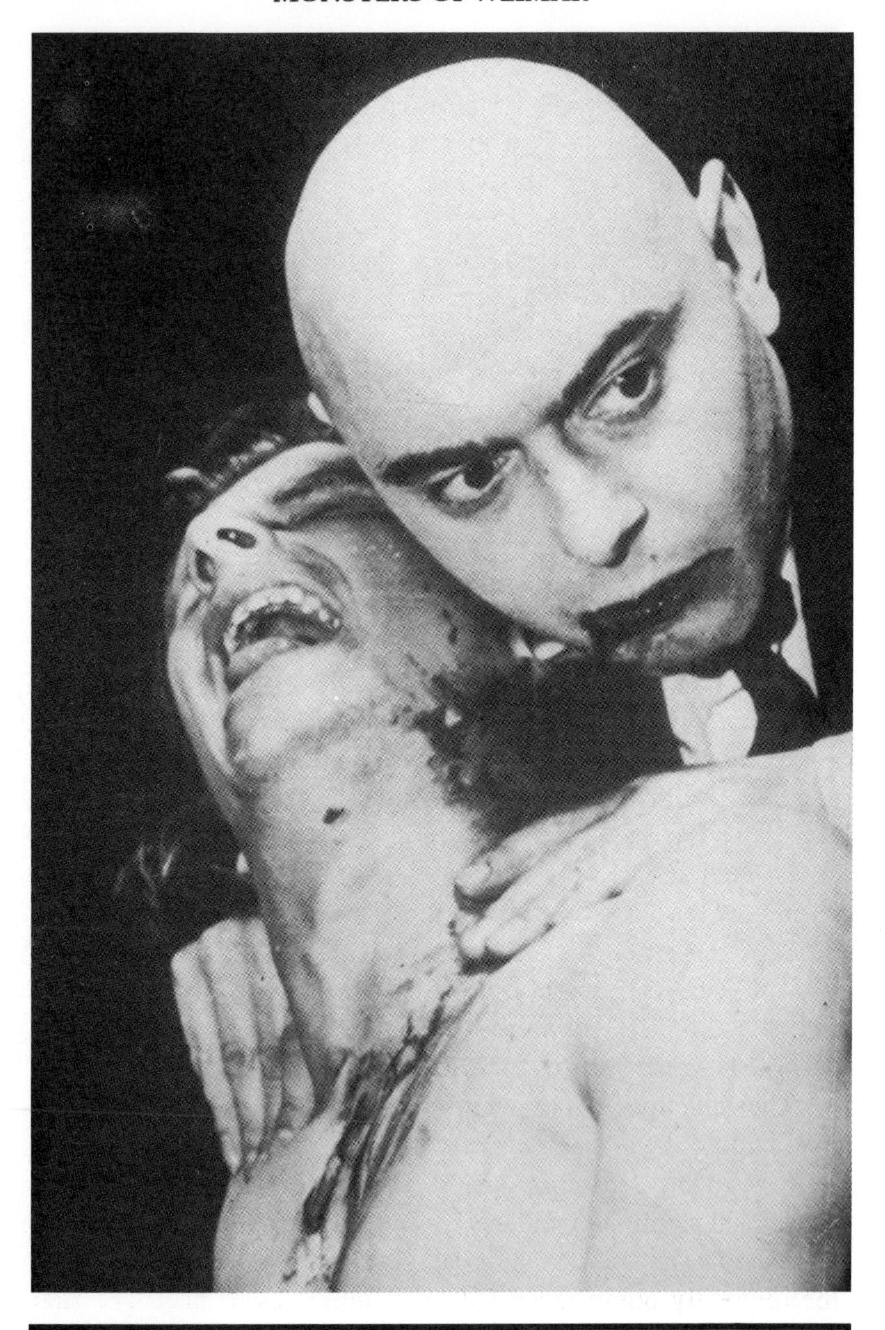

Haarmann (Kurt Raab) claims a young victim in a state of bloody ecstasy, in Uli Lommel's disturbing TENDERNESS OF THE WOLVES.

2. ***Tenderness of the Wolves*** (1974)

Uli Lommel's erotic arthouse horror movie is, perhaps surprisingly, the only film to have been based directly on the Haarmann case. Despite its rich visual sensibility and overtly decadent style, it is also remarkably faithful to the facts as recounted in Lessing's ***Story of a Werewolf.***

Pre-credits, the camera takes us into the shabby boarding house where Haarmann lived (apparently shot on location in Hannover),making its drabness more appealing to the eye by soaking it in the film's dominant deep red and brown shades. An aging female neighbour bangs on the unseen Fritz's wall to ask for "meat", and a quote appears from the killer - "Gladly I yield my death and blood unto God's arms and mercy."

The opening credits suggest a film deep in Fritz Lang territory - Haarmann's strolling shadow is tracked down a long street while Bach plays on the soundtrack - but this is a much more visceral, sexually subversive work. Both its erotica and its violence are steeped in the "decadence aesthetic" of the '70's.

Haarmann, as played by Kurt Raab, is a rather dour, effete figure, not at all the garrulous, fur-lipped Teuton described by Lessing in his book. It's the movie's most major departure from the bare facts. When we first see him, roused from bed with a naked boy, he most resembles Peter Lorre in Karl Freund's ***Mad Love*** (1935) - bald-headed and soft-faced. This interruption by the police brings him into the station on a morals charge, where Lommel makes explicit from the start his hand-in-glove relationship with the police: "We're going to let you go - on the condition you work for us as an informer."

The seductions of the young boys, which become gradually more intense until they reach murder pitch, are the central images of the film. Most are played out against basic Christian icons, such as the devotional paintings and the large crucifix hanging on Haarmann's wall, emphasising both the "werewolf's" religious upbringing, and the implicitly homo-erotic nature of much divine art. The first seduction (the young boy who wants "to run away to sea") is followed by a scene of Haarmann taking along "eight-and-a-half pounds of pork" to his cronies, fixing in our minds the idea that when sex transpires murder is never far away. "He only necks with boys," comes a sly remark from one of his associates, presumably a grim pun.

Though a fascinating work for everyone interested in the bestial side of human nature, ***Tenderness...*** certainly has a gay film's eye for "nice boys in nice clothes". Hardly surprising, perhaps, given the fact that gay film-makers (besides Lommel as director, Rainer Werner Fassbinder takes both a production and acting credit) are dealing with the subject of homo-eroticism turning to sex murder. There's precious little authenticity in the costumes department, however, most of the cast coming dressed in styles that take in every era but the 1920's - though the urchins and rooming houses all look suitably shabby. The beloved Hans Grans appears as a coiffured 70's smoothie, modelling the type of white suit/black shirt combination that Bryan Ferry would be found in that same year. Whether these touches are deliberate anachronisms or due to budget restrictiions is anyone's guess.

The question of Grans's complicity in Haarmann's crimes is dealt with ambiguously, though in one scene (where a lover's tiff ends with Grans shouting "Murderer!" at Haarmann) there's every indication that the film-makers believe he knew more about the murders than Lessing credits. Grans's sexual versatility is also shown as a source of torment to the devoted Haarmann, who bristles with jealousy when Grans dances with pretty young whores, and clearly does not appreciate a black railway porter urging Grans to come to Algiers ("Beautiful women, beautiful men."). At one point, he cuts up rough on Grans and one of the girls, to be pushed back in his place by the surly, fat, leery Wittowski (Fassbinder).

The violence of the film, stemming obviously from the illicit sex, is merely implied at first, though the connections are always clear. Police detectives receive a gift of sausage and meat, after a scene showing Haarmann approaching a pretty blond boy. The scene where the little ten-year-old comes looking for Haarmann, to be told by Frau Lindner, "Go away - he's not for you," has its gruesome aftermath left unshown, but is suggested by neo-expressionist technique. Frau Lindner sits listening to the bangings and clatterings coming from Haarmann in the attic, clutching her throat and enswathed in shadow. She follows him to the river, and watches him dispose of suspiciously-shaped parcels which, incredibly, Haarmann is happy to let float away on top of the water.

By the time explicit violence is shown, it's bound up with the wolf's peculiar religious fetishism (earlier, Haarmann appears particularly pious when begging for clothes in a priest's cassock). This aspect is taken to bizarre extremes when the killer is seen handing out "Hail Mary"s to a young lover while dressed in drag. The grotesquerie becomes progressively nastier, as Haarmann starts to throttle the androgynous, flaxen-haired young man, climaxing (quite literally, as both are in paroxysms, whether of passion or pain) with the bloody, vampiric biting-through of the jugular vein and trachea. Afterward comes the erotic worship of the boy's naked corpse ("He's sleeping," Haarmann tells a female visitor, though the by-now cold young man has a blanket over his face).

When Frau Lindner has amassed enough evidence for an official complaint against Haarmann, the police are reluctant to pounce: "You're a useful man, Herr Haarmann," they tell him after he has been instrumental in apprehending a gang of black marketeers. But, eventually, public outrage acts as the spur. The mass discovery of skulls (offscreen) leads to a call for action from the military police, and even a suggestion that the Nazis might be responsible (whether this political comment is a deliberate anachronism is again unclear - the National Socialists were certainly active in '24, with their tinpot demagogue back on the streets, but they were not the potent, feared force they would become in the late-'20's/early-'30's).

Haarmann is finally trapped by a decoy, an episode apparently not grounded in fact. With Grans's collusion, this stout-hearted young man has his throat gored beyond the call of duty, before the police burst in to arrest the killer. Even then, Haarmann's maniacal passion is irreversible, and he has to be restrained from the wounded boy's neck while under arrest. Then, arm-in-arm, a procession of characters formerly in cahoots with Haarmann, such as Grans and the police detectives, as well as the whores, march the pathetic "werewolf" down the the street to his fate.

"There are victims you don't know about...", the endquote tells us. "They were by far the most beautiful."

The potent mix of homicidal impulse and perverse sexual passion displayed in this film remains just as controversial today (young German Jörg Buttgereit has taken such elements to the extremes in his excessive, but always fascinating, low-budget films). ***Tenderness of the Wolves***, currently without a distributor or a video release, is ripe for rediscovery. It may displease the type of overzealous lobbyist who protested against the "negative image of gays" portrayed in near-namesake ***Silence of the Lambs*** (a matter of contention, since the character Buffalo Bill, though the most extreme type of transvestite - he wears women's skin - is not shown to be homosexual in any conventional sense); but a realist accepts that a person's sexual orientation is about as profound a guide to their qualities as a human being as whether they prefer sweet or savoury food. And in a world where homosexuality permeates all professions, all social classes and all walks of life ('twas ever thus, but it didn't used to be allowed to speak its name), it is inevitable that some gay men will also join the legions of the great 20th century anomaly, the serial killer - as did Fritz Haarmann, Dennis Nilsen and Jeffrey Dahmer.

Paul Anthony Woods

KNOCKIN' ON JOE
(Voices from Death Row) -
edited by Sondra London

(ISBN 1 897743 05 x - £7.50)

The most controversial True Crime book of the year. The mercurial Ms. London has collected stark tales of crime and punishment, guilt and innocence, violence and pain, straight from America's Death Rows and maximum security prisons.

Among the many with stories to tell are:

Joe O'Dell - *an innocent man, condemned to die?* Read his Prison Diaries and Letters, and make your own judgement.

Bobby Fieldmore Lewis - the only man ever to escape from Florida's Death Row; he writes with disarming candour about his life of crime, his time on the Row, and the time he spent with the hated *Ted Bundy*.

G.J. Schaefer - a notorious murderer, discussed by Robert Ressler in his book ***Whoever Fights Monsters***;
Schaefer escaped the death sentence and became a legal clerk on Death Row, witness to the executions of other men. Here, he writes unflinchingly about it - included amongst his tales is the infamous ***Nigger Jack***.

Ottis Toole - deranged partner of *Henry Lee Lucas,* who tells of his gothic nightmare childhood.

Danny Rolling - one of the most dangerous men in the USA today, currently on trial for his life. His stories start to make sense of the bleak road that leads to nowhere, while Ms. London speaks candidly of her love for Rolling - the love which has outraged American TV viewers.

Carl Panzram - classic jailhouse writer / subject of a new film.

WARNING - DUE TO THE INTENSE NATURE OF THIS BOOK, IT IS SUITABLE FOR ADULT READERS ONLY.

THE FAMILY
by Ed Sanders
(ISBN 1 8987743 15 7 - £9.99)

They were children of the '60's. Of free love and psychedelia. Of a better world waiting to be born. But in *Charles Manson* they found a daddy, a lover and a saviour...
All they needed was his word, to ignite the violence within them, and to end the love generation in a tragic rampage of murder and hate.

THE FAMILY has been updated to the present day, with five new chapters. Published in a 500-page edition by **NEMESIS**, this classic case history tells the only complete story of the *"Manson family"*, This new edition contains rare, exclusive stills, many from the shocking new movie, *CHARLIE'S FAMILY* - plus an introduction by the film's director, Jim Van Bebber, who tells why *THE FAMILY* is the only truly essential volume for readers fascinated by the madness of Manson and his followers.

"Ed Sanders has done nothing less than risk his own life...
It is only fitting that such a risk should produce such a terrifying book!" -
THE NEW YORK TIMES

ED GEIN - PSYCHO!
by Paul Anthony Woods
(ISBN 1 897743 00 9 - £5.99)

The story of the incredible real-life ghoul, the "Womanskinner of Wisconsin", and his outrageous crimes. Also contains an entertaining look at Gein's bizarre effect on popular entertainment, in books and films such as *Psycho, The Texas Chainsaw Massacre* and *Silence of the Lambs*.

WARNING - CONTAINS EXTREME ILLUSTRATIONS

"An excellent and absorbing work" -
COLIN WILSON